ROMANS

WORD and SPIRIT COMMENTARY ON THE NEW TESTAMENT

SERIES EDITORS

Craig S. Keener, Asbury Theological Seminary

Holly Beers, Westmont College

ADVISORY BOARD

Gordon D. Fee[†], Regent College

J. Ayodeji Adewuya, Pentecostal Theological Seminary

Lisa Marie Bowens, Princeton Theological Seminary

Jacob Cherian, Centre for Global Leadership Development

Robert Menzies, Asia Pacific Theological Seminary

VOLUMES NOW AVAILABLE

Romans   Sam Storms

2 Corinthians   Ben Witherington III

ROMANS

Sam Storms

Baker Academic
a division of Baker Publishing Group
Grand Rapids, Michigan

Published by Baker Academic
a division of Baker Publishing Group
Grand Rapids, Michigan
BakerAcademic.com

Printed in the United States of America

Library of Congress Cataloging-in-Publication Data
Names: Storms, C. Samuel, 1951– author.
Title: Romans / Sam Storms.
Description: Grand Rapids, Michigan : Baker Academic, a division of Baker Publishing Group, [2024] | Series: Word and spirit commentary on the New Testament | Includes bibliographical references and index.
Identifiers: LCCN 2024004940 | ISBN 9781540964137 (paperback) | ISBN 9781540968395 (casebound) | ISBN 9781493447817 (ebook) | ISBN 9781493447824 (pdf)
Subjects: LCSH: Bible. Romans.
Classification: LCC BS2665.53 .S75 2024 | DDC 227/.107—dc23/eng/20240316
LC record available at https://lccn.loc.gov/2024004940

Baker Publishing Group publications use paper produced from sustainable forestry practices and post-consumer waste whenever possible.

24   25   26   27   28   29   30   7   6   5   4   3   2   1

Contents

Series Preface

In the foreword to Roger Stronstad's 1984 volume *The Charismatic Theology of St. Luke*, Clark H. Pinnock wrote, "The young Pentecostal scholars are coming!"[1] That was a generation ago, and now the Pentecostal scholars are here, many of them having grown up alongside the explosive global growth of charismatic and Pentecostal traditions. Such growth has been well documented,[2] with the number of adherents estimated at more than half a billion. In many places, Bible teaching has not been able to keep pace with this growth. Because of this reality, there is a clear need for a balanced commentary series aimed at Christians who identify as Spirit-filled, including renewalists, charismatics, and Pentecostals, as well as others who want to learn more from this sphere of the church.

Because so many within these traditions often use wider evangelical literature, this series is sensitive to those intellectual and academic standards. However, others mistrust what they see as "purely intellectual" approaches, and they will find that this series also focuses on how the same Spirit who inspired the text speaks and works today. In this way the series offers a conversation for the church rather than operating primarily as a forum for discussion among scholars.

The commentary proper in each volume engages the biblical text both in its ancient setting and with regard to its message for Spirit-filled Christians

1. Clark H. Pinnock, foreword to *The Charismatic Theology of St. Luke*, by Roger Stronstad (Peabody, MA: Hendrickson, 1984), vii.
2. For example, Peter L. Berger, "Four Faces of Global Culture," in *Globalization and the Challenges of a New Century: A Reader*, ed. Patrick O'Meara, Howard D. Mehlinger, and Matthew Krain (Bloomington: Indiana University Press, 2000), 425; Robert Bruce Mullin, *A Short World History of Christianity* (Louisville: Westminster John Knox, 2008), 211 (cf. 276); Mark A. Noll, *The New Shape of World Christianity: How American Experience Reflects Global Faith* (Downers Grove, IL: IVP Academic, 2009), 32.

today. The commentaries often integrate exegesis and application, as readers in charismatic and Pentecostal traditions tend to move naturally between these categories rather than separating them. In other words, such readers traditionally blend the ancient and modern horizons so as to read themselves within the continuing narrative of salvation history—that is, as part of the ongoing biblical story (not part of ancient culture but as theologically/spiritually/eschatologically part of God's same church).

As part of the blending of horizons, distinctive interests for Spirit-filled audiences are addressed when relevant. These include—but are not limited to—the reality of the new birth, healing and other miracles, spiritual gifts, hearing God's voice, the working of the Spirit in daily life, spiritual warfare, and so on. Not all biblical texts, and thus not all exposition, focuses on these points alone, and our authors do not artificially impose these topics on passages that do not naturally address them. In other words, our authors observe how God works in the biblical texts and how Christians can expect God to be working today, even if in new or culturally surprising ways.

However, each author also writes from within a charismatic, renewalist, or Pentecostal context across the broad spectrum of the Spirit-focused tradition, and the authors often refer to such spaces in their writing. The range of voices includes denominational Pentecostals, Reformed charismatics, charismatic Methodists, and others. They also reflect a range of cultures, including Spirit-filled voices from multiple continents.

The authors "preach" their way through the texts, hosting a conversation both as trusted insiders for their own home traditions and as hospitable guides for others who wish to listen again alongside the ancient audiences for the Spirit's voice in our time and contexts. The commentaries are written with other distinctives of the tradition(s), including the incorporation of testimony and sidebars that feature connections to Pentecostal/charismatic/revival history, teaching, and practice.

Other sidebars focus on biblical background and lengthier points of application. The series has adopted the NIV as the default text, as it is widely used in contexts that identify as Spirit-filled. However, our authors will often reference other translations, including their own. Quoted biblical texts from the New Testament book(s) under discussion will be highlighted in bold. Greek words are transliterated.

We offer this series to the church, and we pray that it testifies to the creative work and restorative goodness of the triune God.

Holly Beers, Westmont College
Craig S. Keener, Asbury Theological Seminary

Abbreviations

Old Testament

Gen.	Genesis	2 Chron.	2 Chronicles	Dan.	Daniel
Exod.	Exodus	Ezra	Ezra	Hosea	Hosea
Lev.	Leviticus	Neh.	Nehemiah	Joel	Joel
Num.	Numbers	Esther	Esther	Amos	Amos
Deut.	Deuteronomy	Job	Job	Obad.	Obadiah
Josh.	Joshua	Ps(s).	Psalm(s)	Jon.	Jonah
Judg.	Judges	Prov.	Proverbs	Mic.	Micah
Ruth	Ruth	Eccles.	Ecclesiastes	Nah.	Nahum
1 Sam.	1 Samuel	Song	Song of Songs	Hab.	Habakkuk
2 Sam.	2 Samuel	Isa.	Isaiah	Zeph.	Zephaniah
1 Kings	1 Kings	Jer.	Jeremiah	Hag.	Haggai
2 Kings	2 Kings	Lam.	Lamentations	Zech.	Zechariah
1 Chron.	1 Chronicles	Ezek.	Ezekiel	Mal.	Malachi

New Testament

Matt.	Matthew	Eph.	Ephesians	Heb.	Hebrews
Mark	Mark	Phil.	Philippians	James	James
Luke	Luke	Col.	Colossians	1 Pet.	1 Peter
John	John	1 Thess.	1 Thessalonians	2 Pet.	2 Peter
Acts	Acts	2 Thess.	2 Thessalonians	1 John	1 John
Rom.	Romans	1 Tim.	1 Timothy	2 John	2 John
1 Cor.	1 Corinthians	2 Tim.	2 Timothy	3 John	3 John
2 Cor.	2 Corinthians	Titus	Titus	Jude	Jude
Gal.	Galatians	Philem.	Philemon	Rev.	Revelation

General

AT	author's translation	HR	historical remnant
ca.	*circa*	KJV	King James Version
ESV	English Standard Version	NASB	New American Standard Bible
FR	future restoration	NIV	New International Version

Introduction

Paul's Epistle to the Romans, notes N. T. Wright, "dwarfs most of his other writings, an Alpine peak towering over hills and villages."[1] Its global influence over the past two thousand years is undeniable, and its contemporary relevance is unrivaled. But we must not think of Romans as a theological encyclopedia or merely a summation of Christian doctrine. Although it is thoroughly theological and covers a wide range of Christian truth, it is also a letter "written by a particular person to particular people in a particular time and place."[2]

There is also a sense in which Romans provides us with the consummation of God's redemptive purposes in Christ Jesus. The epistle begins with the declaration that what the prophets of old had promised concerning God's Son has now come to fruition in the gospel that Paul proclaims (1:1–6) and concludes with much the same message (16:25–26). In this way, Paul roots the truths of this epistle in the narrative of God's dealings with Israel in the old covenant and the prophesied fulfillment of his plan to redeem a people for himself. Romans is not an isolated or stand-alone document of theological truths; it is organically and inextricably connected to the overall narrative structure of God's purposes that began with Adam (5:12–21), were confirmed by means of a covenant with Abraham (4:1–25), and are now fulfilled in the person and work of Christ Jesus himself.

Authorship

The authorship of Romans is undisputed. Virtually everyone acknowledges that Romans was written by the apostle Paul (1:1). Paul, however, did employ

1. Wright, "Letter to the Romans," 395.
2. Moo, *Encountering the Book of Romans*, 4.

1

an amanuensis, named Tertius (16:22), the ancient equivalent of a modern-day secretary, who actually put pen to parchment. Some argue that Paul only communicated his ideas to Tertius, who later formulated them in his own words. But as Thomas Schreiner notes, "It is intrinsically unlikely that Paul would surrender the specific contents of Romans to Tertius. The letter was of great import to Paul, and its careful structure suggests that he fussed over the details."[3] Another possibility is that Tertius wrote in something akin to shorthand and later reproduced a longhand copy. Thus, the general themes of the letter originated with Paul, but its specific features came from Tertius. The most likely view is that Paul dictated to Tertius *syllabitim*, syllable by syllable, a not uncommon practice in ancient times.

Occasion and Date

Paul has completed the collection of money for the impoverished church in Jerusalem and is now prepared to deliver this much-needed resource (cf. 1 Cor. 16:1–4; 2 Cor. 8–9). We read in Rom. 15:22–29 that his immediate plans involve going to Jerusalem and then to Rome on his way to Spain. This reinforces the likelihood that Romans was composed close to the conclusion of Paul's third missionary journey. It was then that the apostle made plans to return to Jerusalem (Acts 20:3–6) in the company of representatives of the churches he had planted. Paul likely wrote this epistle during the three months he spent in Greece before he embarked on his journey home.[4]

Paul probably would have stayed in Corinth while in Greece (cf. 2 Cor. 13:1, 10). Confirmation that he wrote Romans while there comes from several statements. There is, first of all, his commendation of Phoebe, who lived in Cenchreae, a seaport adjacent to Corinth (Rom. 16:1–2). Second, it has also been noted that the man named Gaius who sends his greetings in Rom. 16:23 is probably the same Gaius who was baptized by Paul at Corinth (cf. 1 Cor. 1:14). Third, Erastus, Timothy, and Sopater are said to be with Paul when Romans was written (Rom. 16:21, 23); they were also with him when he was in Greece (Acts 19:22; 20:2–4). Finally, "according to Acts 20:3 Paul spent three months in Greece towards the end of his third missionary journey prior to his departure for Jerusalem with the collection. In Greece he would have been most likely to stay in Corinth in fellowship with the church he had founded there."[5]

3. Schreiner, *Romans*, 2.
4. Moo, *Romans*, 2–3.
5. Kruse, *Romans*, 13.

C. E. B. Cranfield makes a strong argument that, given what we know of Paul's movements, the letter was written during the late winter or early spring in one of the years between AD 54 and AD 59.[6] He favors the winter of AD 55–56. Virtually every other commentator identifies a year within that temporal framework. What this means is that Paul wrote his Letter to the Romans while Nero was emperor (AD 54–68). However, it is important to remember that during the first five years of his reign Nero was a decent ruler. It was not until AD 60 that he became the sadistic and barbaric tyrant for which he is notorious.

Recipients

The church in Rome most likely began with the return to that city of certain Jews who were converted on the day of Pentecost in Jerusalem (see Acts 2:10). "Accordingly, the earliest Christian community in Rome would have been Jewish in character."[7] However, this did not last. Luke tells us that "Claudius had commanded all the Jews to leave Rome" (Acts 18:2 ESV). Most believe that this order was issued in AD 49. The Roman historian Suetonius (d. AD 130) attributed this decree to the fact that the Jews were responsible for certain "disturbances" traceable to "Chrestus" (undoubtedly a misspelling of *Christos*, "Christ") (*Divus Claudius* 25.4). Joseph Fitzmyer draws this conclusion:

> Suetonius, then, would have been referring to a conflict between Jews and Jewish Christians of Rome in the late 40s; the constant disturbances would apparently have been caused by Jews who opposed those who accepted Jesus as the Messiah or Lord, and who consequently differed in their interpretation of the law and threatened thereby ethnic unity and identity. These disturbances were happening so frequently . . . that they became the reason for the imperial banishment of Jews and Jewish Christians from Rome. Among the latter would have been Prisca and Aquila, who left Italy for Corinth (Acts 18:2).[8]

There is no support for the tradition that Peter founded the church in Rome. Paul says clearly in Rom. 15:20 that he will not build "on someone else's foundation" (ESV). This makes it highly unlikely, if not altogether impossible, that Paul would have planned a visit to a church that was founded by Peter, and far less likely that he would have written an inspired epistle to it. The Roman Catholic tradition that Peter founded the church in Rome is based on much later speculation. Eusebius (early fourth century) alleges that Peter went to Rome

6. Cranfield, *Romans*, 1:12–16.
7. Cranfield, *Romans*, 1:2.
8. Fitzmyer, *Romans*, 31.

to preach the gospel in the second year of the reign of Claudius (i.e., AD 42). The *Catalogus Liberianus* (AD 354) also speaks of Peter as having started the Roman church and serving it for some twenty-five years. Both of these assertions have been shown by scholars to lack support, especially when compared with what we know of Peter's movements from Acts and certain references in Paul's writings (cf. Gal. 2:7–9). Interestingly, the following conclusion is drawn by Fitzmyer, one of the more prominent and widely respected Roman Catholic New Testament scholars of our day: "Hence there is no reason to think that Peter spent any major portion of time in Rome before Paul wrote his letter, or that he was the founder of the Roman church or the missionary who first brought Christianity to Rome. For it seems highly unlikely that Luke, if he knew that Peter had gone to Rome and evangelized that city, would have omitted all mention of it in Acts."[9]

Purpose[10]

Unlike other of Paul's writings, such as Galatians, 1 and 2 Corinthians, and the Pastoral Epistles, there is little in Romans to alert us to any peculiar or urgent circumstances in Rome that evoked Paul's words.[11] Whereas Paul undoubtedly addresses issues that were pertinent to the believers in Rome, the structure or flow of his argument is dictated more by the internal logic of his theology than by any special needs in the church itself.

Certainly Paul was concerned with the relationship of Jews and Gentiles in the redemptive purpose of God, as well as matters such as the role of the law, the nature of justification by faith, the struggle of the Christian life, the believer's responsibility to the state, the nature and limits of personal freedom, and more, but it would be unwise to single out any one of these themes as the overall purpose for which he wrote. Those who find in Romans a summary of Paul's theology cannot explain the surprising omission of any reference to the Lord's Supper, only brief allusions to the doctrine of the church, and virtually nothing of eschatology.

Leon Morris lists no fewer than twelve theories on the purpose of the letter, none of which is without problems. Yet Morris does point out that we may discern at least three things Paul specifically says he wanted to accomplish by his letter: "First, he wanted to prepare the way for a visit to Rome (1:13; 15:22–24).

9. Fitzmyer, *Romans*, 30.
10. A helpful resource addressing the purpose of Romans is Donfried, *Romans Debate*.
11. The one exception to this is the disagreement among those who identified as "strong" and those whom Paul refers to as "weak." See the commentary on Rom. 14 for how Paul addressed the issue.

Second, he wanted to secure the support of the Roman Christians for his Spanish mission (15:24). Third, he sought the prayers of the Romans, specifically prayers that he might be delivered from unbelievers, that the Jerusalem church would welcome the gift he was bringing, and that he might come to Rome 'in joy' (15:30–32)."[12]

In the second half of the twentieth century, debate erupted about the primary issue that Paul addresses in this epistle. For the past five hundred years or so, following the lead of the Protestant Reformer Martin Luther (d. 1546), most have read Romans as a treatment of individual soteriology. Paul's focus, so Luther believed, was the gracious provision by God of the righteousness of Jesus Christ to those who believed, thereby making it possible for the sinner to be restored to a right relationship with God.

As articulated by scholars such as Krister Stendahl, E. P. Sanders, James D. G. Dunn, and N. T. Wright, a "new perspective" on Paul has arisen that places more attention on the tense relationship between Jew and Gentile. Stendahl was the first to popularize the notion that the focus on individual salvation was more the result of the excessively introspective conscience of Western culture than anything that Paul himself envisioned.[13] Thus, it isn't so much soteriology that concerns the apostle as it is ecclesiology. The most pressing question isn't how to gain entrance into the people of God but what are the markers that identify those who already are and how might they remain in the covenant. Sanders insists that the Jews of Paul's day were not legalists and did not believe in salvation by works.[14] The covenant that God had established with Israel was rooted in grace and based on divine election. If the Jews obeyed the law, it wasn't in order to get saved but rather to stay saved. Entrance into the covenant was by grace. Obedience to the law was necessary to remain within that covenant. In sum, notes Craig Keener, Sanders "argued that nearly all of ancient Judaism affirmed that Israelites as a whole were graciously chosen as part of the covenant, and remained members of the covenant unless cutting themselves off through apostasy. Judaism was thus a religion of grace, and works confirmed rather than earned a place in the covenant."[15]

Thus, the "works of the law" (Rom. 3:20, 28; Gal. 2:16 [3x]; 3:2, 5, 10 ESV) that play such a prominent role in Paul's theology were, purportedly, not legalistic deeds performed apart from God's gracious enablement, designed to merit salvation, but markers or badges of Jewish national identity and privilege, such

---

12. Morris, *Romans*, 17–18.
13. See Stendahl, "Paul and the Introspective Conscience."
14. See Sanders, *Paul and Palestinian Judaism*.
15. Keener, *Romans*, 5–6. The best and most detailed articulation of the argument of Romans from the viewpoint of the "new perspective" is laid out in Dunn, *Romans 1–8* and *Romans 9–16*.

as circumcision, Sabbath observance, and dietary regulations. Works of the law, therefore, were viewed by Paul not as a way for Jews to get in but rather as a way to keep Gentiles out. It is this ethnic exclusivity that Paul seeks to address and overcome by stressing that faith in Jesus alone grants entrance into the covenant community.[16]

Without in any way wishing to diminish the importance of multiethnic unity in the body of Christ, I remain convinced that Paul's primary aim in Romans is to address the question of how one might be reconciled to God. I should also point out that it is misleading to trace this view to the sixteenth century and Martin Luther. The fact is that virtually every prominent theologian and commentator on Romans prior to Luther likewise saw the letter's primary purpose as an articulation of the gospel and the manner in which God has declared us righteous through faith in Christ alone, thereby securing for us the forgiveness of sins and reconciling us to himself. Stephen Westerholm has done an excellent job in documenting the perspective of those preceding Luther, even when they differ on their views of divine election and divine sovereignty and the relation of the former to free will.[17]

Theological Themes in Romans

The Gospel

The gospel plays a massively important role in Paul's Letter to the Romans. He is an apostle, "set apart for the gospel of God" (1:1). This gospel "is the power of God for salvation" (1:16 ESV) and thus pertains to the way in which a person may be reconciled to God. In order to define "gospel" we must look at how it is portrayed in its narrow, focused application and how it also extends to include everything that God has done in Christ to redeem the cosmos and make way for the inauguration of the new heaven and new earth.

So, in one sense, the gospel is the gloriously great good news of what our triune God has graciously done in the incarnation, life, death, and resurrection of Jesus Christ to satisfy his own wrath against us and to secure the forgiveness

16. For a helpful and ultimately persuasive response to this understanding of "works of law," see Schreiner, "'Works of Law' in Paul." For a brief summation and more accessible expression of his argument, see Schreiner, *40 Questions*, 35–51.

17. See Westerholm, *Romans*. Among those cited by Westerholm as defending the traditional perspective on Romans are Origen (185–254), John Chrysostom (347–407), Theodore of Mopsuestia (350–428), Theodoret of Cyrus (393–460), Pelagius (354–420), Augustine (354–430), Peter Abelard (1079–1142), Thomas Aquinas (1225–74), John Wycliffe (1330–84), William Tyndale (1494–1536), John Colet (1467–1519), Erasmus (1466–1536), Martin Luther (1483–1546), Philip Melanchthon (1497–1560), and John Calvin (1509–64).

of sins and perfect righteousness for all who trust in him by faith alone. Christ fulfilled, on our behalf, the perfectly obedient life under God's law that we should have lived but never could. He died, in our place, the death that we deserved to suffer but now never will. And by his rising from the dead, he secures, for those who believe, the promise of a resurrected and glorified life in a new heaven and a new earth in fellowship with the Father, Son, and Holy Spirit forever.

The gospel is fundamentally about something that *has* happened. It is an accomplished event, an unalterable fact of history. But as a settled achievement it also exerts a radical and far-reaching influence on both our present experience and our future hopes. This gospel is not only the means by which people have been saved but also the truth and power by which people are being sanctified (1 Cor. 15:1–2); it is the truth of the gospel that enables us to genuinely and joyfully do what is pleasing to God and to grow in progressive conformity to the image of Christ.

It would not be an exaggeration to say that the gospel is the gravitational center of both our individual experience and the shape of local church life. We see this in numerous biblical texts. For example, the gospel is Christocentric: it is about Jesus, God's son (Mark 1:1; Rom. 1:9). Both Mark (Mark 1:14) and Paul (Rom. 1:1; 1 Thess. 2:8) describe it as the gospel "of God"—he is its source and the cause of all that it entails. Humans do not create or craft the gospel; they respond to it by repenting of their sins and believing its message (Mark 1:15) concerning what God has done in the life, death, and resurrection of Jesus. The gospel, then, is "the word of truth" that proclaims our "salvation" (Eph. 1:13 ESV). It is marked by grace (Acts 20:24), which is to say that it is the message of God's gracious provision, apart from human works, of all that is necessary to reconcile us to himself both now and for eternity.

The gospel is rooted in the call of Israel and is consummated in the Messiah, Jesus of Nazareth, who is the fulfillment of the types and shadows of the old covenant (Rom. 1:1–6; 16:25–27). As such, the gospel must never be thought of as an abstract, ahistorical idea, as if it were disconnected from or unrelated to the concrete realities of life on earth. The life, death, and resurrection of Jesus are thus to be seen as the pivotal chapter in the unfolding story of God's redemptive purpose for humanity.

There are also multiple consequences of the gospel that extend beyond its impact on the individual and their relationship to God. The gospel invariably issues a call for human action. Among the implications or results of the gospel are the cultivation of humility (Phil. 2:1–5), the pursuit of racial reconciliation (Eph. 2:11–22) and social justice (Philem. 8–20), a commitment to harmony and peace among people (Rom. 15:5–7; Heb. 12:14), and the demonstration of love for one another (1 John 3:16, 23). But we must never confuse the content of the gospel with its consequences, or its essence with its entailments.

Finally, whereas the gospel is God's redeeming act in Jesus on behalf of sinful men and women, we must not overlook the fact that it is only because of the gospel that we have a sure and certain hope for cosmic transformation. The good news of God's saving act in Christ is thus the foundation for our confidence in the ultimate triumph of God's kingdom (1 Cor. 15:20–24), the end of physical death (1 Cor. 15:25–26; Rev. 21:4), the defeat of Satan (John 16:11; Col. 2:13–15; Heb. 2:14; 1 John 3:8), the eradication of all evil (Rev. 21:4, 8), and the removal of the curse that rests on our physical environment, followed by the consummation of God's purpose for all creation in the new heaven and new earth (Rom. 8:18–25).

The Righteousness of God

N. T. Wright has rigorously defended the notion that by the "righteousness of God" (Rom. 1:17) Paul had in mind "the expectation that the God of Israel, often referred to in the Hebrew Scriptures by the name YHWH, would be faithful to the promises made to the patriarchs."[18] It is, then, God's loyalty to the covenant with Israel, and not so much that attribute in accordance with which he graciously justifies the individual believer, that is in view by this phrase. Thus, Paul's statement in 1:17 is "about God and God's covenant faithfulness and justice, rather than simply about 'justification'"[19] and the way in which a person may find forgiveness from God.

Others believe that Paul is referring to a status or position that God bestows on those who believe. It is therefore a righteousness that *comes from* God. Martin Luther gave eloquent expression to this view in the sixteenth century. Late in life he recalled how he had been taught that the righteousness of God is an impersonal attribute of God in accordance with which he punishes those who fail to meet his eternal standards. Luther was baffled how anyone, much less the apostle Paul, could call this "good news." In other words, Luther at first believed that the righteousness of God was his enemy, threatening him with eternal condemnation. But he soon discovered that the righteousness that God demands from us God graciously gives to us when the individual believes in Christ Jesus. Luther's conclusion was that the righteousness of God revealed in the gospel is a gift of God given to sinners through faith. This righteousness is purely forensic or legal. It is a matter of our judicial standing before God, not our internal or moral transformation. Thus, Luther's view is that Paul refers

18. Wright, "Letter to the Romans," 398. See Isa. 46:13; 50:5–8; Mic. 7:9.
19. Wright, "Letter to the Romans," 403.

in Rom. 1:16–17 to the righteous status that comes from God in the gospel through faith.

The Plight of the Unevangelized

How can God be just in consigning to hell those who have never heard the name of Jesus or the proclamation of the gospel? This is an issue addressed in Rom. 1:18–32; 2:12–16; 10:14–21. Paul's answer is to assert that God has revealed himself clearly both in creation and in the conscience of every human being. This revelation is sufficiently "plain" (1:19) and unmistakable that to reject it is to leave people "without excuse" (1:20). Thus, no one will be rejected for having failed to believe in a name or a truth of which they know nothing. Rather, they are eternally accountable to God for their willful repudiation of what has clearly been shown to them (1:19) and for their refusal to honor God or give thanks to him (1:21).

The Moral Status of Homosexuality

There is hardly a more controversial and divisive issue in both the church and society at large than that of homosexuality. Although Paul's comments on the matter in Romans are brief and do not address the current debate over the distinction that many draw between orientation and choice, his position is unmistakable. Both male and female same-sex physical intimacy is classified as "impurity" (1:24) and constitutes "the dishonoring of their bodies" (1:24 ESV). Such homosexual passions are "dishonorable" (ESV) and "unnatural" (1:26) and are an expression of the idolatrous exchange by which people serve "the creature rather than the Creator" (1:25 ESV).

Whereas Paul does not speak explicitly to the saving and sanctifying influence of divine grace for those given to this particular sinful lifestyle, his view of the powerful work of the Spirit in delivering men and women from the dominion of sin most assuredly applies to this area of human behavior no less than it does to all others (see 6:5–23; 8:1–11).

Sin and the Human Condition

Paul's perspective on the human condition apart from God's saving grace in Jesus Christ is a bleak one. Original sin, for Paul, is not an abstract notion but rather a concrete reality that accounts for the plight of the human race. It was "through the disobedience of the one man" that "the many were made sinners" (Rom. 5:19). This initial corruption of the human race, consequent upon Adam's transgression (5:12–13), expresses itself in willful, voluntary slavery to the power of indwelling sin (6:15–18) and its many evil facets: idolatry (1:22–25), unrighteousness, covetousness, malice, envy, murder, strife, deceit, gossip, and slander (1:29–32), to mention just a few. Thus, "all, both Jews and Greeks, are under sin" (3:9 ESV) and subject to the sentence of death (6:23). But the good news of what God has done in and through Jesus Christ is that we may be delivered from sin's dominion (6:12–14) and receive "eternal life" (6:22).

Substitutionary Atonement

Foundational to God's saving grace in Christ Jesus is the latter's voluntary sacrifice of himself on the cross. In this way the wrath of the Father was satisfied or appeased—what Paul refers to as propitiation through the blood of Christ (Rom. 3:25; 5:9). This in turn serves as the basis on which believers experience redemption (3:24) and are "justified by his blood" (5:9). Paul's language, to be explained in detail in the subsequent commentary, demands that we view the death of Christ as both penal (he endured the punishment that sin provoked and justice required) and substitutionary (it was in the stead of otherwise guilty sinners that he suffered).

Justification

Largely due to the influence of Augustine (d. 430), the early church until the time of the Reformation envisioned justification as inherent rather than imputed. Justification was viewed as encompassing both the initial event of conversion and faith in Christ and the subsequent process of progressive ethical transformation into the image of the Lord. The traditional Protestant distinction between these two dimensions of salvation, according to which the former is designated justification and the latter sanctification, was entirely foreign to Augustine, who tended to see justification as the all-encompassing renewal of the divine image in humans that begins with initial faith and consummates with the glorified body.

During the late medieval period, the concept of justification was viewed as involving an experiential, ongoing renovation of the sinner that entailed the habit of created grace within the soul, particularly as mediated through the sacramental system of Rome. According to the sixteenth-century Reformers, the righteousness of justification is always both alien and imputed. That is to say, it is *alien* in the sense that it is *Christ's* righteousness, not our own, and it is *imputed* in the sense that it is *legally reckoned to us*, not imparted or infused experientially within us.

It is this latter view that we find in Paul, especially in Romans. Justification is the forensic declaration that the Christian is righteous in the sight of God rather than a process by which he or she is made righteous. It is fundamentally an objective status before God rather than a subjective transformation in one's nature. This status is a gift of God's grace that is laid hold of by faith alone in the person and work of Christ. Justification thus entails both acquittal and acceptance and involves both the forgiveness of sins and the receiving of the righteousness of Christ. God not only declares the believer "Not guilty!"; he also declares the believer "Righteous!" And as Paul will repeatedly make clear in Romans, justification is received by faith, being freely bestowed by God (3:20–24, 28).

The "Christian's" Battle with Indwelling Sin

There is perhaps no more hotly disputed passage in this epistle than Rom. 7:7–25. Does Paul portray for us here what some might call the normal Christian life, or is this a portrayal of what we were before being born again, a condition from which, by the grace of God, we have been delivered? Is the Christian life one of severe struggle and frequent defeat, or is it one of triumph over sin and victory over the flesh? Or are these questions themselves misleading? Is there a third or middle way between these two extremes? The competing interpretive options will be examined in the commentary itself.

Life in the Power of the Holy Spirit

There is widespread misunderstanding of the role of the Holy Spirit in Romans, as many believe its concentrated focus on sin, the gospel, and the saving work of Jesus Christ overrides any emphasis that might otherwise be placed on the Spirit. But the somewhat surprising fact is that "except for 1 Corinthians, Paul's letter to the church in Rome contains the largest amount of Spirit material in the corpus."[20] *Pneuma*, as a direct reference to the Holy Spirit, appears unambiguously in 1:4, 9; 2:29; 5:5; 7:6; 8:2, 4, 5 (2x), 6, 9 (3x), 10, 11 (2x), 13, 14, 15 (2x), 16 (2x), 23, 26 (2x), 27; 9:1; 12:11; 14:17; 15:13, 16, 19, 30. In 8:27 the earlier explicit mention of the Spirit is the subject of the third-person singular "intercedes." There is considerable debate whether *pneuma* in 12:11 refers to the Holy Spirit or the human spirit, but the former is more likely. The adjective *pneumatikos* ("spiritual") occurs three times (1:11; 7:14; 15:27). Of the six occurrences of *charisma* (1:11; 5:15, 16; 6:23; 11:29; 12:6), one refers to the spiritual gift of prophecy (12:6).

We must also remember that there need not be an explicit use of the term *pneuma* for Paul to have the Holy Spirit in mind. Numerous gracious, saving

20. Fee, *God's Empowering Presence*, 472. For an excellent portrayal of pneumatology from a Wesleyan perspective, see Jones, *God the Spirit*.

activities of God are mentioned in Romans that in other texts outside this epistle are clearly attributed to the work of the Spirit. Of one thing we may be certain: the apostle Paul was altogether convinced that whatever degree of success there is in the Christian life, be it in prayer, our battle with sin, our devotion to Christ, our exercise of the *charismata*, or our understanding of the revelation we find in Scripture, the Holy Spirit is absolutely essential.

Election and Predestination

That God has a chosen or elect people is affirmed by all who embrace the authority of Scripture. And no book of the New Testament speaks more directly to the issue than Romans. We find references to election, foreknowledge, and predestination in 8:29–30, 33–39; 9:6–23; 11:1–2, 5–6, 28–29. The dispute among Christians is the basis or ground for God's sovereign choice. Does God elect individuals to inherit eternal life on the basis of his infallible foreknowledge of how they will respond to the gospel, in the exercise of their free will? Or does God choose individuals unconditionally, soley on the basis of his sovereign, good pleasure? Are people elect because they believe, or do they believe because they are elect? Related issues include the extent or intensity of human depravity; the freedom or, conversely, the bondage of the human will; whether or not Scripture teaches prevenient grace; the question of divine justice in the damnation of those who do not believe; and the way in which God's electing purpose serves to glorify his mercy and grace. Regardless of how one interprets the relevant texts, all agree that salvation is entirely of grace and not based on the alleged good works of those who are chosen. At its heart, divine election is the assurance that whatever transpires in the course of redemptive history, God will, in the end, have a people for himself, for his everlasting glory and praise.

God's Purposes for Israel

The role of ethnic Israel and its relationship to the Gentile world constitutes a crucial theme in Romans and in God's purposes in history. The gospel itself is the power of God for salvation "to the Jew first and also to the Greek" (1:16 ESV). Not only is salvation equally available to both Jew and Gentile, but together they will face judgment if they do not obey the gospel (2:9–10). Paul devotes considerable space to answer the question "What advantage is there in being a Jew?" (3:1). Of one thing he is quite certain: neither Jew nor Gentile can be justified by works; both must be reconciled to God by faith alone. What is God's purpose for ethnic Israel in the future? Has he ceased altogether his saving work among the physical descendants of Abraham? Paul devotes an entire chapter (Rom. 11) to answering this question, and the way in which believing

Jews relate to believing Gentiles in the local church is a pressing issue for the apostle and thus must be also for us (see 14:1–15:12).

The Christian's Relationship to Human Government

The relationship to government of both the individual Christian and the corporate body of Christ has never been so much a pressing and relevant issue as it is in our day. But that is not to say it was a minor point when Paul wrote Romans. Chapter 13 clearly asserts that governmental authority has been established by God and that Christians are to "be subject" to it (13:1). How extensive is this authority? Are there exceptions to the believer's responsibility to honor and obey the laws of the land? What happens when the government refuses to fulfill the purpose for which God has placed it in power? These and similar questions are addressed in Rom. 13 and call for considerable reflection.

Textual Integrity

There is little dispute about the integrity of the original text of Romans aside from an ongoing debate over the place of the doxology in 16:25–27. Some Greek manuscripts of Romans omit these three verses altogether, while others place the doxology at the close of either chapter 14 or chapter 15. After careful consideration, most scholars concur that all sixteen chapters of Romans as found in our English versions are an accurate preservation of the inspired original.

Genre

An essential part of exegesis is determining the genre—the type or kind—of literature one is studying. Most scholars acknowledge the presence of at least four basic genres of literature in the New Testament: (1) The *Gospels* are composed of individual units of narrative or teaching. Some would argue that the *parables* are a separate genre within the Gospels that have their own unique characteristics and are thus governed by special rules of interpretation. (2) The book of Acts is composed of shorter *historical narratives*, interspersed within which are a variety of *speeches*. (3) The *epistles*, of which Romans is one, are typically constructed by means of interconnected paragraphs that contain both theological argumentation and ethical exhortation. (4) The book of Revelation is often categorized as *apocalyptic*, in which we find a series of visions that together provide a holistic narrative. On occasion, one genre of literature will appear within another, such as the presence of apocalyptic elements from 2 Thessalonians 2 and 2 Peter 3 embedded within those two epistles.

We should also take note of what some believe is the distinction between *letters* and *epistles*. Letters, so some argue, were written to deal with problems unique to a particular local church and were not intended to be refined literary compositions. Epistles, on the other hand, were literary works written for the benefit of a wider public. Thomas Schreiner suggests that this distinction can be taken too far. Whereas Paul's writings were indeed *occasional* (i.e., they were "occasioned" by some special circumstance in the life of either the author or the addressees), they were "not merely private individual letters."

> Paul wrote them as an apostle, and he expected them to be read in and obeyed by the Christian community (1 Cor. 14:37; 1 Thess. 5:27; 2 Thess. 3:14). Indeed, even though Colossians addressed a specific situation, Paul thought its message would be helpful to the Laodiceans (Col. 4:16). . . . Furthermore, at times Paul clearly said that his words were in fact the very word of God (1 Cor. 14:37–38; see Gal. 1:8). He did not conceive of his letters as mere human advice (see 1 Thess. 2:13). Thus, the letters had a normative and authoritative status from the beginning (which is perhaps why they were preserved), and letters written to particular communities could apply to other churches as well.[21]

The Structure and Literary Features of Romans

Typical of epistles such as Romans are literary features such as introductory formulas (Rom. 1:13; Phil. 1:12; 1 Cor. 1:10; 2 Thess. 2:1), paraenesis or exhortations (Rom. 12:1–15:13; Gal. 5:13–6:10; Eph. 4:1–6:20; Col. 3:1–4:6), and hymns or confessional statements (Eph. 5:14; Phil. 2:6–11; Col. 1:15–20; 1 Tim. 3:16). One especially notable feature in Romans is the *diatribe*, in which Paul anticipates from a hypothetical dialogue partner an objection or question in response to his argument, which he in turn answers. We see this clearly in 2:4; 2:25–3:4; 5:20–6:1; 9:19–20.

The structure of Romans can be seen from this broad outline of the book.

I. Epistolary introduction (1:1–17)
  A. Paul and the principles of the gospel (1:1–7)
   1. The messenger of the gospel (1:1)
   2. The message of the gospel (1:2–4)
   3. The motivation of the gospel (1:5–7)

21. Schreiner, *Interpreting the Pauline Epistles*, 25.

B. Paul and the people of Rome (1:8–15)
   1. The apostle praying (1:8–10)
   2. The apostle planning (1:11–15)
C. Paul and the power of the gospel (1:16–17)

II. The way of salvation (1:18–5:21)
A. Human depravity: the reality of universal sin (1:18–3:20)
   1. The idolatry of the Gentiles and God's judgment on them (1:18–32)
   2. The hypocrisy of the Jews and God's judgment on them (2:1–3:8)
   3. The universality of sin and condemnation (3:9–20)
B. Divine deliverance: the doctrine of justification (3:21–5:11)
   1. Justification by faith: its provision (3:21–31)
   2. Justification by faith: its proof (4:1–25)
   3. Justification by faith: its product (5:1–11)
C. Adam, Christ, and the reversal of the fall (5:12–21)

III. The way of sanctification (6:1–8:39)
A. Freedom from bondage to sin (6:1–23)
   1. Slaves of sin (6:1–14)
   2. Slaves of righteousness (6:15–23)
B. Freedom from bondage to the law (7:1–25)
   1. Severed from the law (7:1–12)
   2. Struggle with sin (7:13–25)
C. Freedom from bondage to the flesh (8:1–30)
   1. Life in the Spirit (8:1–11)
   2. The blessings of sonship (8:12–17)
   3. Groaning for glory (8:18–27)
   4. The divine design for salvation (8:28–30)
D. A celebration of security (8:31–39)
   1. God as sovereign protector (8:31)
   2. God as gracious provider (8:32)
   3. God as spiritual protagonist (8:33–34)
   4. God as powerful preserver (8:35–39)

IV. God's sovereign, saving purpose for Israel and the Gentiles (9:1–11:36)
A. Israel's privileges and Paul's pain (9:1–5)

B. God's electing purpose (9:6–29)

   1. God's purpose (9:6–13)

   2. Humanity's protest (9:14–23)

   3. God's people (9:24–29)

C. Divergent approaches to the law and righteousness (9:30–10:13)

D. The necessity of gospel proclamation (10:14–15)

E. The neglect of gospel privileges (10:16–21)

F. Israel's future (11:1–36)

   1. The principle of the remnant (11:1–10)

   2. The pattern of the restoration (11:11–32)

   3. A concluding doxology (11:33–36)

V. God's principles for living (12:1–15:13)

A. The Christian and life (12:1–21)

   1. Our renewal (12:1–2)

   2. Our responsibilities (12:3–8)

   3. Our relationships (12:9–21)

B. The Christian and law (13:1–14)

   1. Obeying the law of the land (13:1–7)

   2. Obeying the law of the Lord (13:8–14)

C. The Christian and liberty (14:1–23)

   1. Paul's counsel to the weak (14:1–12)

   2. Paul's counsel to the strong (14:13–23)

D. Jew and Gentile in the body of Christ (15:1–13)

   1. The weak and the strong: welcoming one another (15:1–7)

   2. The Jew and the Gentile: together in worship (15:8–13)

VI. God's providence over Paul's life (15:14–16:27)

A. Paul's power in the Spirit (15:14–21)

   1. His confidence in his addressees' character (15:14)

   2. His purpose in penning Romans (15:15–16)

   3. His basis for boasting (15:17–19)

   4. His policy for preaching (15:20–21)

B. Paul's plans for travel (15:22–33)

   1. The plans of Paul under God's providence (15:22–29)

   2. The power of prayer in God's providence (15:30–33)

C. Paul's personal greetings (16:1–24)

    1. A commendation of Phoebe (16:1–2)

    2. Greetings to his friends (16:3–16)

    3. A final warning (16:17–20)

    4. Greetings from his companions (16:21–24)

D. A concluding doxology (16:25–27)

Recommended Resources

Cottrell, Jack. *Romans*. 2 vols. College Press NIV Commentary. Joplin, MO: College Press, 1996.

Cranfield, C. E. B. *A Critical and Exegetical Commentary on the Epistle to the Romans*. 2 vols. International Critical Commentary. Edinburgh: T&T Clark, 1975–79.

Fee, Gordon D. *God's Empowering Presence: The Holy Spirit in the Letters of Paul*. Peabody, MA: Hendrickson, 1994.

Fitzmyer, Joseph A. *Romans: A New Translation with Introduction and Commentary*. Anchor Bible 33. New York: Doubleday, 1993.

Keener, Craig S. *Romans: A New Covenant Commentary*. New Covenant Commentary Series 6. Eugene, OR: Cascade Books, 2009.

Moo, Douglas J. *The Epistle to the Romans*. New International Commentary on the New Testament. Grand Rapids: Eerdmans, 1996.

Murray, John. *The Epistle to the Romans*. New International Commentary on the New Testament. Grand Rapids: Eerdmans, 1971.

Schreiner, Thomas R. *Romans*. 2nd ed. Baker Exegetical Commentary on the New Testament. Grand Rapids: Baker Academic, 2018.

Stott, John R. W. *Romans: God's Good News for the World*. Downers Grove, IL: InterVarsity, 1994.

Thielman, Frank. *Romans*. Zondervan Exegetical Commentary on the New Testament 6. Grand Rapids: Zondervan, 2018.

Witherington, Ben, III. *Paul's Letter to the Romans: A Socio-rhetorical Commentary*. Grand Rapids: Eerdmans, 2004.

Wright, N. T. "The Letter to the Romans." In vol. 10 of *The New Interpreter's Bible*, edited by Leander E. Keck, 395–770. Nashville: Abingdon, 2002.

Paul and the People of Rome

Paul and the Principles of the Gospel (1:1–7)

The unusually lengthy introduction to this epistle is due to the fact that Paul did not found the church in Rome and has never visited it. In order to establish his credentials, he points solely to the fact that he is a **servant** of Christ, a term that "expresses the total belongingness, total allegiance, correlative to the absolute ownership and authority denoted by *kurios* used of Christ."[1] As such, he was **set apart** or consecrated to proclaim the **gospel of God**. The term translated as **gospel** (*euangelion*), or good news, is found seventy-six times in the New Testament, sixty of which are in Paul's letters. Paul's high Christology is seen in his description of Jesus Christ as "Lord," which translates the Hebrew *YHWH* more than six thousand times in the Septuagint (the Greek translation of the Hebrew Old Testament). To speak of Jesus as Lord is to identify him with YHWH, God of Israel, now incarnate in the person of Christ.

Apostleship was not a result of self-promotion; it was the fruit of a divine call (cf. Gal. 1:15–17), which is a primary theme in this opening paragraph. Paul wants to contrast the divine calling by which he became an apostle with human self-appointment by which others claim authority. Not only is Paul an apostle by divine calling, but also the Christians in Rome, loved by God, are **called** to belong to Christ (v. 6) and **called** to be saints (v. 7; for similar assertions,

---

1. Cranfield, *Romans*, 1:50–51. The Greek word *doulos*, here translated as "servant" and elsewhere as "slave," appears no fewer than 130 times in the New Testament. For Paul, freedom is not the opportunity or power to do whatever one wishes, nor the liberty to choose one course of action over another. Freedom for the slave of Jesus Christ is the joy of aligning our will with that of Christ, obeying Christ, doing whatever Christ commands.

see Rom. 14:7–8; 1 Cor. 3:23; 6:19–20; 7:23; 2 Cor. 10:7; Gal. 3:29). This truth applies to **all** the people in Rome to whom the letter is written. We must also take note of the fundamental unity between the two Testaments. Whereas the gospel may well be good news, it is by no means new news, having been **promised beforehand** through the Old Testament prophets (cf. John 5:39–47; Luke 24:25–27, 44–47; Acts 8:32–35).

As for the content or substance of the gospel, it is **regarding** God's **Son**, content that is then unpacked in verses 3–4. There are three primary competing views of this passage, one of the more theologically significant in the book. One view takes verse 3 as descriptive of Christ's humanity or his human nature, whereas verse 4 describes his deity or his divine nature. On this reading, the contrast is between the two components of Christ's person. He is one person with two natures: one human (hence **flesh**, *sarka* [ESV]) and one divine (hence **spirit** [not a reference to the Holy Spirit]). According to yet another view, the contrast between "flesh" and "spirit" is between the outward and the inward. Externally, Jesus may be said to have descended from the seed of David; internally, he was perfected in the spirit (or by the Spirit), which fitted him to be the Son of God with power.

The most likely view contends that the focus of the contrast between verse 3 and verse 4 is not between his human nature and his divine nature but rather between his humiliation and his exaltation. In other words, the contrast is not between two different components in Christ's person but between two successive stages or phases in Christ's experience (cf. Phil. 2:5–11). According to this view, *sarka* refers not so much to the body (far less to the sinful nature) as to the present, natural, earthly realm in which we live. The flesh/spirit contrast is historical; it is a contrast between this present, fallen, earthly, temporal world in which we live and the future, redeemed, heavenly, eternal world that is yet to come.

If true, the phrase "according to the *sarka*" refers not so much to Christ's human nature as to the historical realm/environment with which humanity is necessarily associated. The eternal Son of God entered the sphere of the flesh—that is, this present, fallen, evil age. But as verse 4 goes on to point out, by virtue of his resurrection he has entered the sphere of the spirit, the new age, the heavenly realm where he now lives and reigns.

There is probably little difference between **appointed** (NIV) and **declared** (ESV) (translating the Greek verb *horizō*, from which we get the English term "horizon"). Some insist that it means that the resurrection declares or makes public that Jesus is the Son of God. But in its seven other occurrences in the New Testament it means "determine, appoint, fix as if to mark out a boundary" (Luke 22:22; Acts 2:23; 10:42; 11:29; 17:26, 31; Heb. 4:7). In some sense, then, Christ Jesus was **appointed** Son of God by virtue of his resurrection from the dead.

This would appear to create a theological problem, for how can the eternally preexistent Son be **appointed** Son of God? But Paul says that Jesus was appointed not Son of God but Son of God **in power**.[2] Paul is describing an event in history whereby Jesus was instated in a position of sovereignty and invested with power (cf. Acts 13:33; Phil. 2:9–11). At the resurrection and exaltation Jesus began a new phase of divine sonship. While on earth, Jesus was certainly the Son of God. But he was not the Son-of-God-in-power. Paul is not saying that Jesus became the Son at the time of the resurrection (the heresy of adoptionism). The change is not in the divine nature or in the Son's relationship to the Father, but in Christ's role in redemptive history. After all, it is the **Son** who is **appointed** Son. "The tautologous nature of this statement," Douglas Moo explains, "reveals that being appointed Son has to do not with a change of essence—as if a person or human messiah becomes the Son of God for the first time—but with a change in status or function."[3] The transition from verse 3 to verse 4, therefore, "is not a transition from a human messiah to a divine Son of God (adoptionism) but from the Son as Messiah to the Son as both Messiah *and* powerful, reigning Lord."[4] It is a transition from the Son of God in weakness and frailty and submission and humiliation to the Son of God in power and strength and authority and exaltation.

This is confirmed by the contrasting parallel between **according to the Spirit of holiness** (v. 4 ESV) and **according to the flesh** (v. 3 ESV). As noted, these do not refer to the divine and human natures of Christ, respectively. Rather, as Stephen Wellum points out, "a better suggestion . . . accounts for the framework established by the biblical storyline that governs Paul's identification of Christ: *flesh* and *spirit* mark a contrast between the *old* and *new* eras of redemptive history. The old era is characterized by the covenant mediation of Adam and dominated by sin, death, and the *flesh*; the new era is characterized by the covenant mediation of Christ, the last Adam, and brings forth the blessings of salvation, life, and the *Spirit*."[5] Thus we should understand Paul's contrast as focusing not on the two natures of Christ, the human and divine, "but on the two states of Christ, his *humiliation* and *exaltation*."[6]

The phrase **the obedience of faith** (v. 5 ESV) may mean one of three things, depending on how one interprets the genitive "of faith." If it is an objective genitive, the translation would be "obedience directed toward, or in, [the] faith,"

---

2. With the majority of commentators, I understand "in power" to be modifying "the Son of God." Thus we should read it as saying that he was appointed "Son-of-God-in-power" instead of appointed "with power to be the Son of God."

3. Moo, *Romans*, 48.

4. Moo, *Romans*, 49.

5. Wellum, *God the Son Incarnate*, 173.

6. Wellum, *God the Son Incarnate*, 173.

in which case "faith" would refer to a body of doctrine or the message of the gospel. If it is a subjective genitive, the translation would be "obedience that comes from [or is produced by] faith" (NIV; cf. Rom. 15:18). If it is an appositional or epexegetical genitive, the translation would be "the obedience which is faith." Belief in the gospel can be described as an act of obedience (see Rom. 10:16). I prefer option two. That faith in the gospel to which Paul calls us is the kind or quality that obeys.

However, the salvation of the Gentiles was not the ultimate purpose of Paul's mission. He sought to bring them to the obedience of faith **for the sake of his** [Jesus's] **name** (v. 5b ESV). Fundamental to Paul's endeavors were honor and praise for the glory of Christ's name. Says John Stott, "The highest of missionary motives is neither obedience to the Great Commission (important as that is), nor love for sinners who are alienated and perishing (strong as that incentive is, especially when we contemplate the wrath of God, verse 18), but rather zeal— burning and passionate zeal—for the glory of Jesus Christ."[7]

Paul and the People of Rome (1:8–15)

As is true of his relationship with other believers (see Eph. 1:15–17; 3:14–19; Phil. 1:3–5; Col. 1:3–14; 1 Thess. 1:2–3; 2 Thess. 1:3–4), Paul prays incessantly for the Christians in Rome, included in which is his gratitude for the way that news of their devotion to Christ has spread throughout the inhabited Roman Empire. It is **my** spirit, says Paul, in which he serves, thus likely not referring to the Holy Spirit. That being said, Paul would attribute all his efforts in ministry and prayer to the presence and power of the Holy Spirit in him. Although the words **in preaching** (v. 9) are not found in the original text, Paul is clearly thinking of his faithful proclamation of the good news.

As for his desire to visit Rome (v. 10), Paul doesn't presume to know whether it was God's will for him to do so. Clearly, God's will is not always something that can be ascertained. Regardless of what might ultimately prove to be God's purpose for him, Paul continues to pray and make every effort to get to Rome.

In verses 11–14 Paul gives four reasons why he hopes finally to be allowed by God to come to Rome. The first is his desire to **impart** to them **some spiritual gift** (v. 11). The Greek word translated as **gift** is *charisma*, which here could refer to one of four things: (1) God's gracious gift of eternal life in Jesus Christ (Rom. 6:23), (2) God's gracious gifts to Israel (Rom. 11:29), (3) the Holy Spirit–inspired ability to minister beyond one's natural talents (Rom. 12:6), or (4) some blessing or benefit of a spiritual nature to be bestowed on the Christians at Rome by

7. Stott, *Romans*, 53.

Charismatic Gifts

Paul's expressed desire to impart some "spiritual gift" to the Roman Christians (Rom. 1:11) finds an echo in his reference to a "gift" (*charismatos*) that was "given" (i.e., imparted) to Timothy through the laying on of hands (1 Tim. 4:14). Similar language is found in 2 Tim. 1:6. In her excellent book *Charismatic Christianity* (subtitled *Introducing Its Theology through the Gifts of the Spirit*), Helen Collins demonstrates how spiritual gifts highlight certain assumptions of Pentecostal and charismatic believers about the relationship between God and the world that are then "enacted in their spirituality."[a] These assumptions are "expectancy [enacted and nurtured through the spiritual gift of prophecy], enchantment [as expressed in the gift of miracles], encounter [best seen in the gift of healing], expression [the gifts of utterance of wisdom and knowledge], equality [speaking in tongues], empowerment [particularly associated with the gift of faith], and enjoyment [through what Collins refers to as "the spiritual gift of encouraging exhortation" as found in Rom. 12:8]."[b]

a. Collins, *Charismatic Christianity*, 11.
b. Collins, *Charismatic Christianity*, 11.

God through Paul, which may include apostolic insight into the unity of Jew and Gentile in Christ. Given the use of *charisma* in Rom. 12:6 to refer to what we know as "spiritual gifts" (cf. 1 Cor. 12:7–11), as well as Paul's reference to the impartation of such gifts through the laying on of hands (1 Tim. 4:14; 2 Tim. 1:6), I'm inclined to endorse the third view noted above.

The second reason (v. 12) is to share in mutual encouragement. When Christians see a vibrant and strong faith in their fellow believers, they are encouraged and reminded that God can be trusted in their lives as well. That Paul would happily receive whatever encouragement the Roman Christians might provide is evidence of his humility. Though unknown and inexperienced, these believers have much to offer the apostle, and he is delighted to benefit from it.

His third reason for wanting to visit Rome is that he might **reap some harvest among** the believers there (v. 13 ESV). This is likely a reference to the mutual encouragement just noted in verse 12.

Paul's fourth reason for wanting to make his way to Rome is to fulfill his obligation to make known the gospel **both to Greeks and to barbarians, both to the wise and to the foolish** (v. 14 ESV). By **Greeks** Paul means those who both speak Greek and have adopted its culture, as over against "barbarians." **The wise and . . . the foolish** is simply another way of making the same distinction.

Some see a contradiction between Paul's assertion in verse 15 concerning his eagerness to preach the gospel in Rome and his assertion in 15:20–21 that he desires not to preach where Christ has already been named. However, "Paul undoubtedly wanted to engage in evangelism while in Rome, for even if a church had been planted, he was eager to use every opportunity for winning new converts."[8] Also, it should be noted that for Paul, preaching the gospel entailed more than winning people to Jesus. It also involved strengthening and edifying those who had already come to faith—that is, bringing them into **the obedience that comes from faith** (1:5; 16:26; cf. Phil. 1:27).

Paul and the Power of the Gospel (1:16–17)

The structure of Paul's argument here is important. There are three subordinate clauses that support and/or illuminate the one preceding it. (1) Paul is eager to preach in Rome (v. 15) *because* (*gar*) he is not ashamed of the gospel (v. 16a). And (2) Paul is not ashamed of the gospel (v. 16a) *because* (*gar*) it is in the gospel that one finds God's power for salvation (v. 16b; see also 1 Cor. 2:4–5; 4:19–20; 1 Thess. 1:5; also 2 Cor. 4:7; 6:7; 12:9; Eph. 3:7; and esp. 1 Cor. 1:18). Finally, (3) the gospel has power for salvation (v. 16b) *because* (*gar*) it manifests the righteousness of God (v. 17).

Paul distances himself from the many reasons why people feel **ashamed of the gospel**: fear of losing face, fear of losing friends, fear of being labeled a fanatic, fear of taunting and scorn, fear of losing influence (cf. 2 Tim. 1:8, 16). His pride and confidence in the gospel came from his having seen it do what neither education nor religious zeal nor fame nor Roman military might nor wealth nor ethnic heritage nor anything else can do. The power resident in the gospel, and the gospel alone, can save the lost, give hope to the hopeless, freedom to slaves, guidance to the confused, purity to the polluted, and purpose to those convinced that life has no value.

The power of God for salvation is not unconditionally and universally operative. It must be received, it must be believed, it must be appropriated by the divinely appointed instrument: faith. But what does Paul mean when he says, **to the Jew first** (ESV)? (1) He may be referring to his missionary policy of taking the gospel initially to the synagogues as a starting point for reaching an entire community (cf. Acts 13:46). (2) He also may be alluding to the historical priority of God's revelation to and covenant with Israel. It was through God's

8. Schreiner, *Romans*, 59.

sovereign choice of Abraham and his descendants that the Gentile world would ultimately be blessed. (3) There is a Jewish priority over Gentiles insofar as the former were **entrusted with the oracles of God** (Rom. 3:1–2 ESV; cf. 9:4). (4) The Jews have a priority over the Gentiles insofar as the Messiah, Jesus, came first as a Jew to the Jews (9:5). (5) Paul may also have in mind Jesus's statement to the Samaritan woman: "Salvation is from the Jews" (John 4:22). That is to say, all salvation is salvation through God's covenant with Abraham. But we should also note the ways in which there is *no* Jewish priority. (1) They do not have priority in righteousness. As Paul will say later in the letter, "For there is no distinction: for all have sinned and fall short of the glory of God" (3:22–23 ESV). (2) Neither do they have any priority in how they are saved. Jewish people are saved in precisely the same way Gentile people saved: through faith in Jesus (see 3:29–30; 10:12–13). (3) Neither do they have priority when it comes to participation in the blessings of God's covenant (see Gal. 3:16, 29; Eph. 2:12–13, 19; 3:4–6; 1 Pet. 2:9–10). Gentiles now share equally with Jewish believers in all the covenant blessings and promises.

There is considerable disagreement about what Paul means by **the righteousness of God** (Rom. 1:17). Paul may be referring to an attribute of God, thus the righteousness that characterizes God. This righteousness may be either God's justice (cf. 3:5, 25–26), according to which he always does what is right, or God's faithfulness, according to which he fulfills his covenant promises to his people. Others believe that Paul is referring to a status or position that God bestows on those who believe. It is therefore a righteousness that comes from God. This righteousness is purely forensic or legal. It is a matter of our judicial standing before God, not our internal or moral transformation.

Finally, and more recently, some argue that **the righteousness of God** refers to an activity of God. The righteousness of God is God's action of intervening on behalf of his people to save and deliver them. This idea has strong support from the Old Testament (see Isa. 46:13; 50:5–8; Mic. 7:9). Perhaps all three ideas are involved. God is just and right when he takes saving action to provide a righteous standing for us in his presence. Moo appeals to the imagery of the law court to make the point: "To use the imagery of the law court, from which righteousness language is derived, we can picture God's righteousness as the act or decision by which the judge declares innocent a defendant: an activity of the judge, but an activity that is a declaration of status—an act that results in, and indeed includes within it, a gift."[9]

There is an almost endless list of suggestions as to the meaning of the phrase **by faith from first to last** (NIV) or **from faith for faith** (ESV), the most plausible

9. Moo, *Romans*, 75.

being that this is simply Paul's way of emphasizing that faith, and nothing but faith, from beginning to end, can put us in right relationship with God. Thomas Schreiner explains,

> Most interpretations include the idea of a progression from one kind of faith to another: from the faith of the Old Testament to the faith of the New Testament; from the faith of the law to the faith of the gospel; from the faith of the preachers to the faith of the hearers; from the faith of the present to the faith of the future; from the faith of words we hear now to the faith that we will possess what the words promise; from the faithfulness of God to the faith of human beings; from the faithfulness of Christ to the faith of human beings; from smaller to greater faith; from faith as the ground to faith as the goal.[10]

The list goes on ad infinitum. As for Paul's citation of Hab. 2:4 at the end of verse 17, he means either that the righteous *shall live by faith* or that those who are *righteous by faith* shall live.

Sin and Idolatry among the Gentiles (1:18–32)

Some believe that Rom. 1:18–3:20 is an interruption in Paul's argument, as 3:21 clearly picks up on the "righteousness of God" in 1:17. The purpose of this section is to articulate the necessity for the gospel of grace. The grace of God in Christ, received by faith, can be understood and appreciated only against the dark backdrop of human sin and depravity. Thus, in 1:18–32 Paul paints the grim picture of Gentile corruption, while 2:1–3:8 indicts the Jew. All of humanity, therefore, stands guilty before God (see 3:9).

The principal reason for seeing Gentiles in 1:18–32 is that the knowledge of God rejected by those depicted in these verses comes exclusively through natural revelation—that is, that which God has revealed of himself in creation or the natural order of things. The Jews, on the other hand, are accountable to God primarily on the basis of the special revelation found in the law of Moses and Holy Scripture (cf. 2:12–13, 17–29). Furthermore, this overt form of idolatry was virtually nonexistent among the Jews of Paul's day. The fact that Paul focuses on homosexuality also points to Gentiles, among whom this particular sin was far more prominent and public than it was among the Jews.

For some, the doctrine or concept of **wrath** is thought to be beneath God. Wrath, they contend, is archaic, and Paul's terminology refers to no more than an inevitable process of cause and effect in a moral universe. Divine wrath is

10. Schreiner, *Romans*, 71–72.

thereby reduced to an impersonal force operative in a moral universe, not a personal attribute or disposition in the character of God. But wrath is not the loss of self-control or the irrational and capricious outburst of anger; it is righteous antagonism toward all that is unholy and the revulsion of God's character to that which is a violation of God's will. Indeed, one may speak of divine wrath as a function of God's love for holiness and truth and justice. It is because God passionately loves purity and peace and perfection that he reacts angrily toward anything and anyone who defiles them.

God's wrath **is being revealed** (present tense). Some see this as a futuristic present, hence referring to the final judgment. Others point to the diseases and disasters of earthly life. Given the parallel with verse 17, some have argued that just as the righteousness of God is revealed in the gospel, so too is the wrath of God (i.e., the gospel is the proclamation of both grace and judgment, mercy and wrath). More likely, though, God's wrath is revealed in the deliberate turning over of idolatrous humanity to its chosen way of sin and unrighteousness, described in graphic detail in verses 24–32.

The problem isn't that people don't possess or understand the truth, but rather that they **suppress** it by their unrighteous conduct. The **truth** that they **suppress** is that which God has plainly revealed about himself to all (vv. 19–23). This revelation is both from God and about God. The phrase **plain to them** is better rendered either as "plain in them" or "plain among them," probably the latter; that is, God has made himself known among people (and thus, in a manner of speaking, to them) in his works of creation and providence.

Observe Paul's paradoxical language: in verse 20 he refers to God's **invisible** attributes (cf. 1 Tim. 1:17) as **clearly seen**—an apparent oxymoron. But Paul's point is that the invisible is made visible via creation or nature. Wisdom, power, eternity, and goodness, for example, are not in themselves visible, but their reality is undeniably affirmed and apprehended by the effects that they produce in nature.

These truths about God are made known **in the things that have been made** (v. 20 ESV). From the initial moment of creation itself, God has left the indelible mark of his fingerprints all across the vast face of the universe (see Ps. 19), eliminating all excuse for unbelief. No one anywhere, at any time, can justify their unbelief and idolatry by appealing to ignorance of God's existence. The problem is not a paucity of evidence. The problem is the innate, natural, moral antipathy of humankind to God.

Although they knew God (v. 21a), says Paul, indicating that all people know God. There is a distinction, of course, between a cognitive apprehension of God—that is, knowing that there is a God and that he is worthy of obedience, worship, gratitude—and a saving or redemptive knowledge of God. All people experience the former, whereas only the redeemed experience the latter. Paul does not say that they began in darkness and futility and are slowly but surely groping their way toward the light. Rather, they began with the clear, inescapable light of the knowledge of God and regressed into darkness.

The term **foolish** (v. 21) refers not to intellectual acuity but to moral disposition. The problem with the unsaved person isn't that she can't think with her mind. The problem is that she refuses to believe with her heart. The unsaved person is a fool not because she is of questionable intelligence but because of her immoral refusal to acknowledge and bow to what she knows is true. What Paul has in mind involves a distortion or deliberate mutation when one substitutes something artificial or counterfeit for that which is genuine. Clearly, then, when a person rejects God, she does not cease to be religious. Indeed, she becomes religious in order to reject God. She substitutes for God a deity of her own making, often herself.

Three times Paul declares that **God gave them over** (vv. 24, 26, 28). There is a permissive element involved, as God withdraws divine restraint on human hearts and permits them to have their way. God relinquishes his hold over them and ceases to curb their willful determination to sin. However, God doesn't simply let them go, but also positively consigns them to suffer the consequences of their sin. It is not merely divine relinquishment but also divine retribution as he hands them over to an ever-increasing cycle of sin.

Paul does not say that God himself is the cause of their impurity or idolatry. Rather, God gives them over *to* degrading passions. The act of divine relinquishment presupposes the existence of these sins. God gives them over to what they have already chosen for themselves. That to which God gives them over is not simply their sin but a deeper and more intense cultivation of their sin. In the absence of divine restraint (common grace), sin intensifies and aggravates itself. When God abandons someone to his sin, that sin accelerates.

It would seem, then, that it is idolatry that leads to immorality. People first abandon God, and then God abandons them into the depths of every conceivable vice. Sexual perversion, says Paul, is the result of religious rebellion. This is also seen in the words that Paul employs. Those who **exchanged** (v. 23) God's glory and **exchanged** (v. 25) his truth **exchanged** (v. 26) natural sexual relations for what is unnatural. Simply put, sexual immorality is the consequence of human idolatry. Paul then focuses on homosexual relations because they best illustrate what is **unnatural** (v. 26).

Paul makes it clear in verses 18–25 that once a person denies and turns from God and his moral law, he is subject to no one or nothing other than his own impulses. Whatever he feels is right, whatever brings personal satisfaction is his to pursue because he refuses to acknowledge God's sovereign right to establish morals of right and wrong. Thus, the exchange of God for idols leads to an exchange of heterosexual relations for homosexual relations. A dishonoring of God leads to a dishonoring of oneself.

The word **impurity** (v. 24) is often used by Paul to refer to sexual sin (see 2 Cor. 12:21; Gal. 5:19; Eph. 5:3; Col. 3:5; 1 Thess. 4:7). And the word translated as **relations** in verses 26–27 was commonly used in the ancient world to indicate sexual relations.

Idolatry is clearly contrary to God's design and desire for human beings. Homosexual behavior is the best illustration of what is unnatural in the sphere of sexual conduct. It, too, is contrary to God's design and desire for human beings. In verse 26 Paul refers to women who **exchanged natural relations for those that are contrary to nature** (ESV), and we know that he has in mind same-sex relations because that is what he immediately describes in verse 27. Notice that he says that men **in the same way** (**likewise** [ESV]) gave up what is natural for what is unnatural. Thus, the sin in verse 26 is the same sin described in verse 27. The word translated as **unnatural** (**contrary to nature** [ESV]) in verse 26 is nowhere used in the Bible or in other literature of the day to refer to heterosexual sin, but only to sexual sin with those of the same gender. Neither is it that **unnatural** or **contrary to nature** means contrary to the prevailing customs or social norms of that day and age. Paul is not talking about what may be contrary to our preferences or our feelings or desires or inclinations. He is talking about what is contrary to God's original design in creation.

There is nothing in the passage that would lead us to believe that by **natural** (*physikēn*) Paul means "my" personal, individual nature or inclinations, whatever they may be. "Nature," here, does not mean what seems or feels natural *to me*. It means the way God intended things to be by virtue of creation. Thus, to act against nature or in an unnatural way is to violate the order that God established for human behavior in general, not for our behavior in particular. **Contrary to nature** could also be a reference to the obvious physiological complementarity of male and female and their ability to reproduce in having children, whereas male-to-male and female-to-female sexual contact produces nothing. Just as God's existence and nature are clearly seen in the creation, so also the natural relation of male to female is seen in the way God has constructed the human body.

That Paul has in view a deviation from God's original creative design is evident from the words he uses for "women" and "men." These aren't his normal terms (typically he uses *gynē* for "woman" and *anēr* for "man"). But here he uses *thēlys* for "woman" and *arsēn* for "man." These are the words used in the Septuagint of Gen. 1:27, where it says that God created "male and female." This is confirmed in Matt. 19:4 and Mark 10:6, where Jesus uses these same two terms in quoting from Gen. 1:27. Paul is obviously drawing specific attention to the creation account in Genesis to emphasize the sexual distinction between male and female and that same-sex intimacy is contrary to God's original creative design.

That the word **unnatural** refers to same-sex relations is also confirmed by the fact that in verse 27 Paul explicitly says that this entails men giving up natural relations with women in order that they might engage in sexual relations with other men. This is confirmed yet again when Paul says in verse 27 that men who **abandon natural relations with women** are **inflamed with lust for one another**. One more confirmation that this is the meaning of **unnatural** is that Paul describes such behavior as **shameful acts** (v. 27).

Some who believe that homosexuality is entirely good and permissible argue that Paul is describing what happens when a person who is heterosexual commits homosexual acts. That is, the person who is "naturally" heterosexual acts "contrary to nature" when he or she engages in homosexual activity. But everything just noted argues against this view. Furthermore, all Jewish literature of the day, together with the entire Old Testament, speaks unanimously and with one voice that homosexual conduct is always wrong and sinful, regardless of who engages in it or for whatever reason. Paul says that what is **shameful** is men committing sexual acts **with other men**. He nowhere says that these are heterosexual men committing homosexual acts (see also 1 Cor. 6:9–11; 1 Tim. 1:8–10).

Some contend that Paul is speaking of "pederasty," a word that refers to adult men having sexual relations with young boys. Thus, what Paul opposes is not consensual same-sex intimacy by consenting adults. However, Paul's wording in verses 26–27 is not restricted to a specific kind of homosexual act but is a general prohibition and denunciation of all homosexual activity. It is men engaging in sexual activity with men that he declares is contrary to nature and shameful. Nowhere does he mention sex between men and boys. In addition, there is a particular Greek term that refers to pederasty (*paiderastēs*), and Paul nowhere makes use of it. Furthermore, "the idea that pederasty is in view is contradicted by the reference to the homosexual acts of women in verse 26," and there is no evidence "that women regularly engaged in sexual activity with girls."[11]

Here in verse 28, God once again, for the third time, **gave them up to a debased mind to do what ought not to be done** (ESV). In this case, the sin of humanity is not restricted to sexual immorality but extends to all manner of evil deeds and wickedness, about which we read in verses 29–31. There have been numerous attempts to classify or find some intentional structure in the list of sins that Paul mentions in verses 29–31. The most that can be said is that

11. Schreiner, *Romans*, 105.

the vice list has twenty-one elements. The first set, consisting of four sins, is general in nature and points to the breadth of human wickedness. The second set has five sins listed. Humans are **full** (v. 29 ESV) of such sins. The third set has twelve items and describes not so much the sins committed but rather the people who practice them. There is economic sin (**greed**) and social disorder (**murder, strife, deceit and malice**) (v. 29), the breakdown of the family (**they disobey their parents**) (v. 30), relational sins (v. 31), sins of the mouth (gossip and slander), and so forth. **They know** that such behavior is evil and deserving of divine judgment (v. 32). But worse still, they applaud and encourage others to participate in their sinful conduct.

ROMANS 2

The Threat
of Spiritual Hypocrisy

The Principles of Judgment (2:1–16)

The key to understanding Paul's argument in 1:18–3:8 is his statements in 3:9 and 3:19. Paul is determined to demonstrate that "Jews and Gentiles alike are all under the power of sin" (3:9). The desired result of his argument is "so that every mouth may be stopped, and the whole world may be held accountable to God" (3:19 ESV). That Paul is now, in 2:1–3:8, indicting the Jew as "under the power of sin" (3:9), as he did the Gentile in 1:18–32, is evident from several factors. In his indictment of the Gentile world Paul repeatedly made use of the third-person plural: "What may be known about God is plain to them" (1:19a), "so that people [literally, "they"] are without excuse" (1:20b); "Their thinking became futile and their foolish hearts were darkened" (1:21); and so on all through the remainder of chapter 1. But when he comes to chapter 2, he shifts from the third-person plural to the second-person singular. **You . . . have no excuse, you who pass judgment** on others (v. 1), for **you are condemning yourself** (v. 2), and so on. Most believe that this is one indication that whereas Paul was describing the unbelieving, pagan Gentile world in 1:18–32, now in chapter 2 he turns his attention to the Jewish man or woman.

Paul's use of the second-person singular rather than the second-person plural is likely due to a literary device, noted in the introduction to the commentary, known as a *diatribe*. In a diatribe an author creates an imaginary opponent with whom to dialogue. The author puts questions in the mouth of a conversation partner, and on occasion will portray the individual as voicing objections to the author. That is what Paul is doing here.

There are additional reasons to believe that the apostle is now addressing Jews. They were inclined to judge Gentiles for their religious and moral perversity, so Paul now accuses them of much the same sin. The person addressed in chapter 2 is the recipient of divine kindness, forbearance, and patience (v. 4). Paul's point is that special privilege or advantage does not exempt one from judgment; but this is what many Jews mistakenly believed. Whereas Gentiles are the recipients only of general revelation as seen in creation (1:19–21), those in chapter 2 are the recipients of the special revelation contained in the law of Moses. Finally, in verse 17 Paul specifically addresses the person who calls himself or herself a **Jew**.

Paul begins his indictment of the Jewish person by stating the principles of divine judgment. In verses 1–2 he declares that judgment is universal. Jewish people are not exempt from the same judgment imposed on Gentiles simply because they are Jewish. In fact, he indicts the Jew because she judges others for the very things she herself practices. It is self-righteous hypocrisy that provokes the apostle's words. According to verse 2, this judgment that falls on the Jewish moralist no less than on the Gentile pagan is **based on truth**; that is, it accords with the facts as God sees them. It should be noted, however, that when Paul says that the Jew does **the same things** (v. 3), he does not mean that Jewish people were engaging in overt homosexuality and idolatry as the Gentiles were. He most likely has in view the vices named in 1:29–31.

Judgment is not only universal but also unavoidable (vv. 3–5). Many in the Jewish community evidently believed that their ethnicity exempted them from divine judgment (see Matt. 3:9). During the time of the Old Testament many in Israel who were not living in obedience to the covenant had developed a false sense of security based entirely on their identity as descendants of Abraham.

The criteria for divine judgment are stated in verses 6–15. Judgment, according to Paul, is **according to** each person's **works** (vv. 6–11 ESV). The opening statement in verse 6 and the concluding statement in verse 11 say much the same thing. According to verse 6, God will judge all humankind by their deeds, not by their social group, ethnicity, or educational and financial status. His judgment is and always will be **based on truth** (v. 2). Paul is likely making use of Prov. 24:12, where we read this: "If you say, 'But we knew nothing about this,' does not he who weighs the heart perceive it? Does not he who guards your life know it? Will he not repay everyone according to what they have done?" (Prov. 24:12; cf. Ps. 62:12).

We see this emphasis on judgment according to works in numerous biblical texts, such as Isa. 3:10; Jer. 17:10; Hosea 12:2; Matt. 16:27; 25:31–46; John

5:28–29; 2 Cor. 5:10; 11:15; Gal. 6:7–9; Eph. 6:8; Col. 3:24–25; 2 Tim. 4:14; 1 Pet. 1:17; Rev. 2:23; 22:12. The word in verse 11 translated as **favoritism** (**partiality** [ESV]) literally means "receiving the face." The point is that God does not take into account or treat someone on the basis of external appearance but only on the nature and character of one's deeds. The **distress** awaiting those who reject Christ (v. 9) may refer to the subjective emotional and psychological suffering caused by the **trouble** that is inflicted. This is confirmed by the reference to **peace** (v. 10) that the saved will enjoy. It is the opposite of the **distress** suffered by the lost.

These verses pose an obvious theological problem. Verses 7, 10, 13 appear to say that eternal life is the reward to those who persevere in doing good deeds. But this would prove inconsistent with the doctrine of salvation by grace. Or to put it more bluntly, those three verses appear to be in blatant contradiction with 3:20, where Paul declares that "no one will be declared righteous in God's sight by the works of the law; rather, through the law we become conscious of our sin." The consistent teaching in God's Word is that our salvation and our justification in God's sight come only by God's grace, through faith in Christ. See especially John 3:16, 18a; 6:40; 8:24; 20:31; Acts 10:43; 16:31; Rom. 3:23–24, 28; 4:4–5; 5:1; Gal. 2:16; 3:11, 22; Eph. 2:8–9; Phil. 3:7–11; 2 Tim. 1:9; Titus 3:5; 1 John 5:13.

Some say that Paul is inconsistent—that he does in fact contradict himself. But surely Paul is not so ignorant as to assert in 2:7–13 what he denies in 3:20 (and again in 3:28).

One might choose to argue that the difference between 2:13 and 3:20 is the difference between how salvation was available in the Old Testament and how it is available in the New Testament. In the old era, under the Mosaic covenant, doing the law could justify, but in the new era, under the new covenant, it no longer can. Now, faith alone justifies. There are two obvious problems with this view. First, it makes Paul's point in 2:13 totally irrelevant to his readers, since they live in the present, new-covenant, era. But worse still, Paul clearly and on several occasions insists that obedience to the Mosaic law could never justify (see esp. Gal. 3:21). Salvation in the Old Testament was never based on works of obedience to the law.

Others argue that Paul is speaking hypothetically. He is saying that only perfect obedience would gain a righteousness of which God approves, but such obedience is not practically possible. In other words, he is stating a principle that is true enough in its own right—it is theoretically true—but never practically attained. Moo opts for this view. Note his explanation: "It is a continual seeking after eternal rewards, accompanied by a persistent doing of what is good, that is the condition for a positive verdict at the judgment. Paul never denies the validity of this principle, but he goes on to show that no one meets the conditions necessary for this principle to become a reality."[1] Thus, according to Moo, 2:7 and 2:10 "set forth what is called in traditional theological (especially Lutheran) language 'the law.' Paul sets forth the biblical conditions for attaining eternal life apart from Christ. Understood this way, Paul is not speaking hypothetically. But once his doctrine of human powerlessness under sin has been developed (cf. esp. 3:9), it becomes clear that the promise can, in fact, never become operative, because the condition for its fulfillment—consistent, earnest seeking after good—can never be realized."[2]

Thus, in *principle* obedience to the law justifies one in God's sight (2:7, 10, 13), but in *practice* no one can obey the law (3:10–18). Therefore, no one will be justified through the law (3:20).

A more likely suggestion is that Paul is addressing two different situations. In 3:20 he has in mind one's initial entrance into salvation, that inaugural event when God declares one righteous in his sight through faith in Christ. In 2:13 (on the basis of 2:7, 10), on the other hand, he refers to the final judgment, when one's works or good deeds, being the evidence or fruit of saving faith, will vindicate or reveal the individual to be in righteous standing before God. According to this view, Paul is advocating a judgment based on works. Appeal is made to similar texts in 1 Cor. 6:9–10; Gal. 5:21; 6:8; Eph. 5:5–6. The point is that good works secure entrance into eternal life insofar as they are the product of a true saving faith. A mere profession of faith in Christ without perseverance in good deeds will not avail on the day of judgment. Thus, those who fail to produce works will face judgment, while those who, by the power of the Spirit, live in accordance with God's principles of righteousness will experience eternal life.

In sum, judgment is based on works, not because works merit salvation, but because works manifest faith. Or, as has often been said, "Faith alone justifies, but not the faith which is alone." Earlier, in 1:5, Paul spoke of "the obedience of faith" (ESV), and the likelihood is that he has the same notion in mind here. This is why Paul is not inconsistent in saying that **to those who by patience in well-doing seek for glory and honor and immortality, he will give eternal life** (2:7 ESV). To seek after the **glory** of God is to live by his grace and the power of the Holy Spirit in such a way that our minds are transformed to understand it, our wills are changed to prefer it, and our hearts are made fit to feel it and prize it above all else. But first and foremost, it means that we long to see it displayed in its fullness so that God might be adored and enjoyed forever.

1. Moo, *Romans*, 142.
2. Moo, *Romans*, 142.

Thus, to say that works are necessary for salvation, on the one hand, and that one cannot be saved on the basis of works, on the other, is not contradictory. Judgment is based on works, not because works earn salvation, but because works express faith. This is why it is possible for us to be saved by grace, through faith, not by good works, and yet for us to be judged according to our deeds in the final judgment. It is by means of **persistence in doing good** (v. 7), or endurance in good works, that one inherits eternal life. The present tense of **seek** and the word **persistence** (**patience** [ESV]) emphasize a steady, substantial, and consistent way of life that characterizes those who are truly born again.

Paul also declares that judgment is based on what a person knows (vv. 11–15). His purpose here is to demonstrate to the Jews that mere possession of the law does not, in and of itself, bring salvation and thus does not, in and of itself, constitute an advantage over the Gentiles.

In verse 12 Paul differentiates between two groups of people. All such people have sinned, says Paul, but some do so **apart from the law** while others do so **under the law**. These two phrases likely refer, respectively, to Gentiles and Jews. Gentiles will be judged for their sins, but not on the basis of having violated the law of Moses. They will **perish**, but **apart from the law**, which I take to mean that their disobedience to the law of Moses will not be the grounds for their punishment. God does not hold people accountable for their failure to obey a moral law about which they know nothing. Judgment is always based on a person's response to the knowledge that they possess. Jewish people, on the other hand, those who have lived **under the law** and with full knowledge of what the law contains, will be judged **by the law**.

Clearly, not all people will be judged by the same standard. If Gentiles perish—that is to say, if they suffer judgment on the final day—it won't be because they disobeyed the written law of Moses that we have in our Bibles. Likewise, the people of Israel will be held accountable for how they responded to God's law given through Moses. They will be **judged by the law**. In both cases, for Jew and Gentile alike, judgment will be just. People will be held accountable for how they responded to the revelation given to them.

Although Gentiles do not possess the law of Moses, they are **by nature** (v. 14) aware of the moral principles found in it and yet fail to keep them. Gentiles, therefore, are not entirely without law. The basic moral principles revealed in the law of God (obey your parents, do not murder, do not lie, etc.) are inscribed on their hearts, indelibly embedded in their conscience by virtue of the fact that they are created in the image of God, no less than the Jews are. Unsaved Gentiles, says Paul, manifest an innate awareness of God's moral demands, their conscience either accusing or acquitting them.

An objection often found on the lips of skeptics is that it is unfair of God to hold people morally accountable and to judge them for failure to obey a "law" of which they are ignorant. But no one is utterly without divine law. Everyone will be judged according to their response to the "law" they have received (whether carved in tablets of stone, as with the Jew, or merely on the tablet of one's heart, as with the Gentile).

When Paul speaks of **the work of the law . . . written on their hearts** (v. 15 ESV), he is not alluding to the truth of Jer. 31:33. There the prophet speaks of the time when God's saving work among his people will entail the writing of the law on their hearts. Paul's purpose in verse 15, on the other hand, is simply to demonstrate that the Gentiles have an inner, intuitive awareness of the law and its obligatory force. When Paul says in verse 14 that they are **a law to themselves** (ESV), he has in mind what is intrinsic to human nature by virtue of having been created in God's image, not what is provided by the Holy Spirit by virtue of having been redeemed.

Paul's reference to Gentile obedience to certain divine moral principles does not imply that they are saved or that this is an obedience that secures merit for them in God's presence. In the first place, the text emphasizes that **accusing** thoughts predominate and that **defending** thoughts are relatively rare (v. 15), or at least the exception rather than the rule. Second, the opening statement of verse 12 confirms this point. Although bereft of the Mosaic law, Gentiles are still accountable to God for the law inscribed on their conscience and are subject to condemnation for their failure to obey it.

We read in verse 15 that the works that the law requires are **written on their hearts** (ESV). God has inscribed on the heart and soul of every human being an awareness of the basic and most fundamental principles of good and evil. **Things required by the law** (v. 14) are the basic principles of right and wrong, such as not lying, murdering, committing adultery, stealing, and so on. Paul isn't saying that everything in the law of Moses is inscribed on the hearts of all people but that enough of God's will and his moral requirements is known by them that they are fully accountable and morally responsible in his sight. Indeed, the **conscience** (v. 15) of every human being bears witness to this. The conscience functions as a moral compass of sorts, alerting a person to either the goodness or evil of their actions. The conscience is that facet of the image of God in human beings by which they have an intuitive sense of right and wrong. The conscience says to them either, "You are innocent because you have done what God requires of you," or, "You are guilty because you have disobeyed." The conscience thus brings a mixed verdict. Sometimes you know instinctively that you have done what is right, and other times you know that you have done what is wrong.

An Alternative Interpretation of Romans 2:12–16

N. T. Wright has proposed a reading of Rom. 2:12–16 that, if true, would cast considerable doubt on the traditional understanding of this text.[a] Wright's argument is based on, among other contextual clues, two grammatical observations.

First, he argues that the "for" (*gar*, "indeed" [NIV]) with which verse 14 opens indicates that this verse is an explanation of the principle stated in verse 13. In other words, the "doers of the law who will be justified" (v. 13 ESV) are none other than the "Gentiles" of verse 14. But who are these Gentiles who will be justified by doing the law?

This leads to Wright's second point, which pertains to the word *physei*, translated as "by nature" (v. 14). More traditional views have taken this word with what follows, hence: "When Gentiles, who do not have the law, do by nature things required by the law, they are a law for themselves" (v. 14). On this reading, "by nature" means something like "instinctively" or "by virtue of something in their constitution" as bearers of the divine image. In other words, in some way these unregenerate Gentiles have had the law of God written on their hearts as a constituent element in their status as image-bearers. Though unsaved, they are not without knowledge of what God requires, of the fundamental principles of right and wrong. These they have "by nature." Wright, however, contends that "by nature" should be taken with what precedes and should be translated in a way that is consistent with its usage a mere thirteen verses later in 2:27. In the latter text *physeōs* means what the Gentiles are or have "by birth." Their natural state is that of uncircumcision. My understanding of Wright's interpretation would result in the following translation of 2:14: "For when Gentiles who do not by nature have the law do the things of the law they, not having the law, are a law to themselves." Thus, "By 'nature,' that is, by birth, they are outside the covenant, not within Torah. And yet they 'do the things of Torah' (v. 14)."[b] Although it may seem unusual from a grammatical point of view, a similar construction is found in 14:1 (in which the substantive participle is followed, rather than preceded, by its modifying dative).

These Gentiles, therefore, who by birth did not have the law of God, yet do the things of the law, are *Christian* Gentiles, not unbelievers. This is confirmed by 2:15, which, Wright contends, is in fact a direct allusion to the new covenant in Jer. 31:33 and its promise of God putting his law within his people and writing it on their hearts. Says Wright, "I find it next to impossible that Paul could have written this phrase, with its overtones of Jeremiah's new covenant promise, simply to refer to pagans who happen by accident to share some of Israel's moral teaching."[c]

But if the Gentiles in 2:14 are Christians, what is the meaning of 2:15 and the reference to an inner uncertainty, as it were, concerning their status before God? Says Wright,

> They are not simply lawless Gentiles; but the Jewish law, which is now in some sense or other written on their hearts, and which in some sense they "do," nevertheless has a sufficiently ambiguous relation to them for them to still be concerned that the eventual issue might be in doubt. Hence, as judgment day approaches, they may well find inner conflict as they reflect on their situation. They would not have this inner conflict were they not Christians. The situation would then be the simply [sic] one of verse 12.[d]

Wright concludes that 2:14–15 is not talking about the function of the divine image or conscience in unregenerate Gentiles by which they demonstrate an intuitive knowledge of the law of God. Rather, these are Christian Gentiles who, in fulfillment of the new-covenant promise in Jeremiah, have had the law of God written on their hearts by the Spirit. Although they were born without the law, being outside the covenant God established through Moses, they now have the law in fulfillment of God's promise to establish a new covenant. These are the doers of the law who will find themselves vindicated (justified) at the final judgment.

If Wright's interpretation is correct, the principal textual support for the idea of general revelation in the conscience of humankind is lost.

a. Wright, "The Law in Romans 2."
b. Wright, "The Law in Romans 2," 145.
c. Wright, "The Law in Romans 2," 147.
d. Wright, "The Law in Romans 2," 146.

That God's judgment will take into account not only outward actions but also the hidden things or **secrets** of the heart (v. 16) is because God is omniscient. God knows our secret, unspoken thoughts and desires and motives. On this, see especially 1 Sam. 16:7; 1 Chron. 28:9a; Pss. 7:9; 26:2; 19:14; 139:1–4, 23; Prov. 15:11; Jer. 17:10; 20:12; Ezek. 11:5; John 2:25; Acts 1:24; Heb. 4:12–13; Rev. 2:23.

The Practices of the Jews (2:17–24)

As C. E. B. Cranfield notes, "Paul appears to be deliberately taking up claims which were actually being made by his fellow Jews, echoing the very language in which they were being expressed."[3] They appealed to numerous privileges (vv. 17–18) that were granted to those who traced their descent from Abraham.

These privileges are likely positive rather than negative. There are five of them. First is the name **Jew**, in which they took great pride. There is not a hint of anti-Semitism in this. The name **Jew** as Paul employs it in verse 17 is not used in a pejorative or negative sense. Both Jesus and Paul were Jews. Paul is not attacking the hypocrisy and externalism of the Jew, because he is a Jew. The Jewish people of Paul's day had no monopoly on hypocrisy. The Gentile of Paul's day and our own is no less the target of his denunciation. Paul's point here is that merely bearing the title of **Jew** does not exempt a person from living consistently with the laws that God has laid out for his people.

Second, they appeal to their reliance on the law, which wasn't necessarily a bad thing (see Pss. 19:7–11; 119). Unfortunately, the Jew relied "on it in the sense of thinking to fulfill it in such a way as to put God in his debt or of imagining complacently that the mere fact of possessing it gives him security against God's judgment."[4] Third, they boast in God (cf. Rom. 5:11; 1 Cor. 1:31; 2 Cor. 10:17). Sadly, their boast was exclusivistic: "God is *mine*, not yours, and you can't have him." The fourth and fifth blessings are their unique knowledge of the divine will and the spiritual discernment that comes from it.

They also point to their prerogatives in relation to other people (vv. 19–20). Again, there are five of them: (1) they were spiritual guides to the spiritually blind; (2) they were a light to those in darkness (cf. Isa. 42:6–7); (3) they brought correction to the foolish (practical moral guidance) (cf. Matt. 23:15); (4) they were teachers of the immature; (5) they were possessors of the truth.

In verses 21–24 the argument takes a different turn, as Paul points out how despite their advantages the Jews have failed to live up to their calling. The inconsistency between their claims and their conduct is vivid. Once more, Paul gives five examples: (1) teaching; (2) stealing; (3) committing adultery (cf. Matt. 5:21–48); (4) robbing temples; (5) boasting in the law (he has in mind boasting in the sense of thinking that by obedience to the law one can put God in one's debt, and also in the sense of, on the basis of the former, looking down one's nose at others). Is the reference to robbing temples (v. 22) literal or metaphorical? Probably the former, as "Paul highlights an inconsistency among the Jews. They claim to detest idolatry and spurn any association with idols, yet they are willing to be defiled by profiting from the very idols that they detest."[5] Paul likely had in mind Deut. 7:25, where Moses forbade profiting from the gold and silver taken from pagan temples.

3. Cranfield, *Romans*, 1:164.
4. Cranfield, *Romans*, 1:164.
5. Schreiner, *Romans*, 141–42.

But the apostle isn't suggesting that all Jews are thieves, adulterers, and temple robbers, as it certainly wouldn't apply to him prior to his conversion. "We should recognize that Paul [here] engages in a piece of rhetoric, arguing that the Jews didn't keep the law they possessed and taught. . . . To conclude that these examples charge every Jew of committing these particular sins is a mistake. . . . Paul uses particularly blatant and shocking examples (like any good preacher) to illustrate the principle that Jews violated the law that they possessed."[6] These sins, then, are likely representative of the inconsistency between their claim and their conduct.

Mere boasting in the law of God does not glorify its author. In fact, the name of God is dishonored (**blasphemed**) by those who possess the law but live in willful defiance of its dictates (vv. 23–24; the latter verse is likely a loose citation of Isa. 52:5). It is instructive that Paul describes **breaking the law** of God as dishonoring God (v. 23). Many think of breaking the law in purely horizontal terms, as a violation of a human ordinance or rule. Sin is perpetrating evil against another human being. Evil is done when I am abused or slandered or violated. But Paul says that the essence of sin and evil is dishonoring God. King David in the Old Testament understood this. That is why, in Ps. 51, when he confesses his adultery with Bathsheba and his complicity in the death of her husband, Uriah the Hittite, he says, "Against you [God], you only, have I sinned and done what is evil in your sight" (v. 4a).

Outward Ritual That Lacks Inward Reality (2:25–29)

The problem that Paul then turns to address in verses 25–29 is the belief that an external ritual compensates for, or excuses, the absence of an internal reality. Ritualism and a reliance on the supposed spiritual benefits of certain forms of liturgy are a constant threat to true spirituality. Paul says clearly in verse 25 that circumcision, which was the physical mark in the flesh that was a Jew, is fine if you obey the law. But if you trust in your membership in the covenant people of God and use that as an excuse to disobey God's law, your circumcision is worthless. In much the same way, Paul says in verse 26 that the uncircumcised Gentile who by God's grace and for God's glory strives to live an obedient, law-abiding life will be regarded as if he were circumcised. In God's sight, regardless of whether he has the physical sign in his flesh of being a member of God's covenant people, he is regarded as such. In fact, it is the law-abiding uncircumcised Gentile who is saved and the law-defying circumcised Jew who will be judged by God on the final day (v. 27).

6. Schreiner, *Romans*, 142.

In saying that the uncircumcised Gentile is regarded as circumcised, Paul means that he is part of God's redeemed community notwithstanding the absence of the physical mark in one's flesh. But how can uncircumcised Gentiles belong to the people of God without submitting to the physical rite? Paul's answer in verse 29 is that what constitutes a person as Jewish is circumcision of the heart (likely a reference to regeneration by the Spirit, or the new birth). The true Jew, the true Israelite, is not that man or woman who has Abraham's blood in their veins but the one who has Abraham's faith in their heart. The mark of being a citizen of the kingdom of God is circumcision, not of the flesh, but of the heart. One's ethnic heritage is not decisive in determining who is among the covenant people of God. One's personal faith is.

In these two concluding verses of Rom. 2 (vv. 28–29) Paul clearly defines what it means to be saved and a covenant member of the people of God. Merely having the physical mark in your flesh is no guarantee that you belong to God. He is not saying that physical circumcision is bad. He is merely saying that the external ritual performed on the flesh is of benefit only when it is matched by the circumcision of the heart (see Deut. 10:12–17). It refers to the metaphorical cutting away of the sinful flesh inwardly. The external mark in the physical flesh was always designed to remind the people of Israel that infinitely more important was the renewal and regeneration of their hearts.

When Paul says that **no one is a Jew who is merely one outwardly** (v. 28a ESV), he is not saying that a physical descendant of Abraham, Isaac, and Jacob is not genuinely Jewish. They are still Jewish. But if they have not been circumcised inwardly by being born again of the Holy Spirit, their ethnic identity avails nothing. The Gentile believer in Jesus is actually more "Jewish" than the Jewish person who rejects Jesus. The person who has experienced circumcision **of the heart, by the Spirit, not by the letter** (v. 29 ESV)—that is to say, the person who has been born again and trusts Jesus, regardless of his or her ethnicity—is the true Jew!

Paul is not saying that an ethnic Israelite has no relationship to God. Far from it! He himself was an ethnic Israelite. He is simply saying that mere ethnicity is not what makes one a child of God. Renewal of the heart is the ultimate issue. So, ethnic Jews who are circumcised both in the body and inwardly, in the heart, by the Spirit, are the children of God and heirs to all the promises. But he is also saying that ethnic Gentiles who are circumcised only inwardly, in the heart, by the Spirit, are also the children of God, coheirs of all the promises (see esp. Eph. 2:11–13, 18–19; Gal. 3:16, 27–29).

Ought we then to call the church spiritual Israel or the true Israel? Those who say yes point to the fact that the New Testament authors readily apply to the church titles, honors, and blessings reserved in the Old Testament for ethnic

Israel: the seed of Abraham (Gal. 3:15–29), the circumcision (Phil. 3:1–3), the dispersion (1 Pet. 1:1), chosen race, royal priesthood, holy nation, people for God's own possession, people of God (1 Pet. 2:9–10; see esp. Gal. 6:16; Rev. 3:9). As the true Israel of God, the church, composed of both ethnic Gentiles and ethnic Jews, is the heir of all the promises made to the Old Testament patriarchs. This by no means precludes a possible future ingathering of ethnic Jews (on which, see Rom. 11). What it does mean is that when ethnic Jews are saved, they are incorporated into the church and made one body and fellow heirs with believing Gentiles. There is only one people of God, the church, the true Israel, in which both ethnic Jews and ethnic Gentiles have been circumcised in heart and made heirs to the covenant promises.

ROMANS 3

God's Redemptive Grace in Christ

The Faithfulness of God (3:1–8)

Paul's hypothetical dialogue partner poses three objections to what has preceded, each of which the apostle answers. The first objection is raised in verse 1, followed by Paul's response in verse 2. In Rom. 2:17–29 Paul said that some Jews, notwithstanding their physical descent from Abraham, are not really Jews and that some Gentiles can be Jews, spiritually speaking, even if they are not circumcised. That appears to put in doubt the special position of Israel as God's chosen people (see Deut. 7:6–8; Amos 3:1–2) and calls into question the integrity of the Old Testament Scriptures. If neither physical circumcision nor physical descent from Abraham contributes to one's salvation, and if the law of Moses brings conviction of sin, and if Jews are as liable to judgment as are Gentiles, what benefit or **value** (*ōpheleia*; the verb form was used in 2:25, where the focus is on saving "value") is there in being a Jew at all? If Israel is no better off than pagan Gentiles, the Old Testament promises of God would appear to be invalid. This is the objection that Paul is determined to refute.

Preeminent among all Israel's privileges is that they were made custodians of **the oracles of God** (v. 2 ESV; see Deut. 4:8; Ps. 147:19–20). This phrase may refer to the entire Old Testament Scriptures, but with special emphasis on the promises from God ensuring Israel's ultimate salvation. Paul's words **first of all** suggest that there is to follow a long list of advantages and blessings that God bestowed on the Jewish people during the age of the Old Testament. But he mentions only their being entrusted with **the oracles of God** (v. 2 ESV.).

He then breaks off his argument and resumes it at 9:3–5. His reference to **the oracles of God** or **the very words of God** is meant to awaken in his fellow Jews an awareness of the blessing that is theirs and to stimulate them to humility and repentance and faith in God. Instead, they relied on these many privileges and blessings, such as their ethnicity, as if those alone could guarantee that they are in right relationship with God. They boasted in their possession of **the very words of God** but failed to sincerely believe and obey them.

But if God promised salvation to the people of Israel, how do we account for such widespread unbelief among the Jews? Does their unfaithfulness in rejecting the Messiah mean that God has reneged on his promises to Israel and that he can't be trusted to keep his word? Must we then conclude that God is himself unfaithful?

Not at all (v. 4)! However, Paul doesn't actually answer the objection. He simply shouts it down and declares it invalid. He will later provide his answer to the objection in Rom. 9–11. He does, however, provide something of a response, but one that will in turn provoke yet another objection! The response is found in verse 4. There Paul says that rather than undermining God's faithfulness to his word, human unbelief, rebellion, and sin serve to magnify and intensify the glory of God's justice. To make his point, he cites the words of Ps. 51:4, where David's confession of sin was designed to highlight the justice of God. God's righteousness is seen most clearly against the backdrop of our sin. When we sin or fail God, it isn't because God has failed us. In fact, our failure shines a bright light on God's justice as well as his mercy.

This provokes yet one more objection (vv. 5–8), which is stated three times, on each occasion with a slightly different emphasis. But in each case the central idea is the same. The protest made by our hypothetical dialogue partner is this: "If our sin and unrighteousness, like David's in the Old Testament, magnifies or enhances God's righteousness when he judges us, then we are actually the instruments of God's glory. When we sin, we magnify God's righteousness. If that is true, wouldn't it be unjust of God to condemn us? He would be judging us for the very thing that magnifies his glory as the righteous God!" Paul's immediate response is simply to say, "No, you are very wrong!"

This objection takes on an insidious form when Paul's hypothetical objector pushes back, as he does in verse 8, and says, "Well, then, why don't we just do more evil so that God can benefit from it? If his righteousness as the judge is magnified when seen in comparison with our unrighteousness, let's sin all the more and do God a favor!" The point of the objector is that it would be unfair for God to punish the sinner for something that ultimately works to his advantage. How can God condemn a person when that person's sin actually glorifies God by alerting us to the righteousness of God as judge?

Paul has had enough of this nonsense and feels somewhat embarrassed in even mentioning the objection. He thus adds, somewhat apologetically, **I speak in a human way** (v. 5 ESV). That is to say, he is speaking as a fallen human with distorted reasoning would speak. But we know better. Paul does not really answer the objection. He simply asserts in verse 6 that if the objection were to hold true, how could God judge the world? But we know that God *will* judge the world. Therefore, the objection can't be legitimate. Paul's point is that divine judgment is certain and inevitable. It cannot be challenged or evaded. Therefore, to argue that one's sin should be excused and not judged because it serves to magnify God's righteousness is invalid.

If Paul were to respond more fully to the objection, he might be expected to say something like this: First, the fact that your sin magnifies God's justice when he punishes you for it in no way changes the fact that you have sinned. And the wages of sin is death. Second, there isn't a man or woman alive who has ever sinned with the intention of doing so to glorify and honor God. We sin because we are evil and because we despise and disregard God. Third, it is to God's praise, not yours, that he is wise and powerful enough to bring good out of your evil. It is hardly something for which you can take credit. The bottom line is that you can't blame God for the failures of men and women.

Paul's somewhat indignant response in verse 8 suggests that he believes that the profound absurdity of the objection implies its dismissal. **Their condemnation is just**, says Paul. Anyone who would try to justify their sin by arguing that it really only serves to magnify the righteousness of God as judge is deserving of what comes their way. The principle that undergirds Paul's comments here is the fact that God, in his sovereignty, makes evil serve his purposes. Evil will always be evil. The fact that God can turn it for good does not mean that God is evil, nor does it mean that evil now becomes good. But evil is not outside God's providential sway (see, e.g., Gen. 50:20; Acts 2:22–23; 4:23–28).

The Sin and Condemnation of All Humankind (3:9–20)

To the question in 3:1, "What advantage, then, is there in being a Jew?" Paul answered, "Much in every way" (3:2). But to the question in 3:9, **Do we** [Jews] **have any advantage?** he answers, **Not at all** (3:9). We can avoid this discrepancy "only by clarifying what benefit or 'advantage' he has in mind," notes John Stott. "If he means privilege and responsibility, then the Jews have much because God has entrusted his revelation to them. But if he means favouritism, then the Jews have none, because God will not exempt them from judgment."[1]

1. Stott, *Romans*, 99.

We must take note of Paul's emphasis on the universality of sin. Five times in this section he uses the phrase *ouk estin* (**there is no one**). The one line that lacks this phrase has instead the Greek word *pantes* (**all**), which points to the pervasiveness of sin. Again, in verses 10 and 12 he uses the words *oude heis* (**not even one**) and *heōs henos* (**not even one**). These are emphatic universal negatives. No exceptions allowed.

Note also the structure of this list that follows in verses 10–18. Verses 10–12 describe the universality of sin, similar to what we saw in 1:18–23. Verses 13–14 focus on sins of speech. Verses 15–17 focus on sins in society at large. Verse 18 identifies the ground and root cause of all the sins just noted: the failure to fear God. When Paul says at the beginning of verse 10, **as it is written**, he is unmistakably appealing to Scripture as his authority. He cites six different passages from the Old Testament to make his point. Verses 10b–12 are largely taken from Ps. 14:1–3, which likely has the unbelieving Gentile world in view:

> The fool says in his heart,
>> "There is no God."
> They are corrupt, their deeds are vile;
>> there is no one who does good.
>
> The LORD looks down from heaven
>> on all mankind
> to see if there are any who understand,
>> any who seek God.
> All have turned away; all have become corrupt;
>> there is no one who does good,
>> not even one.

People, apart from God's enabling grace, do not seek God. This inability is due to their unwillingness to submit to his will. But what, then, about the Jewish people? If Paul is indicting all humankind as under sin, including the Jews, how does he prove this from the Old Testament? The answer is found in Rom. 3:15–17. These three verses are a reference to Isa. 59:7–8, which has the people of Israel in view:

> Their feet rush into sin;
>> they are swift to shed innocent blood.
> They pursue evil schemes;
>> acts of violence mark their ways.
> The way of peace they do not know;
>> there is no justice in their paths.
> They have turned into crooked roads;
>> no one who walks along them will know peace.

This is a statement about the spiritual condition of Israel in the days of Isaiah the prophet. In addition, Rom. 3:13a is a reference to Ps. 5:9, which describes the people of Israel. Romans 3:13b is a citation of Ps. 140:3, which describes the enemies of King David from among his own people. The same is true of Rom. 3:14, which is based on Ps. 10:7. Romans 3:18, the final verse in Paul's concluding indictment of the Jewish people, comes from Ps. 36:1.

In verses 13–14 Paul points to the destructive power of the tongue. In saying that **their throat is an open grave** (ESV), he has in mind the deadly effects of human speech. The word **deceit** points to the way people lie and flatter to promote themselves. Again, **The poison of vipers is on their lips** has in view the lethal, cruel way in which we use our speech to destroy others. Such poisonous speech is not occasional; rather, **their mouth is full of curses and bitterness** (v. 14 ESV).

Human wickedness also includes our actions toward others. In verse 15a Paul refers to the widespread evil of murder and killing. **Ruin and misery** (v. 16) refer to the devastation that we inflict on others. In saying **The way of peace they do not know** (v. 17), Paul doesn't primarily mean the absence of peace in our hearts, the anxiety that we so often experience. Rather, he is talking about the violence and warlike ways in which we relate to others. Worst of all, **there is no fear of God before their eyes** (v. 18 [see Prov. 1:7a; 1 Pet. 2:17]). First, we must note that the absence of the fear of God means that at the center or core of sin is the refusal to let God rule our lives. So here again we see that sin is first and fundamentally vertical in its orientation: it is the refusal to honor, reverence, obey, and fear God, a refusal that expresses itself horizontally in the way we defraud and destroy one another.

At minimum, to fear God entails reverence and awe. This is the sort of fear that expresses itself in trembling and amazement and an overwhelming sense of personal frailty and finitude. To fear God means to live conscious of his all-pervasive presence, conscious of our absolute, moment-by-moment dependence on him for light and life, conscious of our comprehensive responsibility to do all he has commanded, fearful of offending him, determined to obey him (Deut. 6:1–2, 24; 8:6; Pss. 112:1; 119:63; Mal. 3:5), and committed to loving him (Deut. 10:12, 20; 13:4). To fear God is to know him (Prov. 1:29; 2:4–5) and to hate evil (Prov. 8:13; 16:6). Fearing God yields confidence (Prov. 14:26), humility (Prov. 3:7; 22:4), and contentment (Prov. 23:17). This, then, is the primary sense in which people do not fear God.

Verses 19–20 are Paul's conclusion to what he has said from 1:18 through 3:18. It is the Jewish people who **are under the law** (v. 19). So how does their failure to keep it imply that **every mouth**, indeed the **whole world**, is guilty before God? How could the whole world be guilty before God because of a law given to the Jews? The answer is that if the covenant people of Israel, to whom the law as well as numerous other blessings have been given, failed to keep it, what reason do we have to believe that anyone else can, including the Gentiles? The law served only to awaken and reveal sin in Jewish hearts, not faith. And if they can't be justified by performing all the good works commanded in the law, then certainly the Gentiles can't either.

Why is it that no one will be able to contend with the verdict of the court? The answer is given in verse 20. The **law** is in itself good and godly, for it reveals the character of God and his will for humanity. But because of our corrupt and wicked nature, it's impossible for us to live up to its requirements. The law serves only to highlight our moral impotence and rebellion. When we see what God requires, we see instantly how we have failed to comply. When exposed to the

APPLICATION

Under the Power of Sin

In Rom. 3:9, what does it mean to be "under the power of sin" (NIV) or simply "under sin" (ESV)? First, we are under sin in the sense that because of our sin we are guilty before God, justly condemned. Sin exerts a condemning influence and authority over us because we have rebelled against God. We have committed cosmic treason. We are subject to the legal penalties that God's justice imposes. Paul will explain this in 3:10–18 as our lacking the righteousness that God's righteousness requires him to demand and failing to seek God and, as he says in verse 18, living with no fear of God in our hearts. Second, we are under sin in the sense that it exerts an experiential power over our lives. We live subject to its promptings. There is a sense in which all humankind is enslaved to sin. Later in Romans Paul will speak of sin as reigning (5:21), enslaving (6:6), ruling (6:12), and exercising lordship (6:14). We go through life carrying this burden on our shoulders and in our souls, one from which Paul will happily declare us free in Rom. 6. Third, as will become evident from 3:13–17, we are "under the power of sin" in the sense that we violate the rights of and treat with contempt other human beings. So, yes, there is a horizontal dimension to sin: we deceive one another with our tongues (v. 13b); out of bitterness we curse one another (v. 14); we shed the blood of other people (v. 15); we ruin other people and make them miserable and strive to destroy peace (vv. 16–17). Both in our speech and in our deeds, we are sinners in our relationships with one another.

law, sin rises up and brings conviction. That is why our only hope is that when we feel that indictment in our souls, that unmistakable sense of moral failure, we must turn to Christ and declare, "I'm trusting in what Jesus did for me. All the guilt and well-deserved punishment for my spiritual and moral wickedness was laid on him, and he satisfied the demands of God's justice in my place."

In sum, Paul has made it clear that no one will be able to mount a defense or make an excuse before God that he or she should be set free and declared innocent. Paul has closed every loophole. He has done it in three ways. (1) In Rom. 1:18–21 he pointed out that creation itself has made God's existence and nature known so that no one has an excuse. (2) He then argued in Rom. 2:12–16 that every human being has been created in the image of God with a conscience that convicts them of their failure to obey God. Each person knows intuitively what God requires. Each person knows intuitively that they have fallen short and are worthy of death (see 1:32). Each person has the law of God **written on their hearts** (2:15). (3) He concludes his argument in Rom. 3:9–20 by pointing to the written law of God, a law that no human, whether Jew or Gentile, can perfectly obey.

The good news is that the infinitely holy God who pronounces us guilty is the same God who loves us in spite of our brokenness and sin. If you are burdened under the oppressive weight of guilt and shame and feel hopeless, the good news of the gospel is that God stands ready, in Jesus Christ, not only to forgive you and cleanse you and lift shame from your soul but also to empower you to live a godly life. You don't have to remain enslaved to shame and guilt and self-condemnation a second longer!

The Divine Provision for Salvation (3:21–26)

Paul's point in Rom. 3:21 is that God's righteousness does not come by obedience to the law. Hence it is **apart from the law**—that is, apart from our doing the works of the law. Douglas Moo explains, "In the new era inaugurated with Christ's death God has acted to deliver and vindicate his people 'apart from' the law. It is not primarily the law as something for humans to do, but the law as a system, as a stage in God's unfolding plan, that is in view here. 'Law' (*nomos*), then, refers to the 'Mosaic covenant,' that (temporary) administration set up between God and his people to regulate their lives and reveal their sin until the establishment of the promise in Christ."[2]

The phrase translated as **through faith in Jesus Christ** (v. 22) has stirred considerable discussion (note the parallel text in Gal. 2:16). Some prefer to

---

2. Moo, *Romans*, 223.

translate it as "through the faith [or "faithfulness"] of Jesus Christ" (a subjective genitive). The NIV rendering **faith in Jesus Christ** finds here a reference to our faith in the Son of God, our trusting of him to save us from sin. On this view, Jesus is the object of our faith (an objective genitive). More recently numerous scholars have argued for the first view (subjective genitive), that this is a reference not to our faith in Christ but to the faithfulness of Jesus himself. If so, Paul's point would be that because Jesus was faithful, because his life was a perfect demonstration of faithful obedience to his heavenly Father, we have a basis for our acceptance by God. We put our faith in the faith(fulness) of Jesus and are thereby justified.[3]

Paul uses the noun "faith" with the genitive of "Jesus Christ" (or simply "Jesus" or "Christ") seven times in his epistles: Gal. 2:16 (2x); 3:22; Rom. 3:22, 26; Eph. 3:12 (pronoun referring to "Christ Jesus" in the preceding verse); Phil. 3:9. Each of these texts would make sense if we translated them as referring to the faithfulness of Jesus himself. Consider Paul's reference to "God's faithfulness" (or "the faith of God") (Rom. 3:3) and "the faith of Abraham" (Rom. 4:16). If the phrase in question is interpreted this way, this would not diminish the importance of *our* faith *in* Christ. Indeed, in Rom. 3:22 Paul promises righteousness **for all who believe** (ESV; see also Gal. 2:16; 3:22; Phil. 3:9). If Paul is thinking of the faithfulness of Jesus as the foundation or basis of our acceptance by God, then justification may, in a sense, be conceived as being both by works and by faith. That is to say, we are justified by faith in the works of Jesus.

Still, it must be noted that much can be said for the traditional interpretation that our faith in Christ is Paul's intent.[4] Thomas Schreiner appeals to four arguments. First, "both Romans and Galatians have a plethora of passages that refer to the faith of believers."[5] Second, "there isn't any unambiguous indication where Paul spoke of the faithfulness of Christ. . . . Granted, the obedience of Christ is an important element in Pauline theology. But nowhere else does Paul describe Christ's obedience in terms of his 'faithfulness' ([*pistis*])."[6] Third, and on the other hand, "there is unambiguous evidence in the Pauline Letters

---

3. This view is defended in depth by Hays, *Faith of Jesus Christ*. Although Hays is concerned primarily with this phrase in Galatians, he addresses the contribution of Romans as well.

4. Paul does not say that we are justified *because* we believe. Human faith is not a work that merits justification. Justification is not *propter fidem per Christum*, or "on account of faith through Christ." Justification is *per fidem propter Christum*, or "through faith on account of Christ." The person and the work of Christ are the grounds or basis of our justification. Faith is the instrument through which we embrace what he did as our only hope. God doesn't justify us because we have faith. God justifies us because of what Jesus did, which we receive through faith.

5. Schreiner, *Romans*, 193. He cites thirty-eight such texts.

6. Schreiner, *Romans*, 193.

that Paul called for faith *in* Christ."[7] Fourth, "the reading 'faith in Christ' also makes the best sense of the flow of thought in Rom. 3:21–4:12."[8]

Paul does not end his message with human sin and depravity and guilt; here begins his glorious declaration that there is forgiveness and redemption and justification by God's grace through faith in Jesus Christ.

For all have sinned and fall short of the glory of God (v. 23) doesn't mean that people are to be as glorious as God and have failed or fallen short in their efforts to attain it. The answer is found in Rom. 1, where we were told that humankind "neither glorified him as God nor gave thanks to him" (1:21). Instead, people "exchanged the glory of the immortal God for images made to look like a mortal human being and birds and animals and reptiles" (1:23). "They exchanged the truth about God for a lie, and worshiped and served created things rather than the Creator—who is forever praised. Amen" (1:25).

Sin is the rejection of God and his glory as the supreme value in our lives. The great sin of humankind is the refusal to treasure, trust, and thank God and worship him above all else. We fall short of the glory of God when we give our allegiance to anything or anyone else, when we fail to make him the foundation and center of our existence.

We turn now to the threefold remedy that God has provided in Christ Jesus. The first is justification. Paul tells us in verse 24 that we are **justified by his** [God's] **grace as a gift** (ESV). Justification refers to God's forensic declaration that the believer in Jesus is righteous in God's sight. It is through the process of progressive sanctification that we are made righteous. But justification is a legal declaration by God, not an experiential transformation in us. It is something that is done outside of us and consists of a legal change in how we are perceived by God. Justification is not a process but a position, a status to which we are elevated. It happens in a moment of time whenever a person puts their faith in Jesus. It is also irreversible. It cannot be lost. God's verdict will never be overturned or appealed to a higher court. All the accusations that Satan can muster will not avail to reverse our standing in God's sight (see Rom. 8:33). Finally, justification is received by faith alone. As Paul says in verse 24, it flows from God's **grace as a gift** (ESV). That is why there can never be any such thing as justification by works.

The second saving blessing is redemption. Justification, says Paul, is **through the redemption that came by Jesus Christ** (v. 24). The word "redemption" is a metaphor that refers to deliverance or release by the payment of a price. Whenever redemption occurs, a ransom has been paid. Humankind was enslaved

7. Schreiner, *Romans*, 193.
8. Schreiner, *Romans*, 193.

and in bondage to sin's power and condemnation, held hostage to the world, the flesh, and the devil. But Jesus graciously offered up the only payment that could effectively set us free: his precious blood, shed on the cross. Jesus himself made this clear in Mark 10:45: "For even the Son of Man came not to be served but to serve, and to give his life as a ransom for many" (ESV).

Paul's third and final word may be the most important of all: *hilastērion* (v. 25) rendered as **propitiation** (ESV) or **sacrifice of atonement** (NIV).[9] There are five other places in the New Testament where this word or a related form appears (Luke 18:13; Heb. 2:17; 9:5; 1 John 2:2; 4:10). In his death Jesus suffered and endured and satisfied in himself the wrath and judgment that was due to sinful men and women.[10] Some English versions translate the word *hilastērion* as "expiation." Many, due to their discomfort with the notion of divine wrath, labor to eliminate the concept of propitiation from the death of Christ. But if God is not angry at sin, if his justice does not require satisfaction, he cannot be holy and righteous. "Expiation" has sin as its object and means to cover or put away or blot out sin so that it no longer constitutes a barrier between us and God. But sin cannot be expiated or wiped out unless the wrath of God against sin is first pacified and appeased. The reason why our sin has been removed is that Jesus, in his suffering, has quenched the wrath of God and satisfied the demands of divine justice.

It is God himself who propitiates his own wrath by his own action of sending his own Son to endure what we deserve. The Father and the Son, in perfect unity and oneness of will, determined to make a way for us to be reconciled to God. And that way was by means of the Father sending the Son in love, and the Son freely embracing the call to die for sinners, and in doing so to answer the demands of divine justice.

So, when Paul says in verse 25 that God put forward Jesus **as a sacrifice of atonement [propitiation (ESV)] through the shedding of his blood**, he means for us to know that it wasn't the life of Jesus that saved us, or his teaching, or his faithfulness, or his good moral example, or his wisdom; it was the shedding of

9. On propitiation, see Stott, *Epistles of John*, 89–93; Morris, *Apostolic Preaching of the Cross*, 125–85; Murray, *Redemption*, 29–33; Nicole, "C. H. Dodd and the Doctrine of Propitiation."

10. The word for "propitiation" may well have as its background the "mercy seat" on which the blood of the sacrifice was sprinkled. In the vast majority of instances in the Septuagint the Greek word *hilastērion* denotes the mercy seat (Exod. 25:17, 18, 19, 20, 21, 22; 31:7; 35:12; 38:5, 7, 8; Lev. 16:2, 13, 14, 15; Num. 7:89). "To propitiate," explains John Murray, "means to 'placate,' 'pacify,' 'appease,' 'conciliate.' And it is this idea that is applied to the atonement accomplished by Christ. Propitiation presupposed the wrath and displeasure of God, and the purpose of propitiation is the removal of this displeasure. Very simply stated the doctrine of propitiation means that Christ propitiated the wrath of God and rendered God propitious to his people" (*Redemption*, 30).

his blood in death on the cross. And this glorious reality is **to be received by faith** (v. 25; cf. 3:21, 22, 26, 28).

In verses 25b–26 we see that when the Father sent the Son to die in our place and the Son, through the Spirit, offered himself up as a sinless sacrifice, God was also acting on his own behalf, for the sake of his own name. What he did for us through Jesus was also an act whereby he demonstrated his own righteousness, his own justice, and thereby vindicated his name in all the earth. Christ's death was **to demonstrate his** [God's] **righteousness** (v. 25). God was determined to make known to all creation that he is just and holy and infinitely glorious and deserving of all our devotion and gratitude and praise.

What possible reason could there be for someone to doubt that God is good and righteous? Paul immediately answers this question in the second half of verse 25: it is because **in his divine forbearance he** [God] **had passed over former sins** (ESV). The Old Testament is a record of a multitude of sins that appear to go unpunished. Justice is not immediately forthcoming. Time and time again people who commit horrible atrocities appear to escape unpunished. If God is just, why does he appear only to wink at sin rather than punish it? This is all due to what Paul calls God's divine **forbearance** (which is not the same as indifference). There were instances when God's judgment fell dramatically, as was the case with the flood during the time of Noah and with the destruction of Sodom and Gomorrah. But for several thousand years it seemed as if very little justice was being meted out. There was no visible, universal manifestation of divine justice and retribution. God's reputation as righteous and holy was open to public slander. We read something similar in the book of Acts. There Paul, speaking to the crowds at Lystra, says, "In past generations he allowed the nations to walk in their own ways" (Acts 14:16 ESV). And during his speech on Mars Hill Paul says, "The times of ignorance God overlooked, but now he commands all people everywhere to repent" (Acts 17:30 ESV).

The death of Jesus was designed not solely to deliver us from sin and condemnation but also to demonstrate the righteousness of God and to vindicate his holiness and glorify his good name. The way that God had governed the world from the fall of Adam to the birth of Christ made it look to many like God was unrighteous and unaffected by sin and indifferent to moral evil. For centuries it appeared that God had been doing what Ps. 103:10 says he does: "He does not deal with us according to our sins, nor repay us according to our iniquities" (ESV).

In order to make known his greatness and the majesty of his holiness, God sent his Son to pay the price for sins committed and thereby vindicated and demonstrated the immeasurable worth of his glory. Paul intends for us to see in the death of Christ, first and foremost, a declaration and demonstration of the unfathomable worth and infinite value of God. God is committed above all else to uphold and make known the glory of his name.

But there appears on the surface to be a miscarriage of justice in the gospel of Jesus Christ. In Prov. 17:15 we read that "the LORD detests" both "acquitting the guilty and condemning the innocent." But if the gospel is that God justifies the ungodly (Rom. 4:5) and acquits the guilty, how does he escape this denunciation? Here we see the twofold challenge that God faces. In the first place, he is committed to proving to everyone that he is in fact just, righteous, and holy. But second, he also desires to justify sinful men and women. How can he do both and declare as righteous people who have belittled him and disregarded him and despised him? How can he be **the one who justifies** (3:26) fallen and rebellious people and at the same time be seen as just and righteous himself?

The solution is found in the death of Jesus as our substitute. The just God requires the maximum punishment for those who have despised him. And Jesus endures that punishment. He satisfies the demands of justice. He quenches the wrath of God. And on that basis God is free to impute the righteousness of Jesus to us and declare us justified when we put our faith in him. In Rom. 4:5 Paul describes God as the one "who justifies the ungodly." But how can God declare as godly those who are ungodly? God can do it because a righteous substitute, Jesus, has lived the sinless life that they should have lived and didn't, and he died the sacrificial death that they should have died but now don't have to.

When God set forth Jesus as a propitiatory sacrifice on the cross, he was, as it were, answering his critics. The death of Christ was not only a substitutionary sacrifice for sinners; it was also the public vindication of the justice and righteousness of God himself. God *is* just; God *is* righteous; the wages of sin *is* death; the undeniable public proof of these is the propitiatory suffering of Jesus.

How Faith Excludes Boasting (3:27–31)

Then what becomes of our boasting? asks Paul (v. 27 ESV). **It is excluded,** and for two reasons. First, it is the essence of faith that it looks away from itself to its gracious object. The moment that faith takes its eyes off of Jesus and examines itself and its own quality, it ceases to be faith. Faith, by definition, is the self-denying determination to look to and praise the object of its trust. As soon as faith compliments itself, it ceases to be faith and becomes a work. The second reason is that saving faith is itself a gift from God. We see this in texts such as Eph. 2:8–9; Phil. 1:29; 2 Tim. 2:24–26; 2 Pet. 1:1. The reason why faith cannot boast about itself is that ultimately the only reason we have faith is that God freely and graciously gave it to us. Paul's point is that all boasting is excluded because of the way God saves us. What excludes boasting from salvation is that justification comes to us not by works of law but by faith alone in Christ alone.

This is why God can justify both Jews and Gentiles. **God is one**, says Paul in verse 30 (ESV). By this he means both that there is only one God, not many, and that the one true God—Father, Son, and Holy Spirit—is unified in his character and in his purposes. Thus there is only one way to be put right with God. God does not have two ways of salvation, one for Jews and one for Gentiles. Whether someone is Jewish and has received the mark of circumcision in the flesh or is a Gentile and has not, God will declare both to be righteous through faith in Jesus. There are not many differing ways of getting right with God.

In saying this, has Paul undermined the law of God? If a person can't be justified by obeying the law, of what good is the law? Has Paul in effect nullified the law, rendering it useless? Far from it, says Paul. In fact, it is faith in Jesus Christ that enables us to **uphold the law** (v. 31). In one sense the Old Testament Scriptures testify to justification being by faith alone. It is also true that the law convicts us of sin and awakens us to our need for justification by faith alone. It is also the case that our faith fulfills the law because it is fulfilled in Christ, in whom we believe. But most important of all, those who have faith in Christ will in fact keep (fulfill or **uphold**) the law. The moral norms of the law still function as authoritative for the believer, and saving faith is the kind of faith that works or obeys. If we pursue and practice God's moral law by faith, knowing that we are not justified by obedience but that we obey because we are already justified, our faith upholds and honors the law of God.

ROMANS 4

Justified by Faith

The Examples of Abraham and David (4:1–8)

To the Jewish mind, any discussion of the correct approach to God must consider Abraham, the father of the nation Israel. So the question Paul addresses in chapter 4 is whether the life of Abraham validates and upholds the conclusion Paul reached in Rom. 3:27–28, that righteousness is by faith and not by works. Abraham was the embodiment of all Jewish virtues. If *he* was not justified by works, then no other person could be. If, on the other hand, he was justified by faith, there can be no other justification for any other individual.

So, how was Abraham justified, or on what grounds did he gain acceptance by God? Paul rules out works as the ground for his justification in verse 2. This has been understood in two ways. On the one hand, a person who is justified by works can boast. But Abraham cannot boast **before God** (v. 2). Therefore, Abraham was not justified by works. But more likely Paul is saying that justification by works is impossible or inconceivable in God's presence (**but not before God**), which rules out any possibility that Abraham was justified by anything he did. To prove that Abraham was not justified by works, the apostle quotes from Gen. 15:6 in verse 3: **Abraham believed God, and it was counted to him as righteousness** (ESV).

Abraham gained favor with God not because of his obedience but as a result of his faith that God would fulfill his promise of an heir through whose line the covenant promises would be fulfilled. He looked away from his old and impotent body and put his confidence in God's promise that in spite of his and Sarah's age, they would have a son. On that basis, or through that means, God declared him righteous. Paul then turns in verses 4–5 to illustrate this truth.

If a man such as Abraham could work for his salvation, he could justifiably demand of God that he be paid. God would be compelled to bestow salvation, not as an act of grace, mercy, or love, but as a matter of legal indebtedness. Anyone who insists on relating to God as a worker relates to his employer will most certainly be paid, but as Paul says later in Rom. 6:23, "the wages of sin is death." Paul's aim is to contrast working with believing. Working is the product of one's own efforts and abilities. Believing, on the other hand, looks to another for help. Working involves doing, while believing involves receiving.

Eternal life is granted to the person who doesn't try to earn or merit acceptance by God. It isn't by virtue of one's work but by belief in the God who justifies the ungodly. It is by means of one's faith that God reckons the person as righteous. The belief or faith that Paul has in mind is that act of heart, soul, and mind by which we look away from ourselves and our achievements and trust entirely in Jesus Christ and what he did in his sinless life and substitutionary death.

The individual who is righteous in God's sight does not work with a view to putting God in their debt. Working "*in order* to be accepted by God" and working "*because* you are accepted by God" are two entirely different things. This individual is also **ungodly** (v. 5), which is to say, profoundly unlike God in every respect, with nothing to commend themselves to God. What we are being told is that Jesus Christ didn't die for a single godly person, nor did God ever justify one. But those whom he does justify by faith become progressively more godly as their lives are transformed by the sanctifying influence of the Holy Spirit.

But Paul doesn't stop with the example of Abraham. He also appeals to that of King David (vv. 6–8; see Ps. 32), who knew firsthand the joy and the blessing that come to the person who receives righteousness from God through faith, apart from working for it. The epitome of blessedness, says David, is not some reward for working, but rather the reception of a righteous standing with God by grace through faith. The blessed, says David, are not those who have good works laid to their account, but rather those whose sins and bad works are *not* laid to their account.

The word **blessed**, used twice, once in verse 7 and again in verse 8, is the same Greek word that we find in Jesus's beatitudes, which pronounce as "blessed" people who display certain grace-given characteristics (Matt. 5:3–9). Jesus also declared blessed those who endure unjust persecution (Matt. 5:10–12). To be blessed is to be the object of God's love and favor, together with the assurance that nothing can nullify or undermine that sort of spiritual intimacy.

But why does God not count or reckon our sins against us (Ps. 103:10; 2 Cor. 5:19)? On what grounds does he take such magnanimous and marvelous action?

He does not simply dismiss our guilt or shrug off our rebellion, unbelief, and hostility as if he were indifferent to his own holiness and the demands of justice. The reason why God does not deal with us according to our sins is that he has dealt with Jesus in accordance with what they require. The reason why God does not repay us according to our iniquities is that he has repaid his Son in accordance with what holiness demands (in perfect harmony with the will and voluntary love of the Son himself).

We can confidently rest in the freedom of forgiveness because God has "presented Christ as a sacrifice of atonement, through the shedding of his blood" (Rom. 3:25). God did not cast aside our sins as if they were of no consequence. Rather, he "laid on him [the Son, our Savior] the iniquity of us all" (Isa. 53:6b). He "pierced" Jesus "for our transgressions" and "crushed" him "for our iniquities" (Isa. 53:5). This alone is why we can sing and celebrate that God does not, and never will, deal with us according to our sins or repay us according to our iniquities. The measure of God's steadfast love is the depth of the sacrifice he endured in giving up his only Son to suffer in our stead (see Rom. 8:32).

The Inadequacy of Religious Rituals to Secure a Right Standing with God (4:9–12)

Both Abraham and David, being Jews, were circumcised, the mark in the flesh of God's covenant with the people of Israel. But it was neither their circumcision nor their ethnicity that put them in the position of favor with God. In verses 9–12 Paul appeals to a well-known fact of chronology. He, in effect, asks the question in verse 10: "When was Abraham declared righteous before God? Was it only after and because he had been circumcised, or was it before?" The answer is clear: it was **before** he was circumcised (v. 10b). Circumcision served to seal the reality of his righteousness that he obtained by faith. God made sure that Abraham's justification and acceptance came before he underwent this ritual cutting of the flesh so that, as verse 11 clearly declares, Abraham might be the spiritual father of the Gentiles also, and not just of the Jews.

Paul says, in effect, "You who are Jews insist that only circumcised people, which is to say, only Jewish people, can be justified and saved. But if that were true, Abraham himself would be lost; he would be unjustified." He says this because when Abraham believed God and was accepted as righteous, he had not yet been circumcised! According to Gen. 15:6, the text that Paul quotes in Rom. 4:3, Abraham was eighty-five years old when he believed God and was justified. Abraham was not circumcised until some fourteen years later, as is told in Gen. 17. Abraham was justified by faith when he was eighty-five but wasn't circumcised until he was ninety-nine. Simply put, long before Abraham ever submitted to any religious ritual or ordinance or physical act, he was saved and accepted in God's sight.

What, then, was the purpose of circumcision for the Jewish people? And what is the purpose of water baptism for the Christian in the age of the new covenant? Both circumcision and baptism are signs that serve to seal the righteousness that we receive by faith (v. 11). As a seal these ordinances testify to the reality of our standing with God. A seal confirms the truth of that to which it points. It authenticates and guarantees the genuineness of that reality. When you are baptized in water, you don't gain a righteousness that you didn't have. You bear witness to the reality of that righteousness that you received by faith. A seal of authenticity is placed on your soul as one who is forgiven and who now stands righteous before God by faith alone. A seal like circumcision or baptism is like the wedding ring when a couple gets married. The ring doesn't cause them to be married; it is a visible witness or confirmation that they are now one flesh.

Paul's main point in demonstrating that Abraham was reckoned as righteous while still uncircumcised is to make it clear that he is the father of both Jew and Gentile. Whether or not you are circumcised has no bearing on your relationship to God. It no longer matters, says Paul, if you have Abraham's blood in your veins. It only matters if you have his faith in your heart. Possessing Abraham's DNA is of secondary importance. Of paramount importance is that you **walk in the footsteps of the faith** (v. 12 ESV) that was Abraham's.

The Principle Stated (4:13)

When Abraham was seventy-five years old, God commanded him to leave his home country and travel to the land that God would show him (Gen. 12:1–3). Upon Abraham's arrival in the land of Canaan, God established a covenant with him in which he made three promises. First, God promised to grant him title to the land of Canaan (Gen. 13:14–15). Second, God promised to Abraham an innumerable posterity: "I will make your offspring like the dust of the earth, so that if anyone can count the dust of the earth, then your offspring could be counted" (Gen. 13:16; cf. 15:5). Third, God told Abraham that he would make him a channel or source of blessing for all nations: "I will bless those who bless you, and whoever curses you I will curse; and all peoples on earth will be blessed through you" (Gen. 12:3; cf. 17:6–8; 22:17–18).

It was not through obedience to **the law that Abraham and his offspring received the promise that he would be heir of the world, but through the righteousness that comes by faith** (Rom. 4:13). There were no stipulations to be met, no works to be performed. There was only one responsibility: believe the word of promise. In what sense is Abraham **heir of the world** (v. 13), and not simply of the promised land? God's people, the offspring of Abraham who like him have put their faith in the promise of grace, stand to inherit the world (see 1 Cor. 3:21–23). This surely has in view the new heaven and the new earth described in Rev. 21–22.

The Principle Proven (4:14–16)

Paul does not simply assert the principle; he proceeds to prove it. His proof, found in 4:14–16, consists of a series of disastrous consequences were it not to be the case that the promise comes by faith.

First, if the fulfillment of the promise made to Abraham was based on his works of obedience, then **faith is null and the promise is void** (v. 14 ESV). Faith and promise have no meaning or place in a relationship that is characterized by works and reward. If what you do for me is based on and determined by what I do for you, our relationship is a legal one, not a gracious one. Whether or not I have faith in what you promised is irrelevant. If I perform according to the terms of a legal contract, you must pay me as the discharge of a legal obligation. We saw this in Rom. 4:1–12. If the promise to Abraham is based on his obedience to the law, there won't be any heirs at all because no one can perfectly obey the law. As verse 15 makes clear, **the law brings wrath**, not because the law is defective or evil, but because we are defective and evil. When we are confronted by the law, we transgress, we sin, and thereby provoke God's wrath.

Second, faith alone must be the basis of our relationship with God, for otherwise grace is excluded (v. 16a). If it were by works, none would be saved. And if somehow someone could work to gain God's favor, the individual human being, not God, would get the glory.

Third, everything must be based on faith alone, otherwise assurance is undermined (vv. 16b–17). We can be guaranteed (v. 16) or assured of the certainty of the promise only if it is rooted in faith. If it were by works, we would start asking anxious questions such as: "How many and what kind of works are necessary?" "How long and how thoroughly must I perform them?" The only way we can ever have assurance of our salvation is if it is by God's grace, through faith, that we are accepted in his sight.

In order to be an offspring of Abraham and thus an heir to the promises given to him, one need not be his physical descendant. The only need is to be one who shares **the faith of Abraham** (v. 16). Abraham **is the father of us all** (v. 16), both believing Jews and believing Gentiles. The promise of the land and the innumerable seed was initially given to Abraham and his physical progeny, the Jewish people. But with the coming of Christ, the definition or meaning of what it is to be the seed or offspring of Abraham has expanded to include not only his physical descendants but also his spiritual descendants. Every single believing Jew will inherit the promises of the Old Testament. But so too will every single believing Gentile (Gal. 3:16, 26–29).

Ancestry no longer matters, but only whether or not you are in Christ. And if you are in Christ by faith, you are an heir of all the promises, regardless of your ethnicity. Jewish men and women who reject Jesus as their Messiah and Savior forfeit their promises as Jews. And Gentiles who accept Jesus as the Messiah and Savior become heirs of those promises. What's clear from this is that we are heirs of the world because Jesus Christ is the heir of the world, and we are in him by faith.

The Miraculous Birth of Isaac (4:17–22)

God's declaration to Abraham, **I have made you the father of many nations** (v. 17 ESV; see Gen. 17:1–8), would undoubtedly have struck most as ridiculous. At that time Abram had no child and was ninety-nine years old (see Gen. 17:15–21), and all knew that the name Abram had been an embarrassment, given that this exalted father, this **father of many** (Rom. 4:17), had no children. From a purely human point of view, it might appear ridiculous for God to give him the name Abraham. But God is never restricted by our perspective. Abraham had begotten Ishmael in the power of his sinful humanity. He would now beget Isaac in the divine power of resurrection life. Just as God said, "Let there be light," and light broke forth out of the darkness (Gen. 1:3), so also would he say, "Let there be Isaac," and Isaac would be conceived in the womb of a woman, Sarah, who was far beyond her childbearing years (21:1–3). At first, however, she was unconvinced (18:9–15).

Paul's twofold description of God is important. He is the one **who gives life to the dead and calls into existence the things that do not exist** (Rom. 4:17b ESV). This is what sustained Abraham when all looked hopeless. The primary thought in Paul's mind is the quickening of the bodies of Abraham and Sarah. The promise that Abraham would be the father of an innumerable people looked foolish, given that both Abraham and Sarah were well beyond the years when they might conceive children (Abraham was ninety-nine and Sarah was ninety). But that was no obstacle to God. The statement at the conclusion of verse 17 has been interpreted in two ways. Some insist that this refers to God's creative activity by which he called the world into existence out of nothing. However,

Paul's focus is not on God's past creative work but on his determination to provide a worldwide family for Abraham. Thus, this phrase points to God's promise to bring nations and innumerable descendants from Abraham when as yet none existed. The promise that Abraham believed was that God would grant him descendants as numerous as the stars in the sky. Abraham had faith that God could effectively call these descendants into existence, even though they did not yet exist. All this, of course, would come about through the miraculous birth of Isaac.

Without the birth of Isaac, the promise to Abraham would have failed. Isaac did not exist and, humanly speaking, could not exist. His father was ninety-nine years old. His mother was ninety and barren. She was now postmenopausal. But Abraham considered the fact that **his body was as good as dead** and yet did so **without weakening in his faith** (v. 19). He trusted God to do the humanly impossible. Paul does not say that by faith Abraham denied his circumstances. Rather, he defied them. When Paul says that against all hope Abraham **in hope believed** (v. 18a), he means that from a human perspective it was hopeless; it was contrary to all reasonable hope that he and Sarah would have a child. But he defied every obstacle and trusted in God's word.

Instead of turning a blind eye to his and Sarah's physical inability to have a child, Abraham **faced the fact** (v. 19) that **his body was as good as dead** and **Sarah's womb was also dead**. He stared directly at the human obstacle to the fulfillment of God's promise and chose instead to trust that God would do what he said he would do. The phrase **he did not waver through unbelief** (v. 20) does not mean "that Abraham never had momentary hesitations, but that he avoided a deep-seated and permanent attitude of distrust and inconsistency in relationship to God and his promises."[1] After all, it says in Gen. 17:17 that when told by God that he would have a child with Sarah, "Abraham fell facedown; he laughed and said to himself, 'Will a son be born to a man a hundred years old? Will Sarah bear a child at the age of ninety?'" Her incredulity is recorded in Gen. 18:9–15. Thus, Paul is not denying the presence of at least some degree of doubt in Abraham's heart but rather is focusing on the overall, settled disposition of his trust in what God has said. After all, though Abraham was a great man, he was still a sinful man.

There are two clauses in verses 20–21 that modify and describe the statement that Abraham **grew strong in his faith** (ESV). First, he grew strong in faith and **gave glory to God**, which should be rendered as "by giving glory to God" (an adverbial participle expressing manner or means). Ascribing honor and praise to God as the one who alone has the ability to fulfill his seemingly

---

1. Moo, *Romans*, 284–85.

impossible promises actually generates stronger faith in our hearts. By faith we acknowledge God as all-powerful and true to his word, which in turn nurtures an even greater measure of faith in his ability to perform what he has promised. Second, Abraham grew strong in faith by **being fully persuaded that God had power to do what he had promised**. Again, the full assurance in Abraham's faith came from his contemplating the power of God. Meditating on God's omnipotence intensifies our confidence in him and deepens our assurance in the certainty of his word.

Abraham's faith consisted of his realization that the very real and imposing natural barriers were no hindrance to God. In effect, Abraham said to himself, "I'm too old to produce a child. Sarah is too old to bear a child. But God is not hindered or restricted by our physical limitations. What may appear hopeless to me, what may be utterly beyond and against hope as far as we are concerned, as far as our natural abilities are concerned, is of no consequence whatsoever to God!" Faith doesn't declare the circumstances and natural barriers to be nonexistent. Faith simply declares that God is not shackled by them.

Abraham's Justification and Ours (4:23–25)

It was in response to Abraham's faith that God credited to his account the righteousness that is required for acceptance by God. However, this entire story was not merely for Abraham's benefit alone but was ultimately designed to communicate to believers today that the only way to be reconciled to God is by faith. Note again what Paul says in verse 23b: the narrative about how Abraham's faith was **credited to him** wasn't included in Scripture for his sake alone **but also for us**. This entire story has as its ultimate aim to lead us to that faith which alone will secure on our behalf the righteousness that God's righteousness requires him to demand.

But faith itself is only as good as the object of its focus. And that is Paul's point in verses 24–25. The faith that results in God reckoning or imputing or counting righteousness to us is that faith which is rooted in and directed toward Jesus, **who was delivered up for our trespasses and raised for our justification** (v. 25b ESV). In saying that Jesus was delivered up **for** (*dia*, "because of") our transgressions, Paul indicates that our sins were the reason for his death. But Paul also says that Jesus was raised **for** (*dia*, "because of") our justification. Some object to the suggestion that Christ's resurrection from the dead was somehow dependent on our justification, as if the latter was the cause or ground of the former. They render the second use of the Greek preposition *dia* as "with a view to," which is to say, Jesus was raised from the dead so that we might be justified. I suspect that Thomas Schreiner's explanation comes closest to what the apostle had in mind:

> Jesus's resurrection authenticates and confirms that our justification has been secured. . . . The resurrection of Christ constitutes evidence that Jesus has been vindicated. At Jesus's resurrection, God declared that Jesus was in the right . . . so that his work on our behalf has been completed. Since believers are united to Jesus Christ in baptism (cf. Rom. 6:1–10), his death is their death and his resurrection is their vindication. Therefore the resurrection of Jesus constitutes their justification. The death and resurrection of Christ fulfill the promise of universal blessing made to Abraham, since they are the means by which all peoples enter into the new people of God.[2]

2. Schreiner, *Romans*, 252.

Adam and Christ

The Blessings of Justification (5:1–5)[1]

The opening word of chapter 5, **therefore**, is Paul's way of linking the previous discussion in 3:21–4:25 to what now follows in this chapter and the remainder of the letter. "Since" should be used when rendering of the causal participle *dikaiōthentes*—**since we have been justified by faith** (ESV)—and combined with the inferential conjunction **therefore** (*oun*) it reminds the reader that there are certain inevitable deductions and implications that follow or flow from the fact that we are reckoned as righteous in God's sight.

This justification, or being declared righteous in God's sight, comes by faith and not by works. The faith that justifies will work and produce the fruit of obedience to God's revealed will. But Paul never confuses the cause and the effect. The cause of justification, or, better still, the means by which a person is declared righteous, is faith. The effect of justification, the fruit that it bears, is a life devoted to God, a life that gradually over time reflects more and more the moral and spiritual image of Jesus in us.

First, to be at **peace with God** is a result of justification, which means that prior to justification we were at war with God.[2] Peace with God implies a cessation of

---

1. It should be noted that there is a break in Paul's argument between chapters 5 and 6. Others prefer to place 5:1–11 with chapters 1–4 and link 5:12–21 with chapters 6–8. Thomas Schreiner has argued for a major break between chapters 4 and 5, so that chapters 1–4 are one major section and chapters 5–8 another.

2. Does Paul say "we have peace with God" (reflecting the indicative *echomen*) or "let us have peace with God" (reflecting the subjunctive *echōmen*)? The difference in Greek is between the short *o* (*omicron*, o) and the long *ō* (*ōmega*, ω). There is manuscript support for both readings, but along with the majority of commentators, I take the indicative to be the more likely rendering.

the hostility that once existed. Something profound had to have happened to remove the hostility that both God and humankind experienced in their relationship with each other. Paul describes the removal of this hostility and enmity in Col. 1:19–22, where we read that through Christ he made peace "through his blood, shed on the cross." To be at **peace with God** means, among other things, that all charges of sin and condemnation have been dismissed. This is to be distinguished from the peace "of" God. Peace "with" God is descriptive of an objective, legal relationship that we sustain to him. The peace "of" God is a subjective feeling of experiential tranquility that we experience as a result of that relationship (see Phil. 4:7).

It must be emphasized yet again that genuine, fruitful, and lasting peace with God comes only, as Paul says, **through our Lord Jesus Christ** (Rom. 5:1). There is no peace with God that is not grounded in the person and work of Jesus. It is only because of what he has done at the cross for sinners and their unqualified faith and trust in the sufficiency of who he is and what he has accomplished that we can have peace with God. The **faith** by which we are justified is faith in **Jesus**. Jesus is the one **through whom** we have access into grace (v. 2). And all this is possible, as verse 6 will make clear, because **Christ died for the ungodly**. **Christ died for us**, Paul declares in verse 8. **We have now been justified by his blood** (v. 9a ESV), the blood of Jesus. And we will be saved now and in the future **through him** (v. 9b). We are reconciled to God **through the death of his Son** (v. 10a) and shall **be saved through his life** (v. 10c). And Paul concludes the paragraph in verse 11 by saying that we rejoice in God **through our Lord Jesus Christ**. Our salvation and relationship with God are decidedly Christocentric.

Elsewhere Paul talks about our being granted access to God. In Eph. 2:18 he says that it is "through him," Christ, that "we both have access in one Spirit to the Father" (ESV). The word "both" here is a reference to Jew and Gentile alike. But in Rom. 5:2 it is into **this grace** that we have been granted access. And it is **in** this grace that we **stand**. And it isn't simply into grace that we have been given access, but into **this** grace, a reference to the grace that Paul has been explaining in the first four chapters of Romans, the grace of God by which we are justified (3:24). At minimum it means that throughout the whole of our lives we are surrounded and engulfed by God's grace. The grace in which we stand is the assurance that at the final judgment we will survive. But it is also a grace that we presently experience. It is the realm or domain or state of being in which all believers live. It is that privileged position we have in Christ.

And it is in this grace that we **stand** (v. 2a), which points to a posture of triumph and victory. To stand in God's grace means that we don't believe or embrace worldly wisdom, values, goals, means, tactics, or strategies. We don't rely on human strength or cater to human desires. It means that we are reliant on divine strength, living in accordance with divine standards of right and wrong, seeking God's goals and judging success by how God defines it. It is **this grace** that alone accounts for the power to bear witness to Christ's resurrection and to give generously to one another in the local church (see Acts 6:8; 13:43). Peter reminds us that we are to "grow in the grace and knowledge of our Lord and Savior Jesus Christ" (2 Pet. 3:18), suggesting that grace is something (an experience, a power, etc.) in which we can deepen and expand and develop.

Yet another effect of having been justified is the ability to **rejoice in hope of the glory of God** (v. 2b ESV). Numerous Pauline texts speak of God's glory as something that we will experience, enjoy, and be engulfed by at the second coming of Jesus (e.g., Rom. 8:18, 21; 2 Cor. 4:16–17; Col. 3:4; 2 Thess. 1:10). But why, then, are believers still subject to suffering (Rom. 5:3), and even called upon to glory in it? Does Paul mean that we find joy in spite of our suffering, or does he mean in the midst of our suffering? Or could it be that it is because of our suffering that we rejoice? The latter is most likely, but not because the apostle is a religious masochist. We can exult or rejoice on account of our trials and adversities because we know that suffering sets in motion or produces a chain of linked virtues that ultimately produces renewed hope and assurance. Again, we see here the counterintuitive nature of Christian living. It would appear at first glance that suffering would undermine or at least greatly weaken our hope. But Paul says just the opposite!

That **we also glory [rejoice (ESV)] in our sufferings** (v. 3a) is not something expressed by Paul alone, for we hear it from Jesus (Matt. 5:10–12), James (James 1:2–4), and Peter as well (1 Pet. 1:6–7). The word translated as **sufferings** actually means "tribulation" or "affliction," but it can encompass virtually anything we face that threatens to undermine our confidence in God's goodness and sovereignty. The primary reference is to the hardships we endure and the opposition we face and the pain we suffer simply for being followers of Jesus, be it physical beatings or verbal assaults or financial loss or some form of cancellation. In the first place, we can rejoice in our suffering because no matter what we encounter that is painful and distressing, we encounter it from a posture of standing in grace (v. 2). Whatever pain and tribulation come our way, they strike us as we **stand** in grace, covered by God's unmerited favor and sustained by the power of his Holy Spirit. The grace in which we stand does not work magically in our lives. Its power comes from truth. We see and know and believe the truth of what God says, and in this way we find strength to hold on. But second, we can rejoice in our sufferings because suffering sets in motion a chain of events that changes us and ultimately concludes in even greater hope.

Suffering, says Paul, **produces perseverance** or endurance (v. 3). Those who suffer are strengthened so that they are able to bear up under the afflictions of life that come their way. The key to this is found in the participle translated as **because we know** (v. 3). Suffering accomplishes nothing good in us if we don't reflect on the fact that God uses it to build endurance and perseverance in our hearts. We can rejoice in our suffering **because we know** that God makes use of it to produce within us a never-say-die mentality. The way one resists the temptation to quit, the way one perseveres and endures, is by knowing that suffering produces endurance.

Perseverance is of value because it produces **character**, and character in turn produces **hope** (v. 4; cf. 1 Pet. 1:6–7). Just as gold is purified of dross and every alloy when it passes through the fire in a furnace, so also our faith and confidence in God's goodness and sovereignty deepen and expand when we persevere through suffering. And it is that enduring faith that Paul has in mind when he speaks of **character**. He means that our determination to stay true to the gospel and our strength to resist temptation grow and deepen as the fire of hardship and tribulation burn away the hypocrisy and superficiality of our relationship to Jesus.

And how does **character** produce **hope** (v. 4)? When a person is transformed by enduring faithfully in the midst of hardship, it demonstrates to their soul that God is real and that their faith in his promises is not misplaced. The believer in Jesus need not anticipate feelings of shame or regret when the day of judgment comes. We know this and can be assured of our future because God has poured out his love for us into our hearts through the Holy Spirit (v. 5). **God's love** is literally "the love of God," which could refer either to our love for God or his love for us. The latter is certainly the proper understanding, and for two reasons. First, the love of God is designed to be a proof of the security of our hope. How can our love of God do that? Our love for God is fitful and often faint. Second, verses 6–11 are an obvious expansion of the nature of the love spoken of in verse 5. There it is clearly God's love for us as demonstrated by the gracious gift of his Son to die in our stead.

This love **has been poured into our hearts** (v. 5 ESV). The verb "poured out" is used elsewhere of the spilling of wine (Luke 5:37), the shedding of Christ's blood (Matt. 26:28), the pouring out of the Holy Spirit at Pentecost (Acts 10:45), and with reference to the fate of Judas (Acts 1:18). Paul is emphasizing the unstinting lavishness with which God has flooded our hearts with a sense of his love for us. "The hearts of believers," writes John Murray, "are regarded as being suffused with the love of God; it controls and captivates their hearts."[3] This exuberant impartation of the love of God, writes Charles Hodge (quoting Friedrich Adolf Philippi), "does not descend upon us as dew in drops, but as a

---

3. Murray, *Romans*, 165.

stream which spreads itself abroad through the whole soul, filling it with the consciousness of his presence and favour."[4] God wants our hearts to be inundated by wave after wave of his fatherly affection, so effusively poured out that we feel compelled to request that he pull back lest we drown in his passion! Paul is talking not "of faint and fitful impressions," says J. I. Packer, "but of deep and overwhelming ones."[5] It's also important to note that Paul uses the perfect tense of the verb. This implies, Packer explains, "a settled state consequent upon a completed action. The thought is that knowledge of the love of God, having flooded our hearts, *fills them now*, just as a valley once flooded remains full of water. Paul assumes that all his readers, like himself, will be living in the enjoyment of a strong and abiding sense of God's love for them."[6]

The Holy Spirit works to evoke and stimulate in our hearts the overwhelming conviction that God loves us. The amplitude and the immensity of God's devotion are not abstract and generic but concrete and personal, not for everyone in general but for each believer in particular.

Paul is not talking about knowledge that we gain by inference from a body of evidence. Neither deduction nor induction can account for what he has in mind. Empirical observation doesn't yield the assurance of being God's beloved. We aren't dealing here with a logical truth that can be concluded from certain premises. Paul is describing a profoundly subjective and experiential sense awakened in the heart by the work of the Spirit. Paul appeals not to an argument but rather to a sensation produced in our hearts by the Holy Spirit. He does not say that God has enlightened our minds or that he has taught us by means of irrefutable reasoning that God loves us. He says, instead, that God has poured out into our hearts, through the Holy Spirit, the reality of his love for us. This is an altogether subjective, experiential reality. It is an awakening in our deepest emotions and feelings of the reality of God's abiding and joyful affection for his children. You won't always be able to explain it in intelligible terms, but you know undeniably and inescapably in your heart that God really does love you![7]

This doesn't mean that this love has no objective foundation. The objective proof or ground for this love is precisely what Paul will proceed to say in verses 6–8. There he points us to the sacrificial, substitutionary death of Jesus in our place. We must never think that our hope is only as good as our ability to experience or feel God's love for us. He most assuredly wants us to feel it, but even

4. Hodge, *Romans*, 135.
5. Packer, *Knowing God*, 118.
6. Packer, *Knowing God*, 118.
7. For a helpful discussion of Christian mysticism in the context of revival, see Poloma, *Main Street Mystics*.

when we don't, we can know his love is real and sure and certain by reminding ourselves of the lengths to which God went in making us his children: the death of his own Son on our behalf (see 2 Thess. 3:5).

Note also in verse 5 the difference in the Greek text between two phrases that in English are the same. Observe that God's love **has been** poured (perfect passive indicative) into our hearts through the Holy Spirit, who **has been** given to us. The Holy Spirit **has been** given (aorist passive participle) to all of us, at a singular point in time, once and for all when we first come to faith in Christ. But the experience of God's love that **has been** given to us through the Spirit can occur repeatedly throughout the course of our Christian lives.

The Love of God in Christ for His Enemies (5:6–11)

The connection between verses 6–11 and what has preceded in verse 5 is important. Paul states in verse 5 that our hope in God will never prove futile, disappoint, or let us down. We know this because God loves us, a love that he has poured out into our hearts through the Holy Spirit. Our hope is as secure as God's love is immutable. But there is more. Since God has demonstrated his love for us by sending Jesus to die for our sins, it follows that he will do everything necessary to make certain that we are safely and securely preserved all the way to the end. The historical, empirical, objective foundation of our confidence in the reality of God's love is unpacked in verses 6–11 and the death of Christ for sinners.

It was **at the right time** (v. 6 ESV) that Christ died for us. The death of Jesus was no accident, no quirk of fate. In Gal. 4:4 Paul says it was "when the fullness of time had come" (ESV) that God sent forth his Son to die. Both of these phrases mean that it was in God's time, when the Father determined for him to die. But knowing when Christ died is of secondary importance to understanding the nature of those for whom he gave his life.

Paul gives us a fourfold description of the kind of women and men for whom Jesus died. (1) They are **powerless** or weak people (v. 6; "without strength" [KJV]), by which Paul means spiritually and morally impotent people, unable to prepare themselves, unable to prove themselves worthy of Christ's sacrifice, helpless to do or say anything that might attract God's love. (2) They are **ungodly** people (v. 6). Jesus didn't die for nor did the Father justify a single "godly" person (4:5). To be **ungodly** means not only that we are unlike God but also that we stand opposed to God. (3) They are **sinners** (v. 8) and (4) **enemies** (v. 10): rebellious, insolent, haughty, arrogant, self-righteous, repulsive, disobedient, and defiant toward God and all that he represents and says.

Who are the **righteous** and the **good** persons for whom someone might die (v. 7)? By **righteous** and **good** Paul is speaking in purely human terms (recall 3:10–18). The righteous person is the civil, law-abiding individual who fulfills their duty, meets their obligations, and fulfills their promises. This is the kind of person who evokes your respect, but not necessarily your affection. It is unlikely that you would give your life for that individual. The good person is one for whom you **might possibly** die. This person evokes your admiration and your affection, both your respect and your love. For such a person, **perhaps** (ESV), you might be willing to die. You are slightly more inclined to sacrifice your life for that kind of individual than you would be for those who, in the eyes of others, are merely righteous.

But God (v. 8) shows or demonstrates and puts on public display his love for us in sending his beloved Son to die, not for righteous people, not for good people, not for intelligent, hard-working, church-attending people, but for sinful enemies! What you and I would do only reluctantly for a good person, God joyfully and spontaneously and abundantly and freely does for evil people. The love of God thus runs counter to every known or implied rule of human behavior. The cross of Christ is the demonstration of God's love, not its procuring cause. Christ's death on the cross isn't what moved God's heart to love sinful people. It was God's heart of love for them that led and stirred him to send his Son to die.

In Rom. 5:5 Paul was not speaking in strictly logical terms, as if he wanted to prove a point. He described there an experience. It wasn't an argument that he was attempting to prove but a feeling that the Holy Spirit awakens in us of the reality of God's love. But in verses 9–10 Paul most assuredly does make a logical argument, and it is irrefutable and airtight. He begins in verse 9 with a proposition. He reasons or makes his case on the basis of God's greatest expression of love for us. God justified us on the basis of the shed blood of Jesus. On the basis of this truth, Paul can assure us that when the day of final judgment comes, we will still **be saved from God's wrath** (v. 9b). God the Father himself has worked in the past decisively through the death of Christ and will therefore work in the future infallibly through the life of Christ to rescue us from his wrath (v. 10). In fact, it is **much more** certain that we will be saved and delivered from God's wrath on that day.

The form of logical argumentation that we see in verse 10 is reasoning from the greater to the lesser (a fortiori), such as we find in Rom. 8:32, where Paul writes, "He who did not spare his own Son, but gave him up for us all—how will he not also, along with him, graciously give us all things?" If the greatest and most costly thing God could do for us was to send his Son to suffer and die on a cross, it stands to reason that he would then do those things to keep us saved that, by comparison, are far easier and far less sacrificial and far less demanding.

But there is more to the argument here in verse 10 than that. It isn't just for good, loving, and holy people that God does this. It is for weak, ungodly, and sinful enemies that he does this. If the greater task was for God to send his Son to die for us while we were his hate-filled enemies, how much more easily and more readily would he save us from the coming wrath now that we are his friends, indeed, his sons and daughters? If Christ died for his enemies, he will surely save his friends! Will the God who loved us and saved us when we hated him turn his back and desert us now that we love him? How can we possibly suggest that God was willing to do the greatest thing for us but is now unwilling to do that which is far less?

When Paul says that we will be saved **by his** [Jesus's] **life** (ESV), he likely has in view both the resurrection of Jesus and his heavenly intercession on our behalf (for the latter, see Heb. 7:25).

The same verb used twice, first in verse 2 and again in verse 3 to describe our joyful boasting and exultation (*kauchaomai*), is the very same word now used in verse 11 to describe our joy and exultation in God for all he has done for us in Jesus. But note carefully how and on what basis this is done: it is **through our Lord Jesus Christ**. There is no such thing as acceptable, God-honoring worship that is not grounded in and focused on and accomplished by means of the person and work of Jesus Christ.

Two Men, Two Deeds, Two Destinies (5:12–21)

The only exceptions in human history to the reality of physical death are Enoch and Elijah. This compels us to ask: Why do all sin? Why do all die? Romans 5:12–21 is the most extensive answer to that question and alerts us to the truth of what is known as "original sin," by which I do not refer merely to the first sin of the first human, Adam, but also to the effect or results of that sin on us, Adam's posterity, and to the fact that we are all born spiritually dead and alienated from God. The purpose of the following discussion is not simply to teach us about the fall of Adam and the ruin and depravity that his sin unleashed on the human race. It is also designed to explain our justification in Christ, the last Adam, by contrasting it with our condemnation in the first Adam. Paul aims to describe the magnitude of the blessing we have in Christ by comparing and contrasting it with the curse we have from Adam.

Paul begins with a crucial proposition in verse 12, followed by his conclusive proof of the proposition in verses 13–14. This is followed in verses 15–21 by the contrasting parallel between the first Adam and the last Adam.

There are five phrases in verse 12 that call for comment. The first is **through one man**. Adam was a historical figure who lived in space-time just as we do, in a geographical location no less than you or I. The importance of affirming the literal, historical existence of Adam is seen in other texts as well (see Matt. 19:4; Mark 10:6; Luke 3:23–38, esp. v. 38; 1 Cor. 15:20–22). The second crucial phrase is **sin entered the world** or, more graphically, "sin invaded the world." This does not mean that Adam was the first sinner; Eve was. It does not mean that sin began its existence at that time in the garden of Eden. Paul says that sin **entered** the world, not that it began to be for the very first time. Sin already existed as a result of Satan's rebellion. This text speaks of sin's inaugural entry into the world of humanity. Sin, therefore, is portrayed as an intruder. It was not a constituent element in the original creation.

Third, as a result of the action of Adam, there came **death through sin** (see Gen. 2:17; Ezek. 18:4; Rom. 6:23; James 1:15). Death in Scripture is threefold: (1) spiritual death (the alienation of the soul from God and the subsequent spiritual corruption of the whole person; cf. Eph. 2:1–2); (2) physical death; (3) the second death (which is the perpetuation of spiritual death into eternity; eternal separation and alienation from God; cf. Rev. 2:11; 20:6). The remedy for spiritual death is regeneration, or the new birth. The remedy for physical death is the bodily resurrection. There is no remedy for the second death. It is irremediable, irrevocable, and eternal.

Sin is the cause of death. Thus, death is a penal evil; it is punishment. Death was not inevitable for Adam and Eve. It was the punishment for rebellion. Death in Rom. 5:12 refers primarily to spiritual death, the alienation of the soul from God and the subsequent spiritual corruption of the whole person. In Eph. 2:1–2 Paul speaks of all humanity as being dead in trespasses and sins. But Paul also likely had in mind physical death, which is the result of our being dead to God.

Fourth, **death spread to all men** (ESV). Adam's sin and its consequences did not stop with him. Death is universal. But why do all die? The answer is in the fifth phrase: **because all sinned**.[8] In what sense have **all sinned**? This is one of the more enigmatic and highly disputed phrases in all of Scripture. We will focus on the major views.

We begin with the doctrine of *Pelagianism*.[9] According to this view, the only reason people die is that they themselves personally sin. It is true, of course, that we die because we sin. But this view argues that the only link or connection between Adam's sin and us is that he set a bad example that we have unwisely followed. Each one of us individually reenacts Adam's transgression in our own experience. There are several objections to this view.

8. The best defense of this rendering of the phrase *eph' hō* is found in Johnson, "Romans 5:12."
9. Named for Pelagius (350–425), a British monk who engaged in theological conflict with Augustine.

It is historically and experientially false: not all die because they voluntarily sin (infant deaths being the obvious example). In verses 15–19 Paul says six times that only one sin, the sin of Adam, is the cause of death. Furthermore, if all die because they are guilty of actual transgression, then they die because they sinned like Adam did. But verse 14 says that some did not sin that way. The Pelagian interpretation would also destroy the analogy or parallel that Paul draws between Adam and Jesus in verses 15–21. If Pelagianism were correct, Paul would be saying that since all people die personally because they sin personally, so also they become righteous personally because they obey personally. But the point of these verses is that just as we died because of the sin of one, so also we live because of the obedience of one. Finally, this view cannot explain why every human being (except for Jesus) does in fact sin. It would appear that there must be something inherent in human nature that causes everyone, without exception, to decide to turn to idols rather than the true God.

Another view is the doctrine called *realism*. This view asserts that all of humankind was present in Adam naturally, biologically, physically, or seminally. It is from Adam and Eve that all have descended. Thus it may be said that we were all in his loins. Even as you were biologically and physically in the loins of your father before you were ever conceived, so too the whole human race was in the loins of our first parent, Adam. Therefore, when Adam sinned, we were really present, being in Adam, and thus we participated in his transgression. When he partook of the fruit, we partook of the fruit. Augustine advocated this view based on his reading of Rom. 5:12 in the Latin translation of the New Testament. According to the latter, the final phrase of verse 12 is rendered, "in whom [a reference to Adam the "one man" of v. 12a] all sinned," not "because all sinned." There are also problems with this view.

But how can we act before we exist? How can we personally and individually sin before we are individual persons? If this view were correct, would we not also be guilty of all Adam's subsequent sins? Again, it is the sin of one man, not of all people in Adam, that accounts for death. Realism says that all die because all really sinned in Adam, but this again destroys the parallel in verses 15–21. Surely it cannot be said that all live because all personally obeyed. We were not physically or seminally in Christ when he obeyed. The point of verses 15–21 is that just as people are justified for a righteousness not their own, so also are they condemned for a sin not personally their own. Paul's point is that death came by **one man** so that life might come by **one man**.

Finally, there is the doctrine known as *federalism* or *covenant representation*. In verse 12 Paul says that all die **because all sinned**. But in verses 15–19 Paul says all die because *Adam* sinned. In both statements Paul is saying the same thing. But how can it be that the sin of one man, Adam, is also the sin of all people? The answer is that there is some kind of union or solidarity between Adam and his posterity. It can't simply be a physical or natural union, as the realists contend. It must be a legal or representative union—that is, a covenant union. God entered into covenant with Adam as representative head of the human race. God dealt with one man, Adam, in the garden of Eden, concerning sin and death, the same as he dealt with one man, Jesus Christ, the last Adam, on Calvary's tree concerning righteousness and life.

Thus, Adam's posterity became guilty of Adam's sin and suffer its penalty, not because we personally committed a sin like Adam's sin (as Pelagians argue), nor because we sinned in Adam as our physical or biological root (as realists argue), but because Adam served in the capacity as covenant head of the human race. Similarly, we become righteous because of Christ's obedience, and experience the life that it brings, not because we personally obeyed, but because our covenant head, Jesus, obeyed (see 1 Cor. 15:21–23).

Two men, two deeds, two destinies. Adam ruined us. Christ renewed us. As we are condemned for the sin of the first Adam, we are justified for the obedience of the last Adam. This is why Adam is called the **type** (*typos*) of Christ in verse 14. According to this view, God has not dealt with people as with a field of corn, each standing for himself, or as grains of sand on the shore, each person isolated and independent of all others. Rather, he has dealt with us as with a tree, all the branches sharing a common root. While the root remains healthy, the branches remain healthy. When the axe cuts and severs the root, all die.

The principal objection to the view of federalism or covenant representation is what appears to be the injustice of it. To indict the entire human race for the sin of one of its members seems morally inconceivable.

We must also openly admit that verses 13–14 are among the most difficult verses to interpret in all of Paul's letters. Paul is talking about that period in Old Testament history stretching from Adam to the Mosaic law. During this period people certainly sinned. But in the absence of law, their sin was not imputed to them or registered against them (v. 13). Nevertheless, they died. But why did they die, if God did not impute or count their sins against them? The answer seems to be this: they died because of the sin of another, someone who had indeed violated a divinely revealed law. That other person, of course, is Adam.

Moreover, says Paul, death reigned even over those who did not sin like Adam did. In other words, there is a class of people who never sinned against an explicitly revealed divine law like Adam did. These are the people who lived in the time between Adam and Moses. Many believe that Paul is referring to infants. If infants don't sin voluntarily and personally against a divinely revealed law, why do they die? If death comes only as a penalty for sin, why do infants, who commit no sin, still die? It must be because of the sin of another. It must be that those who die in infancy, before they commit conscious, personal sin, die because of the sin of their representative head, Adam. That is one way of interpreting these verses.

The problem with this view is that it fails to take into consideration what we read in the book of Genesis concerning sin and death in the period between Adam and Moses. Two examples will suffice. Consider the great flood in the days of Noah. Clearly, those destroyed in the flood were judged, condemned, and put to death because of their personal sin (see Gen. 6:5, 11–13). The second example comes from the story of the tower of Babel as told in Gen. 11:1–9. In both of these cases that occurred between the time of Adam and Moses, God held people accountable for their sin and judged them because of it. They died because of their personal sin.

This is confirmed by what Paul said in Rom. 2:12: "All who sin apart from the law will also perish apart from the law." He is talking about Gentiles, who weren't given the law of Moses but still were held accountable by God and judged by God for having violated the moral standards and norms revealed in creation and indelibly imprinted on their conscience (see Rom. 1:18–23, 32; 2:14–16). Paul wants us to understand that we all enter this world as sinners because of our connection with Adam in his fall. But we also are held accountable and judged because of our own personal sin and not simply because of Adam's sin. If that is the case, what does Paul mean in verse 13 when he says that **sin is not counted where there is no law** (ESV)? In other words, he needs to answer the question of how those who never had the law of God can be charged as guilty of sin. Obviously, he is not saying that their sins were not counted against them in any sense. The people who lived between Adam and Moses were held accountable to God for their sin and were judged because of it.

Paul's point appears to be that although they sinned, their sin was not counted against them the same way as Adam's was. Adam's sin was in defiance of a clear commandment from God. His sin was registered against him in a truly technical and legal sense. It was, therefore, more explicitly defiant and rebellious than the sins of those who did not have access to divinely revealed commandments. Although people who lived after Adam and before Moses also sinned, it wasn't sin that was registered or accounted in the same way as Adam's sin or the sin of those who would later rebel against the law of Moses.

Instead of trying to explain all the details in verses 15–21, we should observe a series of parallels between the first Adam and the last Adam, between the Adam of Eden and Christ Jesus. As bad as what Adam did was, greater still is what Christ has done. The consequences of Adam's sin on the human race cannot compare with the glory and consequences of what Christ has done to reverse the effects of the fall. Paul's aim is to magnify the saving work of Jesus by comparing and contrasting it to the condemnation brought on us by the work of Adam. In verse 14 Paul said that Adam was a **pattern** (*typos*) or **type** (ESV) of Jesus Christ, a foreshadowing, if you will. In other words, there is a parallel that we are to see in the two men. He wants us to look at the work of the last Adam, Jesus, alongside the work of the first Adam. In doing so we will come to marvel and rejoice in the superior saving work of Christ.

The point of verses 15–21 is also to show how Christ is *not* like Adam. Notice the words **not like** in verse 15 and the contrast between the two highlighted again in verse 16. So, in one sense there is a similarity between the two Adams. But the primary point is that greater still is the dissimilarity. What Adam destroyed by his transgression, Christ has restored by his obedience. We see this not only in the words **not like** (v. 15), but also in the opening words of verse 16, **Nor can the gift of God be compared with the result of one man's sin**, as well as in the twofold use of the words **how much more** (in vv. 15, 17).

The main point of this passage is that what Christ has done for all who are in him by faith is far greater than what Adam did for all who are in him by nature. Consider these contrasts:

Verse 15: The offense of one brought death; the obedience of one brought the free gift of grace.

Verse 16: One (the first Adam) sinned, bringing condemnation; one (the last Adam) obeyed, bringing justification.

Verse 17: Through one offense death reigns; through one act of obedience life reigns.

Verse 18: The offense of one brings judgment; the righteousness of one brings justification.

Verse 19: By virtue of one man's disobedience people are made sinners; by virtue of one man's obedience people are made righteous.

Verse 21: Through Adam sin reigned unto death; through Christ righteousness reigns unto life.

It may also be helpful to remember that only if Adam represents us in the garden can Jesus represent us on Golgotha. It was on the cross that Jesus served as our representative head: his obedience to the law, his righteousness, his suffering the penalty of the law, were all the acts of a covenant head acting in the place and on behalf of his people. If Adam stood for us in the garden, Christ may also hang for us on the cross. If someone insists on standing on their own probation before God, instead of submitting to the covenant representation of Adam, they must also stand on their own in regard to righteousness. In other words, if you fall individually and by your own doing, you must be saved individually and by your own doing.

In verse 18 Paul says that **just as one trespass resulted in condemnation for all people, so also one righteous act resulted in justification and life for all people**. The conclusion that some draw is that Paul is teaching universalism—the notion that every single human being will be saved. Just as every single human being was condemned because of what the first Adam did, every single human being (**all people**) will be justified because of what the last Adam did. Is this what Paul is saying? No.

First, all through Romans up until now Paul has made it clear that only those who have faith in Christ are justified by God: "since we have been justified through faith" (5:1). Justification does not come by any other means. Salvation comes only to the one who "believes" (1:16; see also 3:26, 28; 4:3, 5, 16, 22). Second, we have also seen in Romans thus far that there will be eternal and irreversible judgment under God's wrath for those who refuse to embrace Jesus as Lord. We saw this in 1:18, 32; 2:2, and especially 2:5, where unbelievers "are storing up wrath against" themselves "for the day of God's wrath." The same truth is found in 2:8–9. Paul speaks of God judging the world in 3:5–6. And this accounts for texts only in the first four chapters of Romans. Third, in 5:17 Paul speaks of those who "receive" the grace of God, as over against those who do not. Those who do not receive it but reject it in unbelief are eternally lost. Again, justification is never automatic simply because you are a human. It is a status that God confers only to those who believe.

Fourth, Paul's point is that the obedience and righteousness of Jesus Christ come to all who are connected or related to him, just as judgment comes to all who are connected or related to Adam. Whereas every person is "in" Adam, only those who have faith are "in" Christ. Adam acted sinfully, and because we were connected to him, we were condemned in him. Christ acted righteously, and because we are connected to Christ, we are justified in Christ. Adam's sin is counted as ours. Christ's righteousness is counted as ours. Fifth, we must also reckon with what Paul says later in Romans, after chapter 5. He speaks of "death" coming to those who live according to the flesh (8:13). In 9:22 he speaks of certain individuals as "vessels of wrath prepared for destruction" (ESV). If Paul believed that all would eventually be saved, why does he pray fervently for the salvation of his Jewish brothers and sisters in 9:1–5 and 10:1? Finally, sixth, we should never read what Paul says in one passage without considering what he says about the same subject in other places in his letters. And in numerous other texts he speaks of eternal condemnation for those who reject the gospel of Jesus (e.g., 1 Cor. 6:9–11; 11:32; 2 Cor. 11:15; Gal. 1:8; 5:19–21; 1 Thess. 1:10; 2 Thess. 1:5–12; 2:9–12).

There are several additional reasons why Paul should not be understood to be advocating universalism here in Romans 5. It's important to approach a paragraph such as this in relation to all that Paul articulates elsewhere in Romans about those who profit spiritually from the saving work of Christ. We also see here that the impact of Adam's sin extends to those who are "in" him by virtue of his role as covenant representative of the race. So, too, does the blessing of Christ's obedience extend to those who by faith are "in" him, and the two groups are not coextensive. In order to receive the gift of God's grace and righteousness (v. 17), one must believe in Christ. Those who do not have faith are excluded from the **life** that comes **through the one man Jesus Christ** (v. 17). We see repeatedly in Romans that the **all men** (v. 18 ESV) who are justified are those who are united with Christ through faith, apart from works (1:16; 3:22; 5:1; 10:9). Paul makes it clear that whereas there is no limitation on the number of men and women who suffer the consequences of Adam's transgression, only those who by God's grace place their personal faith in Christ's **one act of righteousness** (v. 18) enjoy the blessing of the eternal life (v. 17) he died to secure.

The Eternal Destiny of Those Dying in Infancy

Whenever the concept of original sin and the moral corruption of human nature is raised, the question is asked, Are those who die in infancy lost? The same question would apply to those who live beyond infancy but, because of mental disability or some other unavoidable limitation, are incapable of moral discernment, deliberation, or volition. Several answers have been given to this question.

Some contend for *the sinlessness of infants*. They are born in a state of moral neutrality or moral equilibrium. They do not possess a sin nature, nor are they corrupt. There is nothing in their souls that is properly the object of divine judgment. Hence all who die in that state are saved for no other reason than that they are not condemnable. However, see Gen. 8:21; Job 15:14–16; Pss. 51:5; 58:3; Prov. 22:15; Eph. 2:3.

Another viewpoint asserts that *all will be saved*, inclusive of those who die in infancy. None will suffer eternal condemnation. God's saving grace extends effectually to the entire human race. Again, several texts refute this view. See Matt. 7:13–14, 21–23; 8:11–12; 10:28; 13:37–42; Luke 16:23–28; 2 Thess. 1:9; Jude 6; Rev. 14:10–11; 20:11–15.

Based on a certain interpretation of 1 Pet. 3:18–19 and 4:6, it is asserted that those who die without having the opportunity to hear the gospel of Christ and make a cognitively and morally informed decision will be granted a "second chance" (it is, in fact, a "first" chance if they never had a legitimate opportunity in this life). However, the two texts on which proponents base their view say nothing about postmortem evangelism for either those who die in infancy or pagans who never hear the name of Jesus.

Certain traditions within Christianity have affirmed *baptismal regeneration*, according to which the waters of baptism are used by God to effect the regeneration, spiritual cleansing, and forgiveness of the infant. Needless to say, this view is only as cogent as is the case for baptismal regeneration, and the case for the latter is poor. The Roman Catholic Church has acknowledged the possibility of a state of natural blessedness or happiness in which unbaptized infants experience a form of eternal peace but not the consummate joy of heaven itself. Rome has neither formally affirmed nor denied this teaching, traditionally known as "limbo." Others have appealed to 1 Cor. 7:14–16 to argue that *the infants or children of a believing parent or parents* are, for that reason, granted special salvific privilege in the kingdom of God.

Some Reformed theologians argue that most who die in infancy are *elect*, and therefore saved, while others are *nonelect*, and therefore condemned. The most likely view is that all those who die in infancy, as well as those who are incapable of making an informed choice, are *among the elect of God chosen by him for salvation before the world began*. The evidence for this view is scant but significant.

In Rom. 1:20 Paul describes people who are recipients of general revelation as being "without excuse." Does this imply that those who are *not* recipients of general revelation (i.e., infants) are therefore *not* accountable to God or subject to wrath? If so, those who die in infancy have an "excuse" in that they neither receive general revelation nor have the capacity to respond to it. There is at least one text that appears to assert that infants do not know good or evil and hence lack the capacity to make morally informed and thus responsible choices. According to Deut. 1:39, they are said to "have no knowledge of good or evil" (ESV).

The story of David's son in 2 Sam. 12:15–23 (esp. v. 23) must be noted. The firstborn child of David and Bathsheba was struck by the Lord and died. In the seven days before the child's death, David fasted and prayed (vv. 16–17), hoping that "the LORD may be gracious to me and let the child live" (v. 22). Following the child's death, David washed himself, ate food, and worshiped (v. 20). When asked why he responded in this way, he replied, "Now that he is dead, why should I go on fasting? Can I bring him back again? I will go to him, but he will not return to me" (v. 23). If "I will go to him" is merely a reference to the grave or death, in the sense that

David, too, will one day die and be buried, one wonders why he would say something so patently obvious. Also, it appears that David draws some measure of comfort from knowing that he will "go to him." It would therefore appear that David believed that he would be reunited with his deceased infant. Does this imply that at least *this one particular infant* was saved? Perhaps. But if so, are we justified in constructing a doctrine in which we affirm the salvation of *all* who die in infancy?

More important still is the consistent testimony of Scripture that people are judged on the basis of sins voluntarily and consciously committed in the body. See 2 Cor. 5:10; 1 Cor. 6:9–10; Rev. 20:11–12. Eternal judgment is always based on one's conscious rejection of divine revelation (whether in creation, conscience, or Christ) and willful disobedience. Are infants capable of either? There is no explicit account in Scripture of any other judgment based on any other grounds. Thus, those dying in infancy are saved because they do not (cannot) satisfy the conditions for divine judgment.

Also, if an infant faces eternal judgment on the basis of Adam's sin alone, he or she would have no understanding of the grounds for being condemned. All such infants would know that they were in hell, but could not account for the reason they are there. The latter seems inconsistent with the accepted principles of justice.

We also may have biblical evidence that at least *some* infants are regenerate in the womb, such that if they had died in their infancy, they would have been saved (see Jer. 1:5; Luke 1:15). This at least provides a theoretical basis for considering whether the same may be true of all who die in infancy. Also, some have appealed to Matt. 19:13–15 (// Mark 10:13–16 // Luke 18:15–17) where Jesus declares, "Let the little children come to me, and do not hinder them, for the kingdom of heaven belongs to such as these" (v. 14). Is Jesus simply saying that if one wishes to be saved, he or she must be as trusting as children—devoid of skepticism and arrogance? Is Jesus merely describing the *kind* of people who enter the kingdom? Or is he saying that these very children were recipients of saving grace?

Finally, Millard J. Erickson insists that notwithstanding Adam's sin, there must be a conscious and voluntary decision on our part to embrace or ratify it. Until such is the case, the imputation of Adam's sin to his physical posterity, as is also true of the imputation of Christ's righteousness to his spiritual posterity, is *conditional*. Thus, prior to reaching the "age of accountability" all infants are innocent.[a]

But if we are born with a corrupt and sinful nature, as Erickson concedes we are, our willing ratification of Adam's transgression and the guilt and corruption of nature that are its effects are themselves inevitable effects of the corrupt nature to which we are now ostensibly giving our approval. In other words, how else *could* a person who is born corrupt and wicked respond but in a corrupt and wicked way—namely, by ratifying Adam's sin? If Erickson is suggesting that such a response is *not* inevitable, one can only wonder why it is that *every single human being* who ever lived (except Jesus) ratifies and embraces the sin of Adam and its resultant corruption of nature. Surely someone, somewhere would have said no. Erickson would have to argue that at the point when each soul becomes morally accountable it enters a state of complete moral and spiritual equilibrium, in no way biased by the corruption of nature and the wicked disposition with which it was born. But that leads to another problem, for it would mean that each of us experiences our own garden of Eden, as it were. Each human soul stands its own probation at the moment the age of moral accountability is reached. But if that is so, what is the point of trying to retain any connection at all between what Adam did and who and what we are? If I become corrupt by my own first choice, what need is there of Adam? And if I am corrupt *antecedent* to that first choice, we are back to square one: my guilt and corruption inherited from Adam, the penal consequence of *his* choice as the head and representative of the race.

In view of several of the arguments cited, it seems reasonable to believe in the salvation of those dying in infancy. If they are saved, it is neither because they are innocent nor because they have merited God's forgiveness, but solely because God has sovereignly chosen them for eternal life, regenerated their souls, and applied the saving benefits of the blood of Christ to them apart from conscious faith.

a. Erickson, *Christian Theology*, 2:639.

ROMANS 6

Slaves of Sin or of Righteousness

Slaves of Sin (6:1–14)

Paul's statement in 5:20 that "where sin increased, grace abounded all the more" (ESV; see also 3:20, 24, 28; 4:5; 5:9–10) evidently led some to conclude that believers should sin all the more so that grace might abound all the more. In Romans 6 Paul responds with righteous indignation to this antinomian[1] error: **By no means!** Christians are people who have **died to sin** (v. 2), which doesn't mean that they are insensitive to sin or unable to sin. The translation **How can we live in it any longer?** is somewhat misleading. It would suggest that it is impossible for us to sin. But the verse more literally says **How shall we continue in sin?** It is not the literal impossibility of sin but the moral incongruity of it that Paul has in mind. It makes no sense for people who have **died to sin** to continue to **live in it**.

The incongruity of living in sin when one has died to it is based on the believer's solidarity or union with Jesus, a truth found repeatedly in verses 3–11:

buried *with him* through baptism into death (v. 4a; cf. Col. 2:11–12)
united *with him* in a death like his (v. 5a)
united *with him* in a resurrection like his (v. 5b)
our old self was crucified *with him* (v. 6a)
now if we died *with Christ* (v. 8a)
we will also live *with him* (v. 8b)

1. "Antinomian" means opposition to the law or at minimum a casual or indifferent attitude and thus neglect of God's law.

Paul's typical language for describing this spiritual solidarity with Christ is that we are "in" him (cf. Rom. 8:1; 1 Cor. 1:30; 2 Cor. 5:17, 21; Gal. 2:17; Eph. 1:3; 2:10), a reality to which public witness is given in water baptism (Rom. 6:3–4). When a person is immersed in water, it symbolizes or portrays our cocrucifixion with Jesus. His death is reckoned as our death. When Jesus was crucified, God saw us in and with him, united as one. When Jesus died under the penalty of sin, so did we. In God's sight, what is true in the experience of Jesus is true of us. By virtue of our covenant solidarity and union with Christ, when he died, was buried, and rose again to a new and glorious life, so did we.

The two rhetorical questions in verses 1–2 are not meant to suggest that Christians can attain sinless perfection in this life. Paul clearly says that a born-again believer in Jesus cannot **go on sinning** or **live** in sin, which is his way of saying that a Christian must not sin as an unchanging, unbreakable pattern in life. He isn't denying that we commit sins but is saying that we should not abide in them or linger in them unrepentant. Paul refers to much the same thing in verse 6, where he says that we are no longer **slaves to sin**, by which he means held in complete bondage and total defeat to the power of sin. Yes, believers sin, but they are not dominated by or enslaved to it. In verse 11 he tells us to **count** ourselves **dead to sin but alive to God**. In verse 12 he says not to let sin **reign in your mortal body** (ESV), and in verse 13 he exhorts us not to **present** our members, our bodies, **as instruments for unrighteousness** (ESV). If we are not still battling against sin and sometimes yielding to temptation, why bother issuing these sorts of commands? Paul's point is that we should instead embrace our new identity as those who are one with Christ, alive from the dead, and by his Spirit present ourselves to God as instruments for righteousness.

Believers' response to this truth is that they must **count** themselves dead to sin and alive to God in Christ (v. 11). Simply put, you must not go on living the life you used to live, because you are no longer the person you used to be. In verse 6 Paul says that **our old self** or, more literally, "our old man" was crucified with Christ. Our **old self** is the person we used to be, the individual who was in Adam. Paul means that we are not under compulsion to sin. Sin is not entirely unavoidable. We are not enslaved to it but now are empowered by the Holy Spirit to serve a new master, Jesus. The verb translated as **might be brought to nothing** (v. 6 ESV) does not indicate becoming extinct or nonexistent. Sin is still very much alive in the Christian, but it has been defeated and deprived of its ruling power. The dominion of sin in our lives has been broken, not in the sense that it is impossible for us any longer to sin, but in the sense that sin is no longer necessary. We now are dominated by a power that brings us victory over temptation.

According to verse 7, **anyone who has died has been set free from sin**. The verb translated as **set free** (*dedikaiōtai*) is used elsewhere in Romans to speak of being justified. Paul's point is that the decisive break with the enslaving and reigning power of sin "is viewed after the analogy of the kind of dismissal which a judge gives when an arraigned person is justified. Sin has no further claim upon the person who is thus vindicated."[2] Furthermore, insofar as we have been identified with Christ in his death, we will also be one with him in the new life of his resurrection. Paul here isn't referring primarily to our bodily resurrection when Christ returns and we are glorified and transformed. That will certainly come to pass. Rather, he has in mind living in the present day as alive from spiritual death (see v. 4). To **live with him** (v. 8b) is to walk in the new power of a new life that we have today because of our unity with him in his new life. We are **alive to God in Christ Jesus** (v. 11b) in the sense that we walk in new freedom, new joy, new power to overcome the allure of sin and temptation.

The phrase **the body ruled by sin** (v. 6b; **body of sin** [ESV]) does not mean that the human physical frame is inherently contaminated or evil. Paul has in view our "sin-dominated body" in the sense that the body is conditioned and controlled by sin, "because sin uses our body for its own evil purposes, perverting our natural instincts, degrading sleepiness into sloth, hunger into greed, and sexual desire into lust."[3]

Romans 6:11 is something of a summary statement. The verb **count** has the sense of "reckon." It does not mean that we are to pretend or somehow convince ourselves of something we know isn't true. Rather, we are to reckon with the fact and meditate on the truth that in Christ we died to sin and that in Christ we are alive to God. Our minds are so to grasp the fact of our death and resurrection with Christ that the very idea of sinning is abhorrent and unthinkable to us.

Paul personifies sin as if it were a king demanding to be obeyed. Do not let sin **reign** in your life as it seeks to establish itself over you as lord and ruler, compelling you to **obey its evil desires** (v. 12b). The true King and Lord whose rule and reign we should happily embrace is God. Surrender your members to him so that he can make use of them to achieve righteousness.

Paul's statement in verse 14 is not an imperative, a veiled exhortation or a command that we do something. It is a statement of assured fact, a divine promise. Paul does not say, "Don't let sin have dominion over you," but rather, **Sin shall no longer be your master**. Thus, verse 14a makes valid and relevant the commands of verses 12–13 and provides the encouragement and incentive for their fulfillment. Obedience to verses 12–13 is achieved by the assurance that God's grace guarantees the realization of what is contemplated in

2. Murray, *Romans*, 222.
3. Stott, *Romans*, 175.

the exhortations. Sin is here viewed as a power, and yet it will no longer be our **master**, for another has taken possession of us. We will never again be left helpless; we are now free and able (by God's Spirit) to fight.

Since you are not under law but under grace (v. 14b ESV) does not mean that Christians are law-less, as if to suggest that there are no divine mandates or laws for us to obey. We are most assuredly under the law of Christ (see 1 Cor. 9:21). As for the meaning of verse 14, one view is that Paul means that we no longer live under law as a way of life. In other words, law-keeping is not the way we seek to relate to God, as if by our obedience we can put him in our debt and win favor and blessings from him. Another view is that we are no longer under the law of Moses as a code of conduct. There is a distinction between the old covenant of Moses and its laws and the new covenant of Jesus Christ and his laws. We see this glorious truth about the new covenant from several prophecies of it in the Old Testament. In this regard, see especially Jer. 31:31–34; Ezek. 36:26–27 (cf. 11:19–20); Heb. 13:20–21. Being **under grace** also means we are no longer under wrath, subject to God's judgment.

But how does being **under grace** guarantee that sin will no longer be our **master**? It does so by supplying us with the power of the Holy Spirit to say no to sin and temptation. But more than that, Paul is assuming that we will embrace and draw strength from the fact that we are united with Christ in his death to sin and in his new life. Your death and resurrection with Christ mean that sin will not reign over you. Therefore, don't let it reign over you! In addition, to be **under grace** also means that we are no longer subject to the paralyzing power of guilt, shame, and condemnation (cf. Rom. 8:1). To be "in" Christ is to live **under** his **grace** and favor. To be **under the law** or subject to its dictates and liable to judgment because of our failure to obey it undermines our energy to resist sin and temptation. We feel hopeless to fight against sin and thus make no effort to change or make progress in obedience.

Slaves of Righteousness (6:15–23)

In verse 15 Paul reiterates his response to the charge that his doctrine of grace empowers sin. Some evidently thought that in saying that Christians are not under the law of Moses and bound by its dictates, Paul was declaring our freedom from any and all moral laws. But all people are slaves, either to sin or to God (vv. 16, 22). Paul appears to be concerned that his use of the imagery of slavery might prove to be offensive to some. Thus, in verse 19 he interrupts his argument and says, **I am speaking in human terms, because of your natural limitations** (ESV). He doesn't want anyone to conclude that he is making light of the reality of slavery. He is not in any way endorsing it or turning a blind eye to its evils. He is using the imagery of slavery in his own day to illustrate the relationship that all of us sustain either to sin or to righteousness.

In verses 1–14 Paul repeatedly affirmed that the reason why we must not continue to live in sin is that we, by virtue of our spiritual union with Christ, have died to sin. Now, in verses 15–23, he says we must not continue in sin, because by God's saving grace we have become slaves to him and to righteousness. The reality of spiritual slavery is unpacked by Paul in verses 16–19. If you give yourself over to your fleshly lusts and follow their prompting, you become a slave to your sin. You obey its dictates. You are held in bondage to its passions and desires. On the other hand, if you choose to give yourself to God and submit your life, thoughts, actions, and words to him, you are his slave. You are held captive to his will and ways (see 1 Cor. 6:10–20; Rev. 5:9).

In sum, you are living either as a slave to sin or as a slave to God. If you choose the former, you should understand that you don't rule sin. Sin rules you. The idea that as long as you refuse to embrace and believe the gospel you remain free, that you remain your own lord and master, is a delusion. There is no person anywhere at any time who has not lived as the slave of someone. There is no such thing as unconditional, unequivocal, unfettered freedom. Either you are a slave to your sin or you are a slave to God and his righteousness (see John 8:34–36).

So, how did we who believe in Jesus enter into this true freedom of which the apostle speaks? Paul answers that in verses 17–18, where he gives thanks to God **that, though you used to be slaves to sin, you have come to obey from your heart the pattern of teaching that has now claimed your allegiance. You have been set free from sin and have become slaves to righteousness** (vv. 17–18). That our newly found freedom is the work of God is affirmed again in verse 22, where Paul states that we **have been set free from sin and have become slaves of God**. God's saving power transforms our minds and writes his law upon our hearts and gives us his Spirit, by whose work we see the beauty of Christ and treasure his ways above those of the world, the flesh, and the devil.

There is still something that we do. As Paul says in verse 17, **you have come to obey from your heart the pattern of teaching that has now claimed your allegiance**. Paul's use of **heart** (*kardias*) highlights the sincerity or depth of the response. It is a glad-hearted and altogether willing obedience. The phrase **pattern** [*typon*; **standard** (ESV)] **of teaching** refers to the well-defined body of Christian truth, both the doctrinal concepts and the ethical precepts of God's word. The phrase **that has now claimed your allegiance** is more literally rendered as "to which you were delivered." The passive form *paredothēte* ("deliver" or "transmit," as in the handing down of a tradition) highlights God's initiative in conversion. It isn't so much that tradition has been delivered to us as it is that we have been handed over to the pattern or form of teaching. The outcome or **benefit** (v. 21a) of spiritual slavery to sin is **death** (v. 21b). Conversely, the **benefit** that comes from slavery to God and his righteousness leads to **holiness**, the result of which is **eternal life** (v. 22). Since the **life** we gain by being enslaved to God is **eternal**, it stands to reason that the **death** one experiences by being enslaved to sin is likewise eternal (i.e., hell).

Paul's statement in verse 21 suggests that there is a proper place for being **ashamed**. It has to do with the way one lived before becoming a child of God by faith in Jesus (cf. Jer. 8:12). He isn't telling believers to be ashamed of who they are or to embrace shame as part of their identity. He is telling us that we should be able to look into our past, into that time when we were enslaved to sin, and say, "Lord, I am truly ashamed of the things I believed and the kind of sinful life I lived. Thank you for forgiving me!"

Paul concludes (*gar*, **for**) on the hopeful and encouraging note of eternal life through Jesus Christ (v. 23). Sin pays a wage, whereas God bestows a gift (in both instances, **wages of sin** and **gift of God**, the genitive is subjective). The wage that sin pays is eternal death. The gift that God bestows is eternal life. You have to work to earn a wage. You only have to believe to receive a gift. You deserve your wages, and sin will pay fully and on time. But you don't deserve a free gift. And it comes to a person only **in Christ Jesus our Lord** (v. 23b). Apart from Christ there is no gift of eternal life.

The Christian's Battle with Indwelling Sin

Sanctification and God's Law (7:1–13)

Paul here (vv. 1–7) is unpacking the significance of his statement in 6:14–15 that "we are not under the law, but under grace." First, for the man or woman who has died with Christ and been raised to walk in newness of life, the law has no **authority over** them; it is not the primary driving force or controlling principle in their relationship with God. Christians are still "under Christ's law" (1 Cor. 9:19–23). But they do not obey law in any form as a way of putting God in their debt, or in an attempt to gain favor from him, or as a way to pay him back for what he has done for them. Second, Paul also has in view the law of Moses in particular. Believers live under the terms and dictates not of the old covenant but of the new covenant. The primary difference between the two covenants isn't that one is characterized by law and the other by grace. There is law in both covenants. But in the old covenant the demands of the law did not promise or provide the power to obey. In the new covenant, together with the commandments of Christ, is promised the power of the Holy Spirit to enable Christians to obey.

Here in Rom. 7:1–6 Paul draws a comparison between a married couple and the Christian's relationship to the law. His point is that when someone's spouse dies, that person is free from any further marital obligations. Paul isn't talking about whether or not there are legitimate grounds for divorce and remarriage. His point is simply this: death puts an end to the relationship and frees one to enter into a new and binding relationship. A woman is bound to her husband as long as he lives. If, while they are still married, she marries another, she is guilty of adultery. However, if her husband dies, the marriage is dissolved, and she is free to marry another man.

Just as physical death terminates a marriage, so spiritual union with Christ's death terminates our bondage to the law. When Jesus died for us under the condemnation of the law, God reckoned us to have died. We are no longer in bondage to the law as far as its condemning power is concerned (v. 4). Since we died in and with Christ when he died, we are set free from the law and can now enter into a new relationship with him. We no longer belong to the law but belong to Christ, just as the widow no longer is married to her deceased spouse and is free to marry another. The point of the analogy is that becoming a Christian involves a complete change of relationship and allegiance. Our identification in and with Jesus in his death, burial, and resurrection is so that we **might belong to another, to him who was raised from the dead** (v. 4), Jesus. And this is in order that we **might bear fruit for God**. We are now enabled to live a life that honors God because we **serve in the new way of the Spirit and not in the old way of the written code** (v. 6 ESV).

Paul evidently anticipated that some would take his comments about our being set free from the law and conclude that the law itself is evil and that we are now free to live however we please. The result of this reaction to Paul's words is antinomianism, to which he responds in verses 7–13. His critics, based on their misunderstanding of what Paul has just said, have concluded that the law is sinful, even lethal. But the apostle points out that the law serves to reveal our sins (v. 7). Were it not for the law shining a light on his sin, he would have continued and persisted in his wickedness. He would never have repented had not the law brought conviction to his heart. Paul appeals to the last of the Ten Commandments, which says, **You shall not covet**, probably because it uncovers the desires and intentions of the heart, rather than simply focusing on external behavior. Covetousness was always there, but Paul didn't feel the force of how evil it is until he heard God say, **You shall not covet**. It was then, after the law alerted him to how covetousness betrays a failure to trust God with what we have and to be content with what he has provided, that he felt the sting of how badly he had failed. Longing to possess what others have was imperceptibly present in Paul's heart. But the wickedness of it, the idolatry that gives rise to it, was not fully felt until he heard from God's law that it was prohibited.

That is why the law is not the answer to our problems, but Christ is. As Paul says in verse 8, it was sin that seized **an opportunity through the commandment** that we should not covet. And it was sin that **produced in me all kinds of covetousness** (v. 8 ESV). Sin is to blame, not the law. So here Paul is saying, "Before I came to know God's law, my conscience was at ease. I was complacent, even self-righteous about the state of my soul, thinking myself to be very much alive and well. But when my life was suddenly exposed to the searchlight of God's perfect law, I died. That is to say, my sense of peace and self-assured tranquility was destroyed. That sense of 'It is well with my soul' came to an abrupt end, as my sinful flesh reared up within me in defiance of God's revealed will." But again, Paul is careful to point out that the law itself is not to blame for this outcome. I am to blame. My sin is to blame. Sin took what God intended for good and distorted and exploited it for evil purposes.

Indeed, **the law is holy, and the commandment is holy, righteous and good** (v. 12; see Pss. 1:2; 119:14–16, 97). Sin used the commandments of God as its weapon. So the reason why we must die to the law isn't that the law is wicked but rather that we are. As Paul says again in verse 13, the laws and commandments of God are good, but they expose our sinful hearts and arouse in us all manner of wicked, self-serving defiance.

Sanctification and Our Sin (7:14–25)

Romans 7:14–25 is one of the more disputed passages in all of Scripture and thus requires closer examination than is possible for other texts in the epistle, together with an appeal to numerous secondary sources. Who is this man or woman whom Paul describes? Is this individual a Christian or a non-Christian? Does Paul portray for us here what some might call the "normal" Christian life, or is this a portrayal of what we were before being born again, a condition from which, by the grace of God, we have been delivered? Is the Christian life one of severe struggle and frequent defeat, or is it one of triumph over sin and victory over the flesh? Or are these questions themselves misleading? Is there a third or middle way between these two extremes?

An Overview of the Interpretive Options

Space limitations allow us to examine only the more widely held interpretations of this passage. One view insists that the person described by Paul in verses 14–25 is regenerate or born again. But there are a number of variations within this perspective, only two of which I'll mention. Some believe that the experience described in verses 14–25 is one that even the most sanctified and mature of believers may expect to encounter until the resurrection of the body. Others insist that Paul is describing an experience that may be overcome through growth and maturity in the faith. The goal is to exchange the conflict in Rom. 7 for the victory in Rom. 8. In other words, verses 14–25 describe the Christian who has failed to avail themselves of the power of the Holy Spirit. It may be "normal" in the sense that many languish in this condition, but it is by no means normative in the sense that God has provided us with everything necessary to live victoriously over such sin.

Another interpretive option is that Paul is describing someone (possibly himself) who is unregenerate. Under this major heading, some believe that this is Paul's autobiographical account of his own preconversion experience, either as seen and understood by him at the time of his non-Christian life or as seen and understood by him at the time he was writing Romans. According to the latter, Paul looks with Christian eyes on his former, non-Christian state. He now discerns a discord or struggle that was actually present then but that he did not see at that time.

Others believe that this is Paul's portrayal, not of himself, but of *humanity* under the law. The "I" is not Paul himself but rather a stylistic form making for a more vivid picture than our colorless use of "one." Thus, this is Paul's analysis of human existence apart from faith, either as seen by the non-Christian or as seen by the Christian, in this case Paul. A somewhat similar perspective, but with a slight difference in emphasis, is the position taken by Douglas Moo. He believes that verses 14–25 describe the situation of an unregenerate person: "Specifically, I think that Paul is looking back, from his Christian understanding, to the situation of himself, and other Jews like him, living under the law of Moses. . . . Now, in vv. 14–25, he portrays his own condition as a Jew under the law, but, more importantly, the condition of all Jews under the law. Paul speaks as a 'representative' Jew, detailing his past in order to reveal the weakness of the law and the source of that weakness: the human being, the *egō*."[1]

The Case for Seeing the Person in Romans 7 as a Christian

There are several things that appear to suggest that Paul has in view the regenerate, born-again Christian here in Rom. 7. We begin with the fact that Rom. 7:7–25 is not parenthetical to Paul's main argument but rather is in the context of his discussion of the Christian life that covers all of Rom. 6–8. If this paragraph is Paul's description of the unbeliever's struggle with the law, it "becomes an unnecessary interruption and digression in Paul's train of thought, much more suited to the context of Rom. 2–3 than that of 6–8."[2]

The most natural way to take the **I** in the paragraph is as an autobiographical reference to Paul. The sustained and vivid use of this first-person singular is not easily explained any other way (especially when taken in conjunction with the intensely personal cry in v. 24). In addition, Paul shifts from the past tense

1. Moo, *Romans*, 447–48.
2. Dunn, "Rom. 7,14–25," 260.

in verses 7–13 (used 9x) to the present tense in verses 14–25 (used 26x). What sounds like past, non-Christian testimony in verses 7–13 becomes current, Christian testimony in verses 14–25. Also, if the struggle in verses 14–25 is Paul's preconversion experience, it would conflict with what he says elsewhere about his life as a Pharisee, especially in Phil. 3:6 and Gal. 1:13–14. Whatever else Rom. 7 might be saying, "there is no hint that Paul, before his conversion, was the victim of such an inward conflict as he describes here [vv. 14–25]; on the contrary, all the evidence is against it. . . . If Paul's conversion was preceded by a period of subconscious incubation, this has left no trace in our surviving records."[3]

Advocates of this view also point out that Paul's description of the I in Rom. 7 is inconsistent with what he says elsewhere of the natural or unregenerate person. Note what Paul attributes to the person or the I in Rom. 7. This person

- hates evil and wish to do good (v. 15);
- concurs with the law of God, acknowledging it to be good (v. 16);
- declares that **it is no longer I myself who do it, but it is sin living in me** (v. 17) (one must ask whether the unregenerate individual is capable of engaging in this depth of self-analysis);
- acknowledges their innate depravity (v. 18);
- wants to do good (vv. 18, 21);
- does not wish to do evil (v. 19);
- joyfully concurs with the law of God (v. 22; cf. Ps. 119:97);
- feels imprisoned by and in bondage to their sin (v. 23); and
- confesses their wretchedness (v. 24).

In summary, the person of verses 14–25 does bad things, but they hate them. They violate the prevailing bent of their will to do the good. In their inner being, the deepest and most fundamental seat of their personality, they love God's law, delight in the good, hate and dissociate their will from evil. Can this be said of the unregenerate? In the unregenerate there may well be a conflict between mind or conscience and the will. The conscience is convicted of sin and recognizes right from wrong. But the will resists and does not wish or want to do what the conscience says is right. But in verses 14–25 the will of the individual in view does want to do good.

Along the same line of thought, Paul's description of the person in verses 14–25 is consistent with what he elsewhere says of the Christian. According to

3. Bruce, *Paul*, 196.

verse 25b, this person, in his mind, is **a slave to God's law**. Likewise, in Rom. 6:18 Christians are they who have become "servants" or "slaves" to righteousness. All admit that Gal. 5:17 is describing the Christian, and yet the struggle between "flesh" and "Spirit" in that passage is seemingly parallel to the struggle in Rom. 7. Would we not say that a struggle as serious as the one in Rom. 7 can take place only where the Spirit of God is present and active? Otherwise, would not an unregenerate person simply acquiesce altogether to the promptings of sin and the flesh?

Another argument in favor of taking the individual as a believer is based on verse 25b, which says that the struggle persists beyond the declaration of victory found in verse 25a. If verses 14–23 refer to a non-Christian who becomes a Christian in verses 24–25a, why does Paul say that the struggle is still a reality? As James Dunn notes, "The antithesis between the inward man and the flesh is not overcome and left behind, it continues through and beyond the shout of thanksgiving—as a continuing antithesis between mind and flesh. The 'I' is still divided. In other words, the struggle so vividly depicted in 7:14–25 does not end when the Spirit comes; on the contrary, that is when it really begins."[4]

We should also note that although Paul moves smoothly from a description of himself in verses 7–13 to the description in verses 14–25, there is a notable difference between the two paragraphs, a difference that seems to demand that in the former he was unregenerate and in the latter regenerate. In verses 7–13 we don't see a struggle. Sin assaulted him and left him for dead. But beginning with verse 14 a war is waged. It is not a consistently victorious fight for Paul, but at least he fights (presumably through the power of the Spirit, as described in Rom. 8:2–11).

Furthermore, in verse 22 the **inner being** would appear to be a Christian, especially in light of what we see in 2 Cor. 4:16; Eph. 3:16; 4:22–24; and Col. 3:9–10. Also, is not the **inner being** identical with the **mind** in verse 23 and verse 25? Note further the contrast between the person in 7:16, 21–22, 25 and the person in 8:7. The former confesses the law of God as good, wishes to obey that law, joyfully concurs with it, and serves it with his mind. The unbelieving individual, however, as described in 8:7, does not subject his mind to the law of God, being hostile to him and it, being unable to sustain any attitude other than one of enmity.

Observe the intensity of language, the unusually strong feeling, found in verse 24. If this is not the cry of Paul the believer, even as he writes Rom. 7, it would be unduly dramatic and overplayed. To the objection that such a cry is inconsistent with the joy of salvation, C. E. B. Cranfield reminds us,

---

4. Dunn, "Rom. 7,14–25," 263. Cranfield, *Romans*, 1:345, agrees.

The farther men advance in the Christian life, and the more mature their disciple-ship, the clearer becomes their perception of the heights to which God calls them, and the more painfully sharp their consciousness of the distance between what they ought, and want, to be, and what they are. . . . The man, whose cry this is, is one who, knowing himself to be righteous by faith, desires from the depths of his being to respond to the claims which the gospel makes upon him (cf. v. 22). It is the very clarity of his understanding of the gospel and the very sincerity of his love to God, which make his pain at this continuing sinfulness so sharp. But, be it noted, v. 24, while it is a cry of real and deep anguish, is not at all a cry of despair.[5]

Finally, in verse 18 Paul declares that **nothing good dwells in me** (ESV), only then to qualify it by saying, **that is, in my sinful nature (my flesh** [ESV]). This seems to indicate that there is more to Paul than a sinful nature—namely, the Holy Spirit. In the unregenerate there is only a sinful nature.

The Case for Seeing the Person in Romans 7 as a Non-Christian

To say that Rom. 7:7–25 must be dealing with the Christian life because Rom. 6–8 does is to beg the question. In other words, if 7:7–25 is not about the life of the Christian, then it cannot be said that all of chapters 6–8 is. Furthermore, 7:7–13 deals in part with Paul's preconversion experience, and 8:5–8 is generally regarded as describing the unbeliever.

The emphatic **I** throughout verses 14–25 need not be taken as proof that Paul is talking about himself in any condition, regenerate or unregenerate. Commen-tators have identified several texts where the first-person singular is gnomic and general (see Rom. 3:7; 1 Cor. 6:15; 13:1–3; 14:11, 14, 15; Gal. 2:18–21).

But what about the shift from the past tense in verses 7–13 to the present tense in verses 14–25? This may be explained on grounds other than that Paul is moving from his past, unregenerate life to his present, regenerate life. For example, it may be that the statement **I am unspiritual** (v. 14b; **fleshly** [ESV]) is present tense because so too is the statement **the law is spiritual** in verse 14a. Paul uses the present tense not because of a shift from preregenerate ex-perience but in order to highlight the contrast with the statement concerning the spirituality of the law. The change in tense may also be due to a change in the point under discussion (from the question of whether the law is evil to the question of one's relationship to sin). But why would a change in subject require a change in tense? Some contend that the use of the present tense to describe vividly the experience of one's past is not unprecedented in Paul's writings. There is at least one example: Phil. 3:3–6. Most agree that, although the present

5. Cranfield, *Romans*, 1:366.

tense in these verses is unexpressed, it must be supplied. True, but the reason for contending that Rom. 7:14–25 is descriptive of Paul's present experience as a believer is precisely because the present tense is sustained and expressed throughout the paragraph.

The description of Paul's preconversion righteousness ("faultless") in Phil. 3:6 is not necessarily inconsistent with the sort of struggle spoken of in Rom. 7:14–25. In Phil. 3:6 Paul speaks not of the inner failures before God but of his acknowledged success before people. According to external standards by which the Pharisees judged their conduct, Paul regarded himself as "faultless." But "to live up to prescribed standards of outward conduct is a very different thing from offering to God that complete obedience in inward thought as well as in outward act which the enlightened conscience knows that it owes to the righteous and all-seeing God."[6] Thus, in Phil. 3:6 Paul is speaking of what others saw of him outwardly, not of what God knew of him inwardly. Only by making the word "faultless" (*amemptos*) in Phil. 3:6 mean "altogether without sin" could we use it to argue against the notion that Rom. 7:7–25 is Paul's portrayal of himself before his conversion.

Perhaps the strongest argument that the individual in verses 14–25 is not a born-again believer is the contrast between what is said of them and what is said of the Christian in other texts in Rom. 6–8. Note the differences between what is said of the Christian in the left-hand column and the person in Rom. 7 in the right-hand column of table 1. Can these two really be describing the same person?

Concerning this last contrast, Robert Gundry contends, "The 'I' in 7:14–25 is not merely unable to avoid a mixture of the good and the bad. It cannot do the good at all, only the bad. Sin has taken over so completely that the 'I' is imprisoned. Contrariwise, those who are in Christ 'do not walk according to the flesh, but according to the Spirit' (8:4). The wording is exclusive."[7]

The fact that verse 25b follows the thanksgiving of verse 25a is not insurmountable for this view. Verse 25a can be what Brice Martin calls "an anticipatory interjection of God's ability."[8] In other words, Paul, as it were, gets ahead of himself in declaring the greatness of that deliverance which he knows God both can and will provide. Better still is the fact that on either view the statement of verse 25b has to be taken as a summary assertion of what has preceded. Paul has essentially finished his discourse with verse 25a and the shout of thanksgiving for God's deliverance. He then pauses to sum up what has been the gist of verses 14–24. Therefore, that verse 25b follows verse 25a does not mean that

6. Mitton, "Romans vii," 100.
7. Gundry, "Moral Frustration of Paul," 238.
8. Martin, "Identity of ἐγώ in Rom. 7:14–25," 41.

the experience it describes persists beyond that deliverance for which Paul gives thanks. It follows verse 25a precisely because it is a summary.

All agree that verses 7–13 describe preconversion experience. But many ignore the fact that Paul then immediately links this description (in vv. 7–13) to verses 14–25 with a confirmatory **for** (*gar*). As Gundry observes, "At this point we would have expected disjunction rather than linkage if Paul had meant to shift to Christian experience. As it is, he immediately announces that he is 'fleshly' (v. 14). This announcement recalls v. 5, 'For when we were in the flesh,'

Table 1. Christian Person in Romans 7:14–25 Compared with Romans 6–8 More Broadly

The Christian in Rom. 6–8 Exclusive of 7:14–25	The Person in Rom. 7:14–25
"how shall we who died to sin still live in it?" (6:2)	"I am . . . serving . . . with my flesh the law of sin" (7:25b)
"that our body of sin might be done away with" (6:6b)	"who will set me free from the body of this death?" (7:24)
"that we should no longer be slaves [*douleuein*] to sin" (6:6)	"I am sold under sin" (7:14c); note also 7:25b and the use of *douleuō*
"for sin shall not be master over you" (6:14a)	"I am . . . sold under sin" (7:14c) and "am serving . . . the law of sin" (7:25b)
"though/when you were slaves of sin" (6:17a, 20)	"I myself . . . am serving . . . with my flesh the law of sin" (7:25b)
"and having been freed from sin" (6:18a)	"sold into bondage to sin" (7:14c)
"you became slaves of righteousness" (6:18b)	"making me a prisoner of the law of sin" (7:23b)
"but now we have been released from the Law, having died to that by which we were bound, so that we serve in newness of the Spirit and not in oldness of the letter" (7:6)	"but I see a different law in the members of my body, waging war against the law of my mind, and making me a prisoner of the law of sin which is in my members" (7:23)
"but now having been freed from sin and enslaved to God" (6:22a)	"I am of flesh, sold into bondage to sin" (7:14c)
"for the law of the Spirit of life in Christ Jesus has set you free from the law of sin and death" (8:2)	"making me a prisoner of the law of sin" (7:23c)
"so that the requirement of the Law might be fulfilled in us" (8:4a)	all of 7:14–25, in which the inability to fulfill the law is fundamental

Note: Here the NASB is used (sometimes with the text from the NASB notes).

which because of the past tense and for the context of vv. 1–6 clearly refers to the unregenerate state."[9] Thus, it would seem only natural that verses 14–25, which confirm the truth of the preconversion experience in verses 7–13, would likewise be descriptive of the unregenerate.

Proponents of this view also point out that the **inner being** in 7:22 is not necessarily to be equated with the renewed believer. It could as easily refer to the nonphysical or immaterial part of all humanity. If the **inner being** and the **mind** in Rom. 7 were descriptive of the regenerated Christian, then surely, as Rom. 12:1–2 indicates, transformed conduct would result. But the person in Rom. 7 is impotent to obey.

Contrary to the argument that the **mind** in Rom. 8:7 is in conflict with the **mind** in Rom. 7:22, 25a, Gundry says that they are the same. But how can this be, if in Rom. 7 the **mind** joyfully concurs with God's law and serves it (v. 25a) but in Rom. 8 it is hostile toward God and unable to subject itself to God's law? Gundry's response is that the **mind** does two things in Romans. First, it serves as a moral monitor by means of which even a pagan can see and delight in God's law (cf. 2:14–15; 10:2–3). But second, it also seeks to establish a righteousness of its own apart from God and thus does not subject itself to his law. Therefore, in one sense the **mind** of the pagan delights in the goodness and rightness of God's law, but in another sense it refuses to subject itself to God's law, seeking rather to establish its own righteousness.

The point is also made that there is a shocking absence in 7:14–25 of references to the Holy Spirit, in contrast to Rom. 8, where the Spirit is mentioned nineteen times. Indeed, the entire tone of 7:7–25 is Spirit-less both in terms of the vocabulary used and the attitude of the individual described. It is repeatedly stated by advocates of this view that Rom. 7:13–25 is suffused with a mood of frustration, even despair, altogether different from the mood of joy and victory in other texts that speak of the normal Christian life.

The assessment that Paul makes in 7:14b, **I am of the flesh, sold under sin** (ESV), conflicts with the assessment of the believer in Rom. 8. In the latter, Paul says that the believer is in the Spirit. Furthermore, the idea that a Christian is **sold under sin** (v. 14b ESV) seems to contradict Rom. 6:14. The phrase **sold under sin**, as it is developed in verses 15–24, speaks not simply of the indwelling presence of sin but of its continuous domination in the life of the person in view. It is a domination that makes impossible that willing should become doing.

There are still additional arguments in support of the belief that Paul here is describing the non-Christian. The verb in 7:24 translated as **will rescue** is especially suited to describe a cry for salvation. Indeed, in 8:2 Paul has been "set

---

9. Gundry, "Moral Frustration of Paul," 236.

free," most likely in consequence of his cry for deliverance in 7:24. On the other hand, the cry in 7:24 may well be a reference to Paul's anticipation of the resurrection (1 Cor. 15:57), when **this body of death** (7:24 ESV), through which sin carries on its warfare, will be transformed into the likeness of the body of Christ.

And what of the emphatic "now" in Rom. 8:1? This would appear to point to a shift in experience from 7:7–25 to 8:1–11—that is, a shift from the wretched, unregenerate, frustrated man in Rom. 7 to the joyous, regenerate, victorious person in Rom. 8. On the other hand, the shift in perspective that begins with Rom. 8 may simply point to the victory over the flesh in Christian experience brought about by the Holy Spirit (i.e., the movement in progressive sanctification out of the defeat portrayed in Rom. 7 and into the victory portrayed in Rom. 8). Or the shift may point to the introduction of that other element in the Christian life: the presence and power of the Holy Spirit, who wages war against the flesh. That is to say, the Christian is one in whom the reality of both Rom. 7 and Rom. 8 is found simultaneously throughout this earthly life.

It should also be noted that Rom. 7 does not present us with the same picture as Gal. 5:16–17. In Rom. 7 the person appears to be wholly impotent, whereas in Gal. 5 those who "walk by the Spirit" are able to triumph over the flesh. In Rom. 7 Paul is not describing merely the presence of sin, but rather its ruling power. It is not that all our good acts are tainted, but that we have no good acts at all! It is willing that fails to issue in doing. Says Herman Ridderbos, "The discord pictured in Romans 7 consists not merely in a certain temptation of the ego (the will to the good, the inward man), but in the absolute impotence of the I to break through the barrier of sin and the flesh in any degree at all."[10] Similarly, in Phil. 2:12–13 "willing" in the believer is accompanied by "doing" in the power of God. But in Rom. 7 "willing" never passes into performance but rather is forever (or so it seems) frustrated.

Another problem for the view that sees a Christian in Rom. 7:14–25 is Rom. 6:14, where Paul declares, "For sin shall no longer be your master, because you are not under the law, but under grace." This statement is not a command or an exhortation or a wish. It is a statement of fact, a divine promise. Thus, as Charles Hodge notes, "It is not a hopeless struggle in which the believer is engaged, but one in which victory is certain. It is a joyful confidence which the apostle here expresses, that the power of sin has been effectually broken, and the triumph of holiness effectually secured by the work of Christ."[11] Simply put, it is difficult to see how Paul's statement of assured fact in Rom. 6:14 can be reconciled with Rom. 7:14–25 if the latter passage is taken as descriptive of the Christian.

10. Ridderbos, *Paul*, 127.
11. Hodge, *Romans*, 205.

Conclusion

If Rom. 7:14–25 is descriptive of the Christian, one of two alternatives must be taken. On the one hand, it may be that Paul is speaking of the immature (possibly young) believer who is relying on self and the law and thus can be delivered out of this bondage and into freedom from sin—that is, out of Rom. 7 and into Rom. 8. This deliverance, of course, is relative, for sinless perfection is not possible in this life.

The other option is to say that, contrary to what appears to be the case, Paul is not describing complete and utter spiritual impotence in Rom. 7. It must be taken as an expression of periodic, or occasional, rather than constant, defeat. Perhaps Paul's emphasis is on the sensitivity to sin that the mature believer feels, a sensitivity that increases as one is being conformed to the image of Christ. In other words, whereas Paul may be describing defeat in the Christian life, it is not total defeat. Observe 7:25b, where service to the law of God with the mind is affirmed of this person. "This thought of service," writes John Murray, "indicates that the devotion given is not merely that of determinate will but also of fruitful action—the determinate will issues in service on the apostle's part."[12] Thus, Murray is led to this conclusion:

> When the apostle says that he did not perform what he willed (cf. v. 15), we are not to suppose that his determinate will to the good came to no effective fruition in practice. This would be universalizing the apostle's language beyond all reasonable limits. It is surely sufficient that in this particular case, where the apostle is dealing with the contradiction which arises from the presence of sin and of the flesh, that he should declare and deplore the frustration of his determinate will to the good without giving us a *statistical* history of the outcome.[13]

J. I. Packer, who argues for the Christian view of 7:14–25, suggests that Paul's statement that he is **sold under sin** (v. 14 ESV) is pictorial rather than theological language.[14] In other words, Paul is articulating quite vividly how the condition being described "feels" rather than expressing it directly in explicit and intentional theological terms. In other words, Packer insists that it is precisely because Paul is a Spirit-filled and Spirit-led man who loves God and his law that such moral failures "feel" as though he were a bond-slave to sin. His heightened sensitivity to sin in his life accounts for this elevated and emotionally intense language. It is not, therefore, a technical affirmation that he is in fact still under the power of sin and under divine wrath.

12. Murray, *Romans*, 270.
13. Murray, *Romans*, 272–73.
14. See his discussion of this text in Packer, "The 'Wretched Man' in Romans 7."

The thanksgiving in verse 25 has for its focus neither one's current state of having been justified nor the enabling power of the Spirit presently enjoyed; rather, it is based on Paul's confidence that in the future he will receive his resurrected body. It is a declaration of personal Christian hope. So, in verses 14–25 Paul is not so much describing defeat, says Packer, but discernment. Paul becomes aware of his shortcoming, that he failed to do what he wanted and intended, and thus his text describes the reality of his frustration at this repeated discovery rather than his despair over a struggle that brings repeated and persistent failure.

Thus, according to Packer, Paul is not describing complete moral failure, as if he never gets anything right or never obeys God's revealed will. His distress and bewilderment are simply the reaction of a heart that fails to attain the perfection it so deeply desires. In other words, Paul is not telling us that the daily experience of this **wretched man** (v. 24) is as bad as it could be, but rather that it is not as good as it should be. On this view, then, Paul himself is the **wretched man** who gives vent to his anguish at not being a better Christian than he is. Paul's obvious emotional anguish as he contemplates his personal experience is not because he is a hopelessly enslaved sinner, with little or no prospect for extricating himself from this wretched condition. Rather, his inner turmoil is due precisely to the fact that he is a mature and ever-growing saint. This is based on the principle that the greater and more influential the presence of transforming grace in one's heart, the greater and more intensely painful the lingering reality of sin proves to be. Whereas a life immersed in sin anesthetizes the soul, rendering it increasingly incapable of feeling genuine conviction, a life in tune with the Holy Spirit and devoted to the supremacy of God's glory is ever more sensitive to even the least degree of sin committed.

Regardless of which view of Rom. 7 one takes, it is crucial that we do not allow the language in this paragraph to fuel despair in our struggle with sin. We must never forget that sin will no longer be our "master," because we "are not under the law, but under grace" (Rom. 6:14). When faced with relentless temptation from the world, the flesh, and the devil, we need to remind ourselves that we "have been set free from sin and have become slaves to righteousness" (Rom. 6:18). There is deep and abiding joy, as well as confidence in the face of the pressures of living in a fallen society, in knowing that "it is God who works in you to will and to act in order to fulfill his good purpose" (Phil. 2:13). Far from conceding defeat in our battle with indwelling sin, we should be greatly encouraged by the truth that "he who began a good work in you will bring it to completion at the day of Jesus Christ" (Phil. 1:6 ESV).

ROMANS 8

Life in the Spirit

The Greek word for "spirit," *pneuma*, occurs twenty-one times in this chapter alone, more often than in any other single chapter in the New Testament (8:2, 4, 5 [2x], 6, 9 [3x], 10, 11 [2x], 13, 14, 15 [2x], 16 [2x], 23, 26 [2x], 27). All but two of these refer to the Holy Spirit (the exceptions being in vv. 15a and 16b). Both the NIV and the ESV insert the English word "Spirit" in verse 27b to clarify that the subject of the third-person singular verb **intercedes** is in fact the Spirit of God. The word *pneuma*, or "spirit," is found only five times in chapters 1–7 and eight times in chapters 9–16. The Holy Spirit is mentioned in Rom. 8 almost once every two verses. Compare that with 1 Cor. 12, the chapter on spiritual gifts, where the Spirit is mentioned once in every three verses.

Living according to the Spirit (8:1–4)

The inferential particle *ara*, translated as **therefore** (8:1), directs our attention to what has preceded in the epistle that warrants the conclusion of **no condemnation**. Many point to the larger paragraph, verses 14–25. Paul's point would be that notwithstanding the ongoing struggle with the power of indwelling sin, those who are **in Christ** can rest assured that there is **no condemnation** that awaits them. More likely still is that Paul is thinking of the whole of Rom. 1–7 and specifically what God has done for us in the life, death, and resurrection of Jesus. There is no condemnation, because the judgment we otherwise deserved has been poured out on Christ and the wrath of God has been propitiated (3:25).

The word translated as **condemnation** (i.e., liability or exposure to the penal sanctions of divine law) is found in only three texts in the New Testament, all of them in Romans (5:16, 18; 8:1). The condemnation that came upon us by virtue of our having been in Adam has **now** (*nyn*) been removed because we are **in Christ Jesus**. No condemnation is not a universal blessing but rather is reserved for those who are in Christ through faith. To be "in Christ" refers to that spiritual solidarity or covenant union that God established between the believer and the Lord Jesus.

The condemnation that all deserved did not simply disappear. The grounds for this declaration of forgiveness (note the **for** [*gar*] with which v. 2 opens) is unpacked in verses 2–4. What Paul called **condemnation** in verse 1, he now refers to as **the law of sin and death** in verse 2. That law is the requirement that whoever fails to live up to the perfect standard of God's holiness must suffer death. But there is another law (rule or principle), **the law of the Spirit of life** (v. 2a ESV), which has secured for us, through Jesus Christ, forgiveness and freedom from all condemnation. The Holy Spirit has set us free from this death and condemnation by working in us faith in the all-sufficient sacrifice of Jesus on our behalf.

The law, **weakened by the flesh** (v. 3), could not remove the condemnation under which all sinners stood. But God did what the law couldn't by sending **his own Son** (v. 3) to endure the condemnation that we otherwise deserved. The phrase **to be a sin offering** is the rendering of the more literal "concerning sin." In this way God condemned sin **in the flesh**, likely a reference to the flesh or body of Jesus. When his body was nailed to a cross, the sentence of death, incurred because of our sin, was carried out in and on the person of Jesus (cf. 2 Cor. 5:21).

By **sinful flesh** (v. 3) Paul refers to fallen human nature. Had he said **in sinful flesh** without the qualifying term **likeness**, one might conclude that Jesus had a fallen, sinful human nature. The word **likeness** (*homoiōmati*) does not mean that the human nature of Jesus was only similar to ours but not identical with it (see John 1:14; Phil. 2:7–8; 1 John 4:2). Neither does it refer to the fact that Jesus never committed sin. C. E. B. Cranfield suggests, "The intention behind the use of *homoiōma* here . . . was to take account of the fact that the Son of God was not, in being sent by the Father, changed into a man, but rather assumed human nature while still remaining Himself. . . . [Thus] the intention is not in any way to call into question or to water down the reality of Christ's *sarx hamartias* [sinful flesh] but to draw attention to the fact that, while the Son of God truly assumed *sarx hamartias*, He never became *sarx hamartias* and nothing more."[1] It can be concluded, says Cranfield, "that the Son of God assumed the selfsame fallen human nature that is ours, but that in His case

---

1. Cranfield, *Romans*, 1:381.

The Person of the Holy Spirit

Many Christians struggle to relate to the Holy Spirit as a person. A student of Gordon Fee once said, "God the Father makes perfectly good sense to me, and God the Son I can quite understand; but the Holy Spirit is a gray, oblong blur."[a]

The Holy Spirit is referred to in the Bible as "he" and "who," not "it." Although the noun *pneuma* ("spirit") is neuter, Jesus uses masculine pronouns to describe the Spirit, not to suggest that the Spirit is male but that he is a person, not merely a power. However, Daniel Wallace has argued that such grammatical arguments for the Spirit's personality are invalid. He argues that in both John 14:26 and 15:26 "[*pneuma*] is apposition to a masculine noun, rather than the subject of the verb. The gender of [*ekeinos*] thus has nothing to do with the natural gender of [*pneuma*]. The antecedent of [*ekeinos*], in each case, is [*paraklētos*], not [*pneuma*]."[b] As for John 16:13–14, again the masculine gender of *ekeinos* is more likely due to *paraklētos* in verse 7 than to any attempt to predicate personality of the Spirit. Wallace also addresses similar cases in Eph. 1:14 and 1 John 5:7–8. None of this is to suggest, however, that Wallace himself denies the personality of the Holy Spirit. He simply argues that it must be established on other grounds.

The Spirit has all the qualities of a personal being: mind or intellect (Isa. 11:2; John 14:26; Rom. 8:27; 1 Cor. 2:10–11); emotions or affections (Rom. 8:26; 15:30; Eph. 4:30; cf. Isa. 63:10; Acts 15:28; James 4:5); and will (Acts 16:7; 1 Cor. 12:11). The Holy Spirit also performs all the functions of a personal being. The Spirit talks (Mark 13:11; Acts 1:16; 8:29; 10:19; 11:12; 13:2; 21:11; 1 Tim. 4:1; Heb. 3:7; Rev. 2:7), testifies (John 15:26; Rom. 8:16), and can be sinned against (Matt. 12:31), lied to (Acts 5:3), tested or tempted (Acts 5:9), and insulted (Heb. 10:29). The Spirit enters into relationship with other persons (2 Cor. 13:14) and encourages (Acts 9:31), strengthens (Eph. 3:16), and teaches believers (Luke 12:12; John 14:26; 1 Cor. 2:13).

The Holy Spirit is also fully divine, equal in glory and majesty with the Father and the Son. What is said of God is said of the Spirit (Acts 5:3–4). The Holy Spirit is identified with Yahweh (Acts 7:51; cf. Ps. 78:17–21; Heb. 10:15–17, quoting Jer. 31:33). The activity of God is the activity of the Holy Spirit (e.g., in creation, conversion, etc.). "God said" = "the Spirit said" (cf. Isa. 6:9 with Acts 28:25). We are the temple of God because the Holy Spirit dwells in us (1 Cor. 6:19; Eph. 2:22). If the Holy Spirit is not God, how could we properly be called the temple of God simply because the Spirit indwells us? Blasphemy against the Holy Spirit is the only unforgivable sin (Matt. 12:31; Mark 3:29).

In addition, attributes and actions of deity are ascribed to the Spirit, such as omniscience (Isa. 40:13–14; 1 Cor. 2:10–11), omnipresence (Ps. 139:7–8), omnipotence (as seen in the Spirit's role in creation [Gen. 1], providence [Ps. 104:30], and regeneration [Titus 3:5]; see esp. Zech. 4:6), eternality (Heb. 9:14), and holiness (used of the Spirit only twice in the Old Testament [Ps. 51:11; Isa. 63:10–11]).

The names of the Spirit point strongly to deity. The Holy Spirit is the Spirit of glory (1 Pet. 4:14), grace (Heb. 10:29), life (Rom. 8:2), truth (John 14:17; 15:26; 16:13), and wisdom and revelation (Eph. 1:17). The Spirit is intimately related to the Father and Son in the triune Godhead (Matt. 28:19; 1 Cor. 12:3; 2 Cor. 13:14).

The purpose of the Holy Spirit is also seen in three metaphors used by the apostle Paul. First, the Holy Spirit is portrayed as a *down payment* (2 Cor. 1:21–22; 5:5; Eph. 1:14). This term (*arrhabōn*) was used in commercial transactions to refer to the first installment of the total amount due. The down payment effectively guaranteed the fulfillment of whatever contractual obligations were assumed. The Spirit thus serves as God's down payment in our lives and the assured guarantee that the future will be realized in fullness.

Second, the Holy Spirit is portrayed as the *firstfruits* (Rom. 8:23). This metaphor is also used of Christ's resurrection as the guarantee of ours (1 Cor. 15:20, 23). Similar to the idea behind *down payment*, the Holy Spirit as "the first sheaf is God's pledge to us of the final harvest. Thus . . . the Spirit plays the essential role in our present existence, as both evidence and guarantee that the future is now and yet to be."[c]

Third, the Holy Spirit is portrayed as a *seal* (2 Cor. 1:21–22; Eph. 1:13; 4:30). A seal authenticates (John 3:33; 6:27; 1 Cor. 9:2) or confirms as genuine and true, including the idea that what is sealed is stamped with the character of its owner. The seal also designates or marks out as one's property. In other words, it declares and signifies ownership (see Rev. 7:3–8; 9:4) and serves to render secure or to establish (i.e., protect [cf. Eph. 4:30; Matt. 27:66; Rev. 20:3]) believers in their relationship with God.

a. Fee, *God's Empowering Presence*, 5–6.
b. Wallace, "Greek Grammar and the Personality of the Holy Spirit," 104.
c. Fee, *God's Empowering Presence*, 807.

that fallen human nature was never the whole of Him—He never ceased to be the eternal Son of God."[2]

The more likely interpretation is that Paul uses the word **likeness** to avoid saying that Christ assumed fallen human nature. He took on flesh like ours, because it was really and truly human flesh, a genuine human nature (John 1:14). But it was only like ours, and not identical with it, because it was unfallen. Paul does not use the word **likeness** to deny or undermine the reality of Christ's human nature, as if to say that his flesh only resembles ours but has no qualitative affinity with it. He uses **likeness** because he feels compelled to use the phrase **sinful flesh** instead of merely "flesh." Had Paul omitted the word **sinful**, he also would have omitted the word **likeness**.

God's purpose in all this was **in order that** (*hina*) the **righteous requirement of the law might be fulfilled in us** (v. 4 ESV). The question about this latter phrase is whether Paul is thinking in forensic terms and has in view the way in which the law was perfectly fulfilled on our behalf by means of the obedient life and substitutionary death of the Son, or if he has in mind the behavioral aspect of righteousness that is produced in us by the Spirit. In support of the first option is Paul's emphasis on the passive **be fully met** (more literally, "be fulfilled") and the preposition **in** (*en*), which is locative, not instrumental—that is, "something that is done for and in us by God himself."[3] But the latter option seems more likely, as Paul is now turning his attention to the way in which the Spirit operates in us practically to fulfill what the law requires. We **live** [literally, "walk" or "behave on a daily basis"] **according to the Spirit**—that is, by means of his empowering presence (cf. Rom. 13:8–10; Gal. 5:14; 6:2).

The Mind Governed by the Flesh (8:5–8)

There are only two types of people in this world: those who are in the flesh and those who are in the Spirit, those who live either **according to the flesh** or **according to the Spirit** (v. 5 ESV). As a result, there are, respectively, two mentalities or outlooks on life. Those who are according to the flesh **have their minds set on what the flesh desires** (v. 5a). Those who are according to the Spirit **have their minds set on what the Spirit desires** (v. 5b). Consequently, there are two destinies or outcomes. For those who set their minds on the flesh, there is **death** (v. 6a). For those who set their minds on the Spirit, there is **life and peace** (v. 6b).

The hostility to God and the inability to please him (vv. 7–8) aren't due to an external power resisting well-meant attempts by those of the flesh to do what

2. Cranfield, *Romans*, 1:382.
3. Fee, *God's Empowering Presence*, 535.

is right. They could do what pleases God if only they would. But they won't. To have one's mind **governed** either by the flesh or by the Spirit is to be preoccupied by and devoted to one or the other. The **flesh** is what dominates one's thinking and demands one's affections and devotion. It prioritizes worldly, earthly, and altogether natural and sinful values and actions and beliefs (see Gal. 5:19–21). The **death** that such a mindset and lifestyle produce is eternal separation from God, what John in the book of Revelation calls "the second death."

The refusal to **submit to God's law** (v. 7) is an act and attitude of rebellion and defiance toward all that God commands. Again, the inability mentioned twice in verses 7–8 is a reflection of one's fallen nature. The only thing keeping such people from belief are their own desires. They are unable to submit to God because they are unwilling to do so. Their will is an expression of their nature, and their nature is altogether of the flesh.

The Mind Governed by the Spirit (8:9–11)

The distinguishing feature of a person who believes, who seeks to please God and longs to submit their life entirely to him, is that **the Spirit of God dwells** (ESV) in them. But how might one know if the Spirit dwells within? Earlier, in verses 5–6, Paul said that the Spirit lives and dwells in those who "have their minds set on what the Spirit desires" (v. 5b). To set your mind on the things of the Spirit, says John Stott, is to make spiritual things, spiritual truths and values, "the absorbing objects of thought, interest, affection and purpose. It is a question of what preoccupies us, of the ambitions which drive us and the concerns which engross us, of how we spend our time and our energies, of what we concentrate on and give ourselves up to."[4]

Later, in verse 13, Paul will say that the person in whom the Spirit dwells is the one who puts to death the deeds of the body—that is, the person who does not live the sort of life that Paul describes in Gal. 5:19–21. Those in whom the Spirit dwells are the ones "who are led by the Spirit of God" (Rom. 8:14a). They are the ones who understand and enjoy their adoption into God's family as his sons and daughters and cry out, "Abba! Father!" (v. 15 ESV). They are the ones to whose spirit the Holy Spirit bears witness that they are true children of God. They are those who willingly suffer with Christ (v. 17).

We should take note in verse 9 of the three ways in which the Holy Spirit is described. He is called **the Spirit** (v. 9a), **the Spirit of God** (v. 9b), and **the Spirit of Christ** (v. 9c). There are not three Spirits but one Spirit, who simultaneously sustains the same relationship to both Father and Son. This one Holy

4. Stott, *Romans*, 223.

Spirit, fully God, is entirely equal in every way to the Father and the Son. But this Holy Spirit is also in intimate and eternal relationship with the Father and is thus the Spirit *of* God. He is in intimate and eternal relationship with the Son and is thus the Spirit *of* Christ.

Paul says not only that the Spirit is **in** us but also that we are **in** the Spirit (v. 9). He means that we live every moment under the influence of the Spirit's power. Just as to be **in the flesh** means that a person is subject to its enslaving influence, to be **in the Spirit** means that he is in control.

Since Christ is in you through the indwelling Spirit (much in the same way that God lives in us "by his Spirit" [Eph. 2:22]), although you must die physically because of sin, you are guaranteed resurrection life (v. 10). Thus, "the presence of the Spirit of God indwelling the believer is the ground of our confidence that God will give life to 'our mortal bodies.'"[5] In other words, the phrase **through his Spirit who dwells in you** (v. 11b ESV) refers not so much to the agency of the Spirit, as if it is by means of the Spirit that God will give life to our **mortal bodies** (although that may in itself be true), but to the Holy Spirit as the guarantee or surety that we will be raised. This, then, is the answer to the cry of 7:24: "Who will rescue me from this body that is subject to death?" When Paul speaks of **life because of righteousness** (v. 10b), he is saying that whereas we die physically because of sin, we are raised and glorified because of the **righteousness** of Jesus Christ that has been imputed or reckoned to us through faith.[6]

What Spirit-Filled People Do with Their Sin (8:12–13)

The relationship between verses 9–11 and verses 12–13 is clear. Since we are in the Spirit and not in the flesh, we are not debtors to the flesh. We have no **obligation** to follow its dictates or live according to its prompting. Our responsibility, instead, is to kill or put to death the sinful deeds of the body.

The NIV identifies what Paul simply calls "the deeds" of the body as **misdeeds** (v. 13). He has in mind the sinful deeds that we carry out by means of our bodies: our minds, mouths, hands, actions, decisions, and so on. These are the "deeds" that we are to kill **by the Spirit**—that is, by drawing on his presence and power and trusting in what he says and how he leads us. You will **die** if you live according to the flesh. Some see here a reason to believe that a believer can sin to such a degree as to lose eternal life. Others would argue that the reality of one's salvation and relation to Christ is displayed, demonstrated, and proven by

---

5. Fee, *God's Empowering Presence*, 551.
6. Some contend that the phrase **because of righteousness** (v. 10) refers to our practical, righteous behavior, similar to what we saw in verse 4.

the war that one wages against sin. Putting to death the sinful deeds of the body leads to eternal life, not because by doing so one earns salvation, but because by doing so one gives evidence that one is already truly saved.

The Ministry of the Holy Spirit (8:14–17)

Here Paul describes numerous ministry activities of the Holy Spirit, the first of which is that the Spirit lovingly leads all **the children of God** (v. 14). In light of the preceding verses, specifically verse 13, we see that the Spirit leads us to put to death the sinful deeds of the body. The leading of the Spirit is his ministry of imparting to us the power and motivation to kill sin in our lives. But the Spirit also leads us in daily decisions we make (see Acts 8:26–40; 9:10–19; 10:1–8; 13:1–3; 16:6–7; 18:9–11; 19:21; 20:22–23). Only those who embrace cessationism[7] would deny the Spirit's currect active guidance in the ways described in these many texts in Acts.

Moreover, the Spirit enables us to recognize and rejoice in our **adoption** as the children of God (v. 15; cf. Gal. 3:26; 4:4–7; 1 John 3:1–2). Christians are called the **sons of God** three times in Rom. 8 (vv. 14, 15, 19 ESV) and **children of God** three times (vv. 16, 17, 21 ESV). Both phrases have nothing to do with gender but refer to privilege and status. The focus is on intimacy of relationship, not whether one is male or female. Thus, women are included as "sons" of God, just as men as well as women are the "bride" of Christ.

The Spirit induces not **fear** but confident faith in knowing that God is our Father (v. 15). Jesus always spoke of God as "my Father," both as a formal designation and as personal address in prayer. The lone exception to this rule is his cry of dereliction from the cross: "My God, my God, why have you forsaken me?" (Mark 15:34). At that moment Jesus regarded his relationship to God as penal and judicial, not paternal. In the Old Testament, apart from texts in which God is compared with an earthly father, the word is used of him only fifteen times. Yet, in not one of those cases does anyone refer to God as "my Father" in personal, individual prayer. Yet, that is precisely what Jesus did and what we are told to do. **Abba**, the Aramaic term lying behind the Greek *patēr*, was used in Judaism to express the intimacy, security, and tenderness in a family relationship. For Jesus to speak of God in this way as "my Father" was something new and unheard of. He spoke to God like a child to their father—simply, inwardly, confidently. Jesus's use of **Abba** in addressing God reveals the heart of his relationship with God.

---

7. Cessationism is the belief that certain, more overtly miraculous, spiritual gifts ceased to be operative at some time in the late first century or soon thereafter.

PENTECOSTAL INTEREST

The Holy Spirit in the Old Testament

The Hebrew term *ruah* ("breath, wind, spirit") appears approximately 377 times in the Old Testament (only 264 of which are translated by the Greek *pneuma* in the Septuagint). Of these 377 instances, 94 refer to the Spirit of God. Gordon Fee has summarized the activity of the Spirit in the Old Testament.[a] The Spirit is responsible for creation (Gen. 1:2; Ps. 104:30) as well as the eschatological renewal of the earth (Isa. 32:15). The Spirit empowers for leadership (Num. 11:17; 27:18; see also Judg. 3:10; 6:34; 11:29; 14:6, 19; 15:14). Saul was empowered by the Spirit to be king (1 Sam. 11:6), as was David (1 Sam. 16:13). The Holy Spirit is the agent of prophetic activity as well as other forms of inspired speech (see 2 Sam. 23:2; 1 Chron. 12:18; 2 Chron. 15:1; 20:14; and esp. Num. 11:29). The Spirit is related to God's work of revelation (Dan. 4:8, 9, 18; 5:11, 14), is described as the very presence of God (Pss. 51:11; 139:7; Isa. 63:10–14), and is the key to Israel's future (Isa. 11:2; 42:1; 59:21; 61:1; Ezek. 11:19; 18:31; 36:26–27; 37:1–14; Joel 2:28–30).

a. Fee, *God's Empowering Presence*, 905–10.

It is by means of the Spirit's ministry within that **we cry** out, **Abba! Father!** (ESV).[8] We don't sigh, we cry! We don't simply say it, we shout it! This cry of **Abba! Father!** isn't the result of logical reasoning. This is more than an arid, ethereal doctrinal affirmation. It is the fruit of the Spirit's powerful awakening within our hearts of an intuitive experiential awareness that we are his and he is ours. Because of the Spirit's work, we approach God not as our boss or slave master but as our Father and thus experience the affection as his children.

The Holy Spirit also **testifies** "to," not "with" (NIV), our spirit that we are God's children and in doing so brings assurance of salvation (v. 16). Assurance comes not only from the promise of Scripture that whoever believes has eternal life (John 3:16), but also from a transformed life that progressively grows in conformity with the image of Jesus (1 John 2:3–6). There is also the inner witness of the Spirit, who awakens us in our hearts to the reality of our relationship with God. Romans 8:16 speaks of this third basis of assurance.

Although in verse 16 the NIV translates the Greek phrase *tō pneumati hēmōn* as **with our spirit** (associative dative), the strong likelihood is that "to our

8. In Gal. 4:6 it is "the Spirit who calls out, 'Abba, Father.'" Clearly, both are true.

Hearing God's Voice

Some would insist that a central feature of the Spirit's leading of the believer (Rom. 8:14), together with the Spirit's role in testifying to the Christian of their salvation (8:16), is hearing God's voice, more often internally and rarely audibly. This is the conclusion of Paul Harcourt in his foreword to Tania Harris's book *The Church Who Hears God's Voice: Equipping Everyone to Recognise and Respond to the Spirit*. He cites Rom. 8:14 and contends that "a relationship with God the Father through Jesus must necessarily be one of intimate two-way communication, involving the Spirit."[a]

a. Harcourt, "Foreword," xiii. See also Harris, "Contemporary Revelatory Experiences"; Luhrmann, *When God Talks Back*.

spirit" (dative of indirect object) is more consistent with Pauline thought.[9] In other words, we know that we are saved not only because of the declaration of Scripture and the fruit of obedience but also because of the inner witness of the Spirit. Paul is describing a witness that is immediate, intuitive, transrational (but not irrational), and beyond empirical observation or verification.

The connection between verses 15 and 16 is a reminder that the knowledge that we are children of God is not a conclusion we draw from the fact that we cry **Abba! Father!** That cry itself is the result or fruit of that conviction which the Holy Spirit has evoked in our hearts. We first receive the Holy Spirit, who then produces in our hearts the unassailable confidence that we are God's children, an assurance that leads us to cry out, in the Spirit's power, **Abba! Father!**

Finally, the Spirit awakens the children of God to their status as **heirs of God and fellow heirs with Christ** (v. 17 ESV). According to Rom. 4:13 (cf. 1 Cor. 3:21–23), because we share the faith of Abraham, we, like him, are heirs of "the world." As God's children, we inherit all that belongs to him, and God owns the world (Ps. 24:1). But most important of all, we inherit God himself. Our greatest expectation and hope is that one day we will see God himself and enjoy and celebrate his glory forever (cf. Rom. 5:2; Rev. 21:3; see also Pss. 16:5; 73:25–26; Lam. 3:24). Paul is also quick to remind us that our inheritance depends upon our willingness to suffer with Christ (cf. Luke 9:23; Acts 14:22;

9. See Wallace, "Witness of the Spirit in Romans 8:16."

2 Tim. 3:12; 1 Pet. 4:12–14), likely a reference to what he will say explicitly in Rom. 8:35 concerning trouble, hardship, persecution, famine, nakedness, danger, and sword (see also Phil. 3:10–11).

The Groaning of Creation, the Christian, and the Holy Spirit (8:18–25)

The shift in focus from verses 1–17 to verses 18–27 is significant. In the former, Paul envisions life in the present age as one of victorious spiritual growth through the power of the Spirit. In the latter, the upbeat tone in verses 1–17 is tempered by the harsh realities of life in a broken world (note Paul's vocabulary of **sufferings** [v. 18], **frustration** or "futility" [v. 20], **bondage** and **decay** [v. 21], **groaning** [vv. 22–23], and **weakness** [v. 26].)

Knowing full well that his comment in verse 17 will undoubtedly have evoked anxiety and fear in the hearts of many, he immediately follows up on that statement with verse 18: **I consider that our present sufferings are not worth comparing with the glory that will be revealed in us**. There is a great disproportion between the sufferings that God's children endure in this life and the glory that is reserved for them in the next (see 2 Cor. 4:16–18).

We will not be mere spectators of this glory. We will actually participate **in** it. It is not something we will only see, but something we will personally experience (cf. Col. 3:4). God's children will in some sense be enveloped in glory, surrounded and saturated with the very glory of God and the blessings of the age to come. By **glory** Paul means the comprehensive, all-satisfying splendor of all that God is in himself and for us in Christ (see John 17:24). This is the glory that will be revealed to us and in us, the glory in which we will participate and that we will experience and enjoy forever. Paul can speak with such confidence about this glory because he has actually seen it (see 2 Cor. 12:1–6).

But prior to being caught up in that **glory**, there is **groaning**. The verb in verse 22 is *systenazō*, literally, "groan with." In verse 23 Paul uses the related verb *stenazō*, "groan." The only difference is that the former verb emphasizes that creation does not groan alone but does so in conjunction with either the rest of creation or in conjunction with Christians. When Paul comes to verse 26 to describe what the Holy Spirit does in and on behalf of weak Christians, he uses the related noun form of these verbs, *stenagmos*.

To make his point, Paul will employ the figure of speech known as personification, wherein some dimension of the material creation is described as if it were a thinking, feeling, choosing person (see Pss. 65:12–13; 96:11–13; 98:8; 148:8). Here in verses 19–22 the inanimate world is portrayed as if it were animate. The nonthinking processes of nature are portrayed as if they could think and feel and make meaningful choices. The entire material creation, all of nature, is described as **groaning** to be set free from the judgment that has been placed on it.

By the word **creation**, found four times in this one paragraph (vv. 19, 20, 21, 22), Paul does not mean the holy or elect angels, for they were not subjected to vanity and corruption. He does not mean Satan or demons, for they do not long for the day of redemption. He does not mean Christians, because they are distinguished from **creation** in verses 19, 21, 23. He does not mean humankind

PENTECOSTAL INTEREST

The Holy Spirit and the Natural Creation

The apostle Paul clearly maintains a metaphysical distinction between the Creator and the natural creation. The latter is not merely an extension of the former, as in many versions of pantheism. And yet, citing the work of May Ling Tan-Chow,[a] Helen Collins describes "the relationship between the natural and supernatural realms as permeable, where the Spirit breaks in and effects things in the world, often in response to prayer."[b] This is what James K. A. Smith refers to as an "enchanted" theology of both creation and culture.[c] While acknowledging the primary role of the Spirit in the origin and preservation of the natural realm, Collins and Smith highlight the Spirit's immanence and operation *within* the created order. Others would simply use the word "supernatural" to describe the Spirit's presence and power in and through material reality. This helps to explain Paul's reference to "the power of signs and wonders, through the power of the Spirit of God" (Rom. 15:19) that characterized his ministry. Such "miracles" are not to be thought of as an interruption or inbreaking of the Spirit into the ordinary operations of the natural realm, far less a "violation" of so-called natural laws. These demonstrations of "power" are instead less common and more concentrated manifestations of the Spirit's sovereignty over, in, and through creation that are designed to draw special attention to God's person and purpose. Collins sums it up well by defining "miracles" as "intense revelations of the Spirit's enchantment that act as clear signs of the kingdom of God."[d]

a. Tan-Chow, *Pentecostal Theology*.
b. Collins, *Charismatic Christianity*, 43.
c. Smith, *Thinking in Tongues*, 39–41.
d. Collins, *Charismatic Christianity*, 63.

in general, because it cannot be said of them that they were subjected to futility by a will other than their own. He does not mean unbelieving humankind in particular, for they, like Satan, do not long for the day of redemption. Thus, all rational creation is ruled out. In referring to the **creation** Paul is not thinking of any being that thinks or that is shaped in the image of God. By **creation** Paul means the earth, nature, nonrational creation, both animate and inanimate—the flora and fauna of nature. He is talking about the material world in which we live, that surrounds us.

Paul tells us to take note of creation's current defilement and suffering, imposed in judgment subsequent to the fall of Adam (see Gen. 3:17-19). The creation was **subjected to frustration** (v. 20) or futility, by which he means the inability and ineffectiveness of something in attaining its goal. The material world in which we live is unable to properly fulfill the purpose for which God brought it into existence. The material world was originally designed by God not only to draw attention to his creative genius and power but also to provide a place for men and women to live and thrive and enjoy the good gifts of God. But creation is prevented from accomplishing this goal, **not willingly** (v. 20 ESV), but by virtue of the judicial act of God in response to the sin of Adam. This futility or judgment is described again in verse 21 as **bondage to corruption** (ESV). The material world, in consequence of the fall of humanity, is enslaved to environmental devastation and plagues and destructive earthquakes and horrific tornadoes and pollution.

This futility or judgment imposed on creation was done **in hope that the creation itself will be liberated from its bondage to decay and brought into the freedom and glory of the children of God** (vv. 20b-21). Indeed, Paul personifies the material realm as waiting **with eager longing** (v. 19 ESV) to be delivered from its corruption when the children of God are delivered from theirs (see Isa. 11:6-9; 65:17). The verb for **waits** (*apekdechomai*) has the sense of someone stretching the neck or craning forward, hoping to catch a glimpse of something. It is as if the material world is standing on tiptoes, looking with anxious expectation for its deliverance from the curse and its entrance into the original purposes for which God made it. Thus, the final redemption both of God's children and of God's material creation is linked not solely in the judgment they currently endure but also in their ultimate freedom.

The imagery takes on yet a different and additional light in verse 22. There Paul says that the whole creation has been **in the pains of childbirth right up to the present time**, groaning under the present burden of sin and death in anticipation of the new life that it will experience when God redeems it. The material creation expectantly waits with eager longing **for the children of God**

to be revealed (v. 19; the meaning of which is clearly seen in 1 John 3:2–3; see also 1 Cor. 15:51–53; Phil. 3:20–21).

The reason for our groaning is once again the work of the Holy Spirit. In this case, the Spirit stirs our hearts and souls to long for the final redemption of our bodies. Paul attributes this inner spiritual ache to the fact that we have **the firstfruits of the Spirit** (v. 23). Here the apostle makes use of an agricultural metaphor and describes the Spirit as the **firstfruits** of the full harvest that is yet to come (the genitive **of the Spirit** is appositional, meaning that the Spirit is the firstfruits). The point is that we have in the Holy Spirit a taste in advance of the feast that is yet to come. We have him completely in our hearts, but we do not yet experience the fullness of the blessings of salvation that he will bring to us when Jesus returns.

Paul says that we **groan inwardly** for the day when the reality of our adoption as the children of God will be fully and finally consummated. This is not so much a groaning under the burden of sin, although that is involved, as it is a groaning for the glory of life in the new heaven and new earth. It is not the groaning of disappointment and frustration but the groaning of anticipation and expectation. These groans are not death pangs but birth pangs. Thus we see the natural, material creation and the spiritual, human creation joining together in a virtual chorus of groaning, a symphony of sighs, as it were, as we together agonize in anxious expectation of that final day of redemption.

When that day comes, we will experience the consummation of our adoption, the full revelation and disclosure of our identity as the children of God, at the heart of which experience will be **the redemption of our bodies** (v. 23b). By **redemption** Paul is referring to that time when we will be so utterly transformed that our souls will be set free from all sinful impulses and our bodies forever delivered from susceptibility to disease, decay, and death (cf. 7:24; 8:11, 17).

Although we are saved by faith, we are also saved **in this hope** of the future complete restoration and resurrection of our entire selves—body, soul, mind, spirit, will, and emotions. One doesn't hope for what can be seen or for what one already possesses (v. 24). Hope is altogether future in its orientation. Notwithstanding the frustration of life in a broken world, **we wait . . . patiently** (v. 25), confident that when Christ returns, we will experience the fullness of our salvation.

The Groaning of God the Holy Spirit (8:26–27)

It is not only the material creation and Christians who groan, but so too does the Holy Spirit (v. 26), specifically in relation to his role in our prayer lives.

Responding to the Danger of Charismatic Gnosticism

Paul's perspective on the final redemption of material creation in Rom. 8:18–25 is a healthy warning against all modern forms of Gnosticism. The latter existed in an incipient form in the first century, as seen, for example, in the response of Paul in his epistle to the Colossians (Col. 2:20–23) and John in his first epistle (1 John 1:1–4; 4:1–5). As Gnosticism developed, its advocates embraced a dualistic view of the world in which physical matter was considered evil and the spiritual realm was good. Hence, the body was despised, leading either to extreme asceticism (deprivation of the body) or to extreme licentiousness (indulgence of the body), and ultimately to a denial of the doctrine of bodily resurrection. They attempted to solve the problem of creation and the origin of evil by positing a Demiurge—a creator or architect of the world, distinct from the Supreme Deity. The Demiurge is the God of the Old Testament, responsible for matter and evil in the cosmos. The Supreme—and utterly spiritual, and therefore good—Deity is separated from the Demiurge by a series of emanations. In creation, an emanation of God descends from pure spirit through layers of reality until it assumes its form as dense matter.

This dualistic view in which physical substance is denigrated and all things spiritual elevated resulted in their denial of the true humanity of Christ. They espoused the heresy known as Docetism (from Greek *dokeō*, "seem, appear"). The work of Christ was primarily designed to deliver humanity from the prison of earthly, material ignorance. Gnostics also laid claim to a special "knowledge" (*gnōsis*) of the truth available only to the elite and initiated, a knowledge regarded as superior to faith.

We must reckon with the fact that there is a strain of Gnosticism in some sectors of the Pentecostal-Charismatic world. Given the latter's emphasis on the immaterial realm, physical creation is sometimes viewed as a threat to true spirituality. Often due to a heightened emphasis on revelatory insight into God and his purposes, an elitist mentality has emerged in which only a favored few have access to the true knowledge of God.

But Paul's emphasis here in Rom. 8 reminds us that God created matter. The physical is spiritual. When he created earth and sea and plant and animal, as well as the human body, he pronounced them "good" (Gen. 1:4, 10, 12, 18, 21, 25, 31). Material substance is not inherently evil.

God intends to deliver the whole of creation from the curse of futility and environmental corruption that was imposed consequent to the fall of Adam. When Christ returns, he will not eliminate the physical realm but will inaugurate a new heaven and a new earth (Rev. 21:1), devoid of the influence of sin but still very much material in nature. When the people of God are fully redeemed and have received their glorified bodies, "the creation itself will be liberated from its bondage to decay and brought into the freedom and glory of the children of God" (Rom. 8:21). Paul simply refuses to permit our focus on the Spirit to diminish the value of the physical and God's creative design for what he has made.

All Christians feel weak at times and wish that there were a way in which our unspoken requests could be made known to God. Simply put, we all need the help of the Holy Spirit.

The phrase **in the same way** (v. 26a; **likewise** [ESV]) connects what Paul is about to say with what has gone before. In verse 18 he encouraged the believer in view of the surpassing glory that will replace our current suffering. Similarly, in verses 19–25 he again encourages the believer to persevere by pointing to the fact that even the material creation is groaning in anxious anticipation of our redemption, because when we receive our glorified bodies at the return of Jesus, the material creation will also experience its final redemption, and the curse of futility imposed on it because of Adam's sin will be lifted. The earth and everything in it will be renewed (see Rev. 21–22). So, verses 18–27 constitute one long exhortation designed to encourage believers to persevere in the midst of hardship and suffering. To that Paul now adds that even when you feel weak and wordless in your prayer life, the Holy Spirit himself intercedes on your behalf to make certain that your deepest desires and needs are brought to the Father in heaven.

The word **weakness** refers not to physical exhaustion or to intellectual confusion but to our not knowing **what to pray for as we ought** (ESV). We know that there is much more that needs to be articulated, but we can't figure out precisely what it is. But it is uplifting to know that my limitations, my lack of knowledge, my inability to decipher precisely how and for what I should pray is no reflection on God's power (cf. Eph. 3:20–21). Paul is talking not about style or posture or manner or length in prayer but about its content. We are ignorant of what we or others may need, ignorant of what God has promised, and unable to put into words the cry of our hearts. But the Holy

Spirit takes up where we, because of weakness, leave off. If we do not know what to pray for, the Spirit does. He intercedes for us **with groanings too deep for words** (v. 26b ESV).

Is this groaning of the Holy Spirit literal or physically audible, or could it be metaphorical? The **groaning** of the material creation is clearly metaphorical. We humans literally and audibly groan as we wait in anxious expectation to be set free from the perishable and painful bodies in which we now live. But Paul says that God the Holy Spirit will also groan as he identifies with our deep, profoundly emotional yet inarticulate yearning for answers to prayers that we feel too weak and ignorant to utter. As our intercessor (vv. 26–27), he intercedes for us **through wordless groans (too deep for words** [ESV; NASB]). The single Greek word behind this translation, *alalētos*, is used only here in the New Testament. Does it mean "ineffable"—that is, incapable of being expressed in human language (cf. 2 Cor. 12:4)?[10] If so, the groans may well be audible, though inarticulate. Or does it mean simply "unspoken," never rising to the audible level at all? If the former is correct, the groanings are probably ours that the Holy Spirit inspires and prompts within us. But the latter is more likely. The groans are from the Holy Spirit himself. He is the one who **intercedes for us.** Douglas Moo explains,

> While we cannot, then, be absolutely sure . . . , it is preferable to understand these "groans" as the Spirit's own "language of prayer," a ministry of intercession that takes place in our hearts (cf. v. 27) in a manner imperceptible to us. . . . I take it that Paul is saying, then, that our failure to know God's will and consequent inability to petition God specifically and assuredly is met by God's Spirit, who himself expresses to God those intercessory petitions that perfectly match the will of God. When we do not know what to pray for—yes, even when we pray for things that are not best for us—we need not despair, for we can depend on the Spirit's ministry of perfect intercession "on our behalf."[11]

Thus, it is the Spirit, not we, who prays. Even if praying in tongues is included in verses 26–27, Paul is in no way exclusively concerned with tongues.[12] Paul may well include tongues in the reality of the Spirit's **groans** within and for us, but he would not restrict the latter to praying in tongues. In other words, Rom. 8:26–27 is a glorious truth that applies across the board to all Christians, both

10. The word for "inexpressible" (*aneklalētos*) is found in 1 Pet. 1:8. It is significant that Paul does not use that word here.

11. Moo, *Romans*, 525–26.

12. For a clear defense of the interpretation that Paul is indeed addressing the experience of praying in tongues, see Fee, *God's Empowering Presence*, 575–86. See also Bertone, "Experience of Glossolalia"; Menzies, *Christ-Centered*, 64–72.

those who pray in tongues and those who do not. We must not overlook the context of verses 18–27, in which all Christians suffer in this present time, all Christians groan under the curse imposed by sin, and all Christians therefore struggle in their weakness to know precisely how and what to bring to God in prayer. The promise of the Spirit's work on our behalf in verses 26–27 thus applies to every believer, every child of God, regardless of a particular spiritual gift they either have or don't have.

Instead of our weakness in prayer bringing discouragement to our hearts, Paul reminds us that **the Spirit helps us in our weakness** (8:26a). Paul's acknowledgment that, in spite of the Spirit's indwelling presence, we are still weak (*astheneia*) runs counter to the triumphalism in certain Pentecostal-Charismatic circles. The only other place in the New Testament where this verb for "help" is used is Luke 10:40, where Martha asks Jesus to tell Mary to "help" her in the kitchen. So, the Spirit helps us by taking our unexpressed desires and petitions and communicating them perfectly to the Father. But does this refer to our groanings, or to the groanings of the Holy Spirit, or in some sense to both? Could it be that the Holy Spirit stirs and elicits these groanings in us such that they are in some sense both his and ours?

Some argue that these can't be the groanings of the Spirit because the Spirit is communicating directly with our heavenly Father. Why would the Spirit need to make use of groanings? The Spirit knows what he is asking on our behalf, and the Father certainly knows what the Spirit is saying. God the Father knows the mind of the Spirit, and the Spirit knows what the will of God is for each of us (v. 27). There is no confusion or uncertainty. But Paul isn't talking about how the Spirit regularly speaks to the Father. He is describing an altogether unique experience when the Spirit intercedes with the Father on our behalf when our hearts and minds are incapable of articulating in prayer what we want him to know. So I am led to conclude that these "groanings" are both ours and those of the Holy Spirit. The Spirit awakens in us or stirs in our hearts groanings that he then identifies with and makes his own. He then carries these groanings to the heart of the Father on our behalf. Such groanings occur in our **hearts** (v. 27), not in our mouths. You can't hear them or feel them. Rather, as God searches the hearts of his children (v. 27), he finds unuttered, unexpressed groanings produced in us by the Spirit.

These requests and needs are taken up by the Spirit in the form of deep groanings and carried by him to the Father. The Father in turn understands perfectly what these groanings mean because when the Spirit conveys them to God on our behalf, he does so in a way that perfectly conforms to God's will. The mind of the Spirit and the mind of the Father are in perfect harmony. So here is the sequence or process that Paul is describing:

In our weakness, we don't know what to pray for.

The Holy Spirit awakens in us and stirs up groans.

The Spirit in turn makes our groans his own,
groans that can't be put into words.

These groans are then taken by the Spirit to God the Father.

↓

God the Father knows perfectly what the Spirit is saying because the Spirit
asks the Father, on our behalf, only for things that align with his will.

God's Purposeful Sovereignty over All Things (8:28)

This one verse contains one of the more precious and powerful promises in all of
Scripture. It assures us that literally nothing can derail God's purpose to fulfill all
his other promises to us. Paul speaks with unassailable confidence (**we know**),
largely based on what follows in verses 29–30. Since God's loving purpose for
our salvation stretches from eternity past into eternity future, there is nothing
that can ultimately do us any spiritual harm or derail God's purpose for our lives.

Paul doesn't say that we know how God does this, but only **that** (*hoti*) he
does it. He is telling us that although our knowledge in this matter is certain,
it is not exhaustive. We may speak with absolute confidence concerning God's
providential power to bring good out of bad. But we will rarely be in a position
to explain how he did it.

Although the main text of the ESV does not identify "God" as the one who
works in this way, the NIV does, and rightly so (likewise, the NASB).[13] The
manuscript evidence is almost evenly divided on this point. But Paul says that
we are called according to a **purpose**, which demands someone who intends
to take the seemingly random and senseless things of life and make of them
something profitable and lasting. Things in and of themselves do not think or
formulate a plan. Furthermore, the basis for Paul's confident assertion in verse
28 is the reality of the divine plan of salvation in verses 29–30. The reason (*hoti*,
for [NIV]; perhaps more accurately, "because") why we are assured that the
things in this life work ultimately for our good is that God is working to bring
us into conformity with his Son (v. 29; see also Eph. 1:11). Thus, our faith and
hope are in God, not in **things**, be they good or bad.

13. Fee, on the other hand, believes the subject of the verb is the Spirit. See *God's Empowering
Presence*, 589–91.

The **all things** in view include not only the blessings and positive experiences of life but also the suffering, tribulation, and challenges we face (as stated in vv. 18–27 and later in vv. 35–36). Paul is saying not that all things *are* good but that God is able to **work together** (ESV) in all such **things** for our **good**. God does not transform evil things into good things. Rather, God can take something inherently evil and make it serve a higher, better, and more spiritually productive end (cf. Gen. 50:20). The **good** in view is identified in verse 29 as conformity "to the image of his Son." It is holiness, not health and wealth, that God has promised. Thus, the promise in verse 28 is not universal in scope but is assured to those **who are called according to his purpose** (ESV). For the Christian, then, for those who love God and are called according to his purpose, there is no such thing as pointless suffering. Our suffering and distress may be altogether random, unexpected, and mysterious, but they never are pointless.

This does not mean that God is sovereign only over that portion of the world that pertains to and affects believers. God is no less sovereign over the lives of unbelievers than he is over ours. But this does not mean that he is orchestrating their lives for their greater conformity to Christ. That happens only for those who are in Christ and not only believe but also **love** God.

God's Gracious Sovereignty in Salvation (8:29–30)

The doctrine of divine election and predestination is pervasive in Scripture. The verb "choose, elect" is used twenty-two times in the New Testament, seven of which refer to election to salvation or eternal life. The adjective "elect" also occurs twenty-two times, seventeen of which refer to men and women chosen or elected to eternal life. The noun "election" occurs seven times, all with reference to salvation. The verb "predestine" occurs six times, four of which refer to people being predestined to salvation (cf. Eph. 1:5, 11).

The first link in this eternal chain of salvation is foreknowledge. Although God foreknows all things from eternity past, here in verse 29 he has in view men and women (*hous*, the relative pronoun rendered as **those** or perhaps **those whom** [ESV]). These he also predestined to be conformed to the image of his Son.

Predestination (*proorizō*, "decide beforehand") is not synonymous with foreknowledge. Whereas the latter focuses on the distinguishing love of God whereby people are elected, predestination points to the decision God made of what he intended to do with those whom he foreknew (see Acts 4:28). Predestination is that act in eternity past (again, note the prefix *pro*) in which God ordained or decreed that those on whom he had set his saving love would inherit

The Sovereignty of God and Divine Foreknowledge

The verb "know" often refers to something more than mere mental or intellectual understanding and cannot be restricted to having knowledge in advance of some particular event. See, for example, Matt. 7:23, where Jesus reveals his future response to false disciples at the last judgment: "I never knew you; depart from me, you workers of lawlessness" (ESV). Clearly, Jesus knew them but never entered into a covenant or saving relationship with them. Thus, "know" is used as a virtual synonym for "love" (cf. Gen. 18:19; Exod. 33:17; Jer. 1:5; Hosea 13:5; Gal. 4:8–9; see esp. Amos 3:2), and it refers to setting one's affection upon or highly regarding or delighting in someone with peculiar interest. The verb "foreknow" (*proginōskō*, the prefix *pro* indicating an event that transpired in eternity past) occurs five times in the New Testament (Acts 26:5; Rom. 8:29; 11:2; 1 Pet. 1:20; 2 Pet. 3:17). The noun "foreknowledge" (*prognōsis*) occurs in two texts (Acts 2:23; 1 Pet. 1:2). For God to foreknow those whom he predestined refers to a knowledge that entails covenant commitment, love, and a relationship of intimacy (see Rom. 11:2). That God foreknew his people is to say that he set his gracious and merciful regard upon them, that he knew them from eternity past with a sovereign and distinguishing delight. Paul does not address here the basis for this foreknowledge, be it foreknown faith or otherwise.

The Arminian[a] approach to foreknowledge takes one of three forms. Foreknowledge may refer to God's knowledge of all men and women from eternity past. In other words, "foreknowledge" is but a synonym for "omniscience." However, all those whom God foreknows he also predestines; therefore, if foreknowledge encompasses every human being, then every human being will ultimately be saved (universalism). Also, Rom. 8:29–30 is the basis for Paul's assertion in verse 28, a verse that concerns those who love God and are called according to his purpose—that is, Christians. Another option is that foreknowledge refers to God's advance knowledge of who would choose or believe in Christ. God elects or predestines unto salvation those whom he foreknows will exercise saving faith in Christ. Election is therefore conditional, insofar as God's decision to predestine a person to eternal life was conditioned upon his foreknowledge that an individual would believe in the gospel.

A slightly different view is the notion of corporate conditional election. God determines to save a class of people, those who trust Christ. Election concerns God's predestination of the believing community to eternal life. Perhaps the best definition is that provided by Paul Marston and Roger Forster: "The prime point is that the election of the church is a corporate rather than an individual thing. It is not that individuals are in the church because they are elect, it is rather that they are elect because they are in the church, which is the body of the elect One. . . . A Christian is not chosen to become part of Christ's body, but in becoming part of that body [by free will, exercising faith] he partakes of Christ's election."[b]

A more recent advocate of this view is William Klein, who contends that "God has chosen the church as a body rather than the specific individuals who populate that body."[c] The concern of the New Testament regarding predestination, says Klein, "is not *how* people become Christians nor *who* become Christians" but "*what* God has foreordained on behalf of those who *are* (or *will be*) Christians."[d]

According to the Wesleyan-Arminian[e] doctrine of prevenient (or preventing) grace, God graciously and mercifully restores to all human beings the freedom of will lost in the fall of Adam. Prevenient grace provides people with the ability to choose or reject God. Thus, there is a measure of free will supernaturally restored to every person. This grace, however, is not irresistible. Whereas all are recipients of prevenient grace, many resist it to their eternal demise. Those who utilize this grace to respond in faith to the gospel are saved. In essence, God's prevenient grace serves to neutralize human depravity and restores in every person the ability to freely believe the gospel.

a. Arminianism derives its name from the Dutch theologian James Arminius (1559–1609).
b. Marston and Forster, *God's Strategy in Human History*, 136.
c. Klein, *The New Chosen People*, 259.
d. Klein, *The New Chosen People*, 185.
e. "Wesleyan-Arminian" describes the version of Arminian theology developed by John Wesley.

eternal life (although some believe that people are predestined unto particular historical blessing and service, but not salvation). There are six verses in the New Testament where the verb *proorizō* is used (Acts 4:28; Rom. 8:29, 30; 1 Cor. 2:7; Eph. 1:5, 11; cf. also John 10:14–16, 24–30; Acts 13:44–48; 2 Thess. 2:13).

God's ultimate purpose was the establishment of a spiritual family, his adopted sons and daughters in union with the Son of God, Jesus Christ. God foreknew us and predestined us to become like Jesus, spiritually, morally, and physically. "The term 'firstborn' . . . refers to Christ's status both as the first human being released from bondage to decay (cf. 1 Cor 15:20–23) and the first in importance among God's children."[14] That to be the **firstborn** (Rom. 8:29) refers to preeminence of status is clear from Ps. 89:27 and Col. 1:15, 18.

14. Thielman, *Romans*, 411.

The Golden Chain of Salvation in Romans 8:29–30

Those in the Reformed theological tradition argue that each link in this eternal chain of salvation is coextensive with every other link. The objects of God's saving activity are the same from start to finish. *Those whom* he foreknew, not one more or one less, *these* also he predestined. Whom did he predestine? Those whom he foreknew. And *those whom* he predestined, not one more or one less, *these* he also called. Whom did he call? Those whom he predestined. And *those whom* he called, not one more or one less, *these* he also justified. Whom does God justify? Those whom he called. And *those whom* he justified, not one more or one less, *these* he also glorified. Whom does he glorify? Those whom he justified. There is a continuity in the recipients of salvation from divine foreknowledge in eternity past all the way through glorification in eternity future.

Those whom God predestined he also **called** (v. 30), a reference not to the mere proclamation of the gospel but to the powerful work of the Holy Spirit by which he effectively secures a response in the sinner's heart (cf. 1 Thess. 1:5). We know this because **those he called, he also justified**. The call in view is that summons by which God not only invites a person externally in the gospel, but also by means of the Holy Spirit internally enables that person to respond to it (Rom. 1:6–7; 8:28; 1 Cor. 1:9).

Those who are called God **also justified**, which, as we have seen repeatedly in Romans, refers to God's forensic declaration that the righteousness of Jesus Christ has been imputed or reckoned to the elect. That Paul would speak in the past tense in saying that those whom God called he also **glorified** (insofar as glorification is yet future in terms of our experience) is likely due to his desire to emphasize its certainty; it is so securely set and sealed in the mind and purpose and predestined plan of God that it may be spoken of as having already occurred.

The Security of Salvation (8:31–39)

To a rhetorical question that Paul poses (v. 31a), he responds with a decisive response: **If God is for us, who can be against us?** (v. 31b). The ways in which God is for us are unpacked in verses 32–39. The question is not suggesting that Christians have no enemies but only that enemies can do no lasting or eternal spiritual harm. Paul knows this on the basis of an unbreakable principle of divine logic (*a maiore ad minus*, "from the greater to the lesser"; cf. Matt. 6:30). The God who is for us is he **who did not spare his own Son, but gave him up for us all** (v. 32a). Similarly to Paul's reasoning in Rom. 5:9–10, the God who has done the incomparably greatest thing can be trusted to **graciously** provide us with all lesser things we need to stay in relationship with him.

Negatively speaking, he **did not spare his own Son**. Positively speaking, he **gave him up for us all** (v. 32). By **all things** Paul means everything essential to knowing and enjoying God and remaining in relationship with him forever. But what of the accusations brought against the **elect** by their enemies and Satan? They are to no avail because God has already justified us (v. 33b). Whatever sins we are accused of have already been atoned for by Jesus, **who died—more than that, who was raised to life** (v. 34b). The sufficiency of Christ's atoning sacrifice for sins and the confirmation given when God raised him from the dead provide the assurance we need that no accusation against us can prevail. In addition to which, Jesus **is at the right hand of God** (the place of supremacy, power, and honor) and is there **interceding for us** (see Heb. 7:25; 1 John 2:1–2). "The argument," notes John Stott, "is that no prosecution can be of any avail if Jesus Christ is our Advocate who pleads our cause, and if God the Judge has already justified us."[15]

Paul again employs a rhetorical question when he asks, **Who shall separate us from the love of Christ?** (v. 35a). There follows a list of the many threats to our spiritual security, none of which can separate us from Christ's love. He mentions **trouble (tribulation** [ESV]) and **hardship (distress** [ESV]). The former refers to physical suffering while the latter has in view the internal and emotional anxiety it can induce. **Persecution** is something with which Paul himself was quite familiar (see 2 Cor. 11:22–29). By **famine** and **nakedness** he likely had in mind what he wrote in 2 Cor. 11:27b: "I have known hunger and thirst and have often gone without food; I have been cold and naked." No degree of **danger**, not even martyrdom (**sword**; cf. Luke 21:16–17), can overturn what God has done for his elect through Christ Jesus. Paul sums up with a citation of Ps. 44:22, where the psalmist declares, "For your sake we face death all day long; we are considered as sheep to be slaughtered."

It is **in** (v. 37) all such attacks, not by evading or avoiding them or being spared the devastation they bring, that we conquer **through him who loved us**. Paul is careful to point out that it isn't through our courage, resolve, endurance, or determination, but rather through the presence of Christ at all times and on the basis of what he has accomplished that we conquer. It is not our hold on him, but his hold on us, that enables us to stand securely through the very worst.

15. Stott, *Romans*, 104.

As if to silence all lingering objections, Paul lists every conceivable threat to the love of God for us. **Neither death nor life** poses a legitimate threat. Death serves only to bring the believer into God's glorious presence, and there is nothing in life, be it tragedy or triumph, nor any manner of success or failure, that can sever our relationship to our Savior. Neither can **angels** or **demons** (*archai*; **rulers** [ESV]) diminish our status as justified children of God. Neither the holy angels who do God's bidding nor the demonic rulers who oppose his will have the power to threaten our security in Christ.

The Role of Angels and Demons in God's Eternal Purpose

Paul's reference to "angels" and "demons" in Rom. 8:38 reminds us of their prominent place in biblical theology and in the experience of God's people.

The word "angel" (*angelos*) occurs in 34 of the 66 books of the Bible: 108 times in the Old Testament and over 165 times in the New Testament, for a total of about 275 times in the Bible. Angels, no less than humans, were created at a point in time (Ps. 148:2–5; John 1:1–3; Col. 1:16). Being direct creations of God, they did not descend from an original pair as humans did, nor do they procreate (Matt. 22:28–30). Angels are characterized by the basic elements of personality: intellect, emotion, will, self-consciousness, self-determination, and a sense of moral obligation (i.e., conscience) and the power to pursue it. They are intelligent but not omniscient (Mark 13:32; 1 Pet. 1:12), experience emotion (Job 38:7; Luke 15:10; Rev. 4–5), and exercise their wills (Rev. 12:7–12).

Although angels are immaterial, incorporeal spirits (Heb. 1:15), they have spatial limitations; that is, they are not omnipresent (see Dan. 9:21–23; 10:10–14, where we find both spatial movement and temporal limitation). They lack gender (Matt. 22:28–30), and yet are typically described as masculine (Zech. 5:9 may be the lone exception). Angels are able to assume the form of and appear as humans: (1) to the naked eye (Matt. 28:1–7; Luke 1:11–13; 1:26–29), (2) in visions and dreams (Isa. 6:1–7; Matt. 1:20), and (3) in human form (Gen. 18:1–8; in this case they were sufficiently physical in their appearance that the men of Sodom and Gomorrah lusted after them; see also Mark 16:5). See also Dan. 10:5–6; Matt. 28:2–3; Rev. 4:6–8 for differing manifestations.

All angelic power is subject to God's power and purpose (Ps. 103:20; 2 Pet. 2:11). They were instrumental in God's destruction of Sodom and

Gomorrah (Gen. 19:12–16), and one angel killed 185,000 Assyrians (2 Kings 19:35). An angel moved the stone from Christ's tomb (Matt. 28:2), while another entered a locked prison and secured Peter's release (Acts 12:6–11). Yet another, "an angel of the Lord," struck down Herod (Acts 12:23).

In addition to the designation "angels," they are called "mighty ones" (Ps. 103:20), God's "hosts" (Ps. 46:7 ESV), "messengers" (NIV) or "watchers" (ESV) (Dan. 4:13, 17), "heavenly beings" (Ps. 89:6), and "sons of God" (Job 1:6; 2:1; 38:7 ESV). There may well be several special classifications or categories or kinds of angelic beings. (1) Cherubim, the highest order or rank, guard Eden and prevent Adam and Eve's return (Gen. 3:24) and hover above the mercy seat (Exod. 25:17–22; cf. "the cherubim of the Glory" in Heb. 9:5; see also Ezek. 10:4, 18–22). Cherubim are never explicitly called "angels" because they are not messengers; they proclaim and protect the glory and holiness of God. (2) Seraphim (literally, "burning ones" [Isa. 6:1–7]; the name speaks of their consuming devotion to God) are "afire" or "ablaze" with adoration of God. Their principal task is worship. (3) Living Creatures (Rev. 4:6–9) could be either cherubim or seraphim or another class altogether.

Only two angels are named: Michael (literally, "who is like God?") is an angel assigned to protect Israel (Dan. 10:13, 20–21). He is the "archangel" (Jude 9) and the leader of the angelic host in their war against Satan (Rev. 12:7). Gabriel (literally, "mighty one of God"), in each of his appearances, communicates or interprets divine revelation concerning God's kingdom purposes (Dan. 8:16; 9:21; Luke 1:19, 26).

As for the number of angels in existence, a "multitude" announced Jesus's birth (Luke 2:13–15 ESV; or "great company" [NIV]). God is Yahweh "of hosts" (Ps. 46:7, 11 ESV), the head over a vast army of angels. Jesus refers to "twelve legions" of angels, hence seventy-two thousand angels (Matt. 26:53). Revelation 5:11 refers to "thousands upon thousands, and ten thousand times ten thousand" angels (cf. Deut. 33:2; Dan. 7:10; Jude 14).

The holy or elect angels (1 Tim. 5:21) worship God (Isa. 6:1–4; Rev. 4:6–11; 5:11–14), serve his will (Ps. 103:19–21; Heb. 1:7, 14), provide guidance and direction for God's people (Gen. 24:7, 40; Exod. 14:19; 23:20; Num. 20:16; Acts 5:17–20; 8:26; 10:3–7, 22), guard and protect God's people (Pss. 34:7; 78:23–25; 91:11; 1 Kings 19:5–7; Dan. 6:20–23; 12:1; Acts 12:15), provide comfort and encouragement (Matt. 4:11; Luke 22:43; Acts 27:22–24), are used by God to impart both revelation and interpretation (Gal. 3:19; Acts 7:38, 52–53; Heb. 2:2), assist in response to prayer (Dan. 9:20–24; 10:1–21), and execute judgment (Gen. 18–19; Exod. 12:23, 29; 2 Sam. 24:15–17; 2 Kings 19:35; Ps. 78:49; Acts 12:23).

Demons appear to be fallen or rebellious angels (Matt. 25:41; 1 Pet. 3:22; Rev. 12:7), although Michael Heiser offers a different interpretation. Basing his view largely on a wide range of Second Temple Jewish texts (i.e., extrabiblical, noninspired documents, especially 1 Enoch and Jubilees), Heiser provides this account of the origin of those entities we know as demons in the New Testament: "Specifically, the disembodied spirits released at the death of the giants [i.e., the Nephilim in Gen. 6:4], the offspring of the union of the sons of God and mortal women, are the demons known in Second Temple texts and the New Testament Gospels."ᵃ

In any case, demons are beyond the possibility of redemption, and that for three reasons: (1) there is no record of such in Scripture; (2) there is no record in Scripture of demonic repentance; (3) the impact of Christ's cross on demons is always portrayed as judgment, never salvation (see Col. 2:11–15; nowhere do we read of justification, forgiveness, redemption, adoption, regeneration, etc. being true of any angelic being). Eternal punishment in the lake of fire has been "prepared for the devil and his angels" (Matt. 25:41).

Demons are described with several differing terms. They are called "principalities/rulers" (*archē*; Rom. 8:38; Eph. 1:21; 3:10; 6:12; Col. 1:16; 2:10), "authorities" (*exousia*; Eph. 1:21; 3:10; Col. 1:16), "powers" (*dynamis*; Rom. 8:38; Eph. 1:21), "dominions" (*kyriotēs*; Eph. 1:21; Col. 1:16), "thrones" (*thronos*; Col. 1:16), and "world rulers" (*kosmokratōr*; Eph. 6:12). "Demon" (*daimōn* or *daimonion*) is used sixty-three times in the New Testament, fifty-four of which are in the Gospels. They are also called "spirits" (*pneuma*; cf. Luke 10:17 with 10:20), "unclean spirits" or "impure spirits" (used twenty-one times, half of which are in Mark; cf. Luke 11:24), and "evil spirits" (only eight times in the Gospels and Acts; cf. Luke 8:2).

Virtually everything true of angels is true of demons: properties, personality, powers, and so forth. The primary difference is that the demons are evil, serving Satan, and the angels are good, serving God. Demons can speak to and communicate with humans (Luke 4:33–35, 41; 8:28–30; Acts 19:13–17), are intelligent (Luke 4:34; 8:28; Acts 19:13–17), and can formulate and propagate their own doctrinal systems (1 Tim. 4:1–3). Demons have emotions and experience a variety of feelings (Luke 8:28; James 2:19). There appear to be differences or degrees in their strength (Mark 9:28–29) and sinfulness (Matt. 12:45). Like the holy angels, demons can appear to us in various forms, both spiritual and physical (Matt. 4:1–11; Rev. 9:7–10, 17; 16:13–16). They can infuse their victims with superhuman strength (Mark 5:3; Acts 19:16). Like the holy angels, demons can move swiftly through space (Dan. 9:21–23; 10:10–14). Normal physical barriers do not restrict their activity (in Mark 5:1–13 a "legion" [six thousand] of demons inhabited one man and then two thousand pigs).

Demons can physically assault someone and/or cause physical affliction (Luke 9:39; 13:10–17). Mark 9:18 (cf. Matt. 17:15) speaks of a demon seizing a young boy. In Matt. 9:32–34 a man's inability to speak is attributed to a demon (cf. 12:22–24; Luke 11:14–15). Demons inspire and energize the false wisdom of the world that all too often infiltrates the church and poisons interpersonal relationships in the body of Christ. James 3:13–18 describes two kinds of wisdom, that which comes from heaven and that which is characterized as "earthly, unspiritual, demonic" (*daimoniōdēs*). Some believe that demons may have been responsible, in part, for the crucifixion of Jesus (1 Cor. 2:6–8). Demons also engage in cosmic-level warfare with the holy angels (Rev. 12:1–12).

a. Heiser, *Demons*, 112n4.

Nothing that we encounter in **the present** or anything that may come our way in **the future** has the potential to undermine our relationship with Christ. Indeed, no **powers**, by which Paul likely means no supernatural force or miraculous event, no matter how strong it may be, can threaten our position as children of God. Paul employs a figure of speech known as merism when he speaks of **height** and **depth**. Simply put, nothing above us or below us or anything in between, **nor anything else in all creation will be able to separate us from the love of God in Christ Jesus our Lord** (v. 39 ESV). This final phrase is designed to shut off and close down any possible loopholes. No being, no thing, no event, nothing that is or ever will be, not even yourself (after all, you are a created thing), will be able to separate you from the love of Christ!

But what if God himself should choose to separate me from his love? But the whole point of Paul's argument in verses 31–34 is to prove precisely the opposite. God has taken the most elaborate, sacrificial, personally painful and costly steps possible to embrace us in his love. Paul's argument is that rather than being against us, God is **for** us (v. 31); rather than taking from us, he gives all things to us (v. 32); and rather than condemning us, he justifies us (v. 33). Furthermore, on what grounds or for what cause would God reject you or separate himself from you? Perhaps you will say, "My sins." But Paul's argument is that Christ died for those very sins (vv. 33–34). Those sins that you fear might separate you from God were the sins for which Christ paid the penalty. That is why no one can bring a successful accusation against you (v. 33). What sin can you possibly commit that might separate you from God's love for which Christ did not already pay the penalty?

ROMANS 9

God's Sovereignty in the Salvation of Jew and Gentile

The Purpose of Romans 9–11

The purpose of Rom. 9–11 is related to an unanswered question raised in 3:1–6. There Paul introduced the problem posed by Jewish unbelief and the apparent threat it poses to the faithfulness of God. Paul didn't directly answer the question. But now, in Rom. 9–11, he does. Furthermore, in 8:28–30 Paul said that God's purpose for his people is dependent on his calling them to himself through faith in Christ. But how can we have any confidence that it will come to pass if God's "call" or commitment to Israel fails? The unbelief of Israel and their separation from Christ appears to call into question or jeopardize the faithfulness of God in fulfilling his word. Thus, Rom. 9–11 is designed primarily to assert and defend the goodness and faithfulness of God in spite of Israel's failure to turn to Jesus as the Messiah.

Romans 9 typically has been a focal point in the debate between those in the Wesleyan-Arminian tradition and those from a more Reformed or Calvinistic perspective. Both views will be explained in what follows, starting with the latter and concluding with the former.

The Importance of Intercessory Prayer (9:1–5)

We begin with verses 4–5, where Paul lists the many benefits and blessings that were granted to Israel as God's old-covenant people. In verses 1–3 Paul describes in graphic terms his love for them and his prayer that they would be saved. We look first at who it is that Paul prays for and why their unbelief poses such a threat to God's faithfulness to fulfill his promises.

In this letter Paul does not hesitate to speak his mind concerning the Jewish nation and their widespread rejection of Jesus (see 2:9, 17–29; 3:9, 29; 4:9–18; 9:25–10:5; 10:19–21). But there can be no question about his love for his fellow brothers and sisters according to the flesh (see 10:1). The depth of Paul's sorrow at the lost estate of his **own race** (v. 3) has produced **great sorrow and unceasing anguish in** his **heart** (v. 2). The reason for describing the privileges of Israel (vv. 4–5) is to show how tragic their condition is. Israel is God's chosen people, with unparalleled privileges, and yet they are accursed and cut off from Christ.

First, they bear the name **Israel**, a general statement of honor designed to sum up and embrace the items that follow (see Gen. 32:22–28; John 1:31, 47, 49; 3:10; 12:13). Second, to them belongs **the adoption to sonship**. It was a theocratic, national, corporate adoption, but still a matter of great privilege (see Exod. 4:22–23). Third, there is **the divine glory**, a reference to "the glory that abode upon and appeared on Mount Sinai (Exod. 24:16, 17), the glory that covered and filled the tabernacle (Exod. 40:34–38), the glory that appeared upon the mercy-seat in the holy of holies (Lev. 16:2), the glory of the Lord that filled the temple (1 Kings 8:10, 11; 2 Chron. 7:1, 2; cf. Ezek. 1:28). This glory was the sign of God's presence with Israel and certified to Israel that God dwelt among them and met with them (cf. Exod. 29:42–46)."[1]

Fourth, it was only Israel that had been given **the covenants**, a reference to the Abrahamic, Mosaic, and Davidic covenants. Fifth, theirs was **the receiving of the law**. It was only to Israel that God provided the Mosaic law. No Gentile nation was so blessed. Sixth, there is **the temple worship** or "the service," a reference to all that was entailed by the temple and the activities that transpired there, especially the sacrificial system described in Leviticus (see Heb. 9:1–7; cf. Exod. 12:25–27). Seventh, **the promises** somewhat overlap with **the covenants** (see Rom. 15:8; 2 Cor. 1:20; Gal. 3:16; Eph. 2:12). Eighth, **the patriarchs** refers to Abraham, Isaac, Jacob, and David, among others.

Finally, **from their race, according to the flesh, is the Christ, who is God over all, blessed forever. Amen** (ESV). The supreme privilege and honor is that the anointed one, Jesus Christ, descended, as far as his human nature is concerned, from the Jewish people. Although he is not less than human, he is assuredly more. He is, as Paul says, **God over all**.

The punctuation of verse 5 is disputed. The likely literal rendering is, "of whom is Christ according to the flesh, who [i.e., Jesus Christ] is over all, God

1. Murray, *Romans*, 2:5.

blessed forever. Amen," or, "of whom is Christ according to the flesh, who [Christ] is God over all, blessed forever. Amen." On either translation, the absolute deity of Jesus is asserted. Others place a full stop after the word "flesh" and read the final phrase as a doxology to God the Father. Hence, "of whom is Christ according to the flesh. He who is God [the Father] over all be [or "is"] blessed forever. Amen." Another variation is, "of whom is Christ according to the flesh. He who is over all is God [the Father], blessed forever. Amen." Others place a comma after "flesh" and a period after "all." Thus, the clause "he who is over all" would refer to Christ, but "God be blessed forever" remains a doxology to the Father. Hence, "of whom is Christ according to the flesh, who is over all. God [the Father] be blessed forever. Amen."

The statement that begins with **for I could wish** (v. 3) is probably a prayer, for three reasons: (1) what Paul wishes for parallels the prayer of Moses in Exod. 32:11–14, 31–32; (2) of the other six occurrences of the verb translated as "wish" (*euchomai*) in the New Testament, five refer to prayer (Acts 26:29; 2 Cor. 13:7, 9; James 5:16; 3 John 2); (3) Gordon Wiles has shown that such wishes are in most cases prayers transposed for use in a letter. Consequently, a wish such as we find in Rom. 9 is simply "the expression of a desire that God take action regarding the person(s) mentioned in the wish."[2]

The Greek imperfect tense fills in for the optative and denotes "a present-time action that is potential or attempted but never carried out."[3] When Paul declares, **For I could wish that I myself were cursed and cut off from Christ for the sake of my people**, he appears to be praying, "If my damnation will save the Jews, so be it." The word translated as **cursed** (*anathema*) refers to something delivered over to divine wrath and eternal condemnation (1 Cor. 12:3; 16:22; Gal. 1:8–9). It means forfeiting one's salvation and being consigned to eternal wrath and perdition. The full extent of what it means to be *anathema* is defined as being **cut off from Christ**—that is, to be eternally excluded from fellowship with Christ Jesus (cf. Matt. 7:23; 25:41).

Some argue that Paul's declaration is hyperbolic and not to be taken literally. Or perhaps the apostle used to pray for this, but then came to his senses and realized that such a petition is inappropriate for a Christian to pray. Others suggest that Paul only contemplated praying for this but never actually did so. Most likely Paul means to say that he *would have* prayed for this *had it been permissible*. Had the end in view been something genuinely attainable by a believer, he would have prayed for it. This is called the desiderative or tendential imperfect: "I could almost wish." One contemplates the desire but does not come to the point of

2. Wiles, *Paul's Intercessory Prayers*, 22. For other examples of "wish-prayers," see Rom. 15:5, 13; 16:20; 1 Cor. 1:8; 1 Thess. 3:11–12; 5:23.
3. Moo, *Romans*, 558.

actually making it the express focus of one's wish. Paul knew all too well that it was, in fact, theologically impossible for him to be severed from Christ and condemned. Several verses earlier he had clearly affirmed this fact (8:31–39).

Also, if it were an obligatory act of Christian love that not only Paul but all of us should pray such a prayer, then those who might be saved as a result would also have to pray such a prayer. The end result would be that no one is saved, because each person would have prayed to be condemned in order that others might be saved. They in turn would pray the same prayer, and the cycle would go on without end. We must also remember that God did not create a world in which a person could be eternally condemned for an act of love. And would hell really be hellish if it were the place to which Paul were assigned for having expressed his most profound and Christlike desire to love his fellow Jews?

Knowing that some would question his sincerity in making a request of God that he knew could never be fulfilled, Paul emphatically affirms the integrity of his prayer in five statements in 9:1. **I speak the truth**, which in itself should have been enough. He speaks truth **in Christ**, a reference to his personal relationship to Jesus as Lord. His union with Christ is the orbit within which his emotions and beliefs move. Somewhat redundantly he says **I am not lying** in order to reinforce the accuracy of what he is about to say. **My conscience bears me witness** (ESV) evokes that faculty or dimension by which we judge ourselves and bring our own souls under moral scrutiny. In declaring that it is **through the Holy Spirit**, Paul confirms and certifies that his conscience in this matter is clear and upright. The grammar here is somewhat awkward. A wooden translation would be, "my conscience bearing witness to me in/by the Holy Spirit" (although "Holy Spirit" has no article, as is typically the case when it appears in the dative case). Paul's intent is that "just as Christ attests to his speaking truth, so the Spirit attests to the trustworthiness of his conscience as it [his conscience] bears its independent witness to his veracity."[4]

Has God's Word of Promise to His People Failed? (9:6–13)

Virtually all misunderstandings of verses 6–13 arise from a failure to see that these verses were written to solve a problem posed by verses 1–5. The question or problem that Paul is faced with is this: If Israel is God's covenant people, to whom so many glorious privileges have been given (vv. 4–5), why are so few Israelites saved? Has the rejection of Jesus Christ by the majority of Israelites thwarted God's purpose? And if God's promises to Israel do not hold true, what reason do we have to be confident that his promises to us will?

4. Fee, *God's Empowering Presence*, 592.

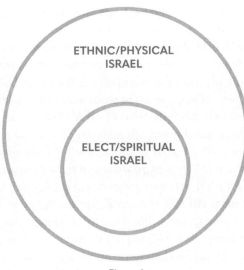

Figure 1

Paul's answer takes the form of a proposition (v. 6a), God's word has **not failed**, which is based on a principle (v. 6b), **for not all who are descended from Israel are Israel**. This in turn is supported by proofs (vv. 7–13).

Grammatically speaking, it is more accurate to translate this statement as "all who are of Israel, these are not Israel." If God's word of promise and covenant is that all ethnic Israelites are to be saved, then clearly his purpose has failed, and his word is void. But Paul denies that God ever intended to save all ethnic Israelites. His purpose has always been to save a remnant within, but not the entirety of, ethnic Israel. There is an Israel *within* Israel. There is a *spiritually elect remnant* within the *physical nation*. (This can be illustrated as in fig. 1.)

The outer circle includes all who have physically descended from Abraham. They are "Israel" according to the flesh. The inner circle points to those who are also chosen by God to inherit eternal life. They are "Israel" according to the promise. The latter constitutes what Paul refers to as the "remnant" (Rom. 9:27; 11:5). The unbelief of those in the outer circle does not jeopardize the redemptive purpose of God, for that promise applied only to the inner circle, the elect remnant within the nation as a whole. Thus, **God's purpose in election** (v. 11b) will not fail. Simply put, not every person who is a physically ethnic Israelite is a spiritually elect Israelite. Douglas Moo summarizes this way:

> If the OT teaches that belonging to physical Israel in itself makes a person a member of God's true spiritual people, then Paul's gospel is in jeopardy. For were this the case, the gospel, proclaiming that only those who believe in Jesus

Christ can be saved (cf. 3:20–26), would contradict the OT and be cut off from its indispensable historical roots. Paul therefore argues in vv. 6b–29 that belonging to God's true spiritual people has always been based on God's gracious and sovereign call and not on ethnic identity. Therefore, God is free to "narrow" the apparent boundaries of election by choosing only some Jews to be saved (vv. 6–13; 27–29). He is also free to "expand" the dimensions of his people by choosing Gentiles (vv. 24–26).[5]

To prove his point, Paul appeals to the families of Abraham and Isaac. In God's dealings with each of these patriarchs we see the principle of verse 6b in operation. Although both Isaac and Ishmael were Abraham's physical descendants, Isaac alone is a true or spiritual Israelite. Likewise, whereas both Jacob and Esau were the physical seed of Isaac (being twins), only Jacob was the spiritual seed whom God purposed to save. Thus, Ishmael and Esau fall within the orbit of the outer circle because they are ethnic, but not elect, Israelites. Isaac and Jacob, on the other hand, fall within the orbit of the inner circle, being both ethnic and elect Israelites.

First, in verse 7a Paul distinguishes between **children** and **descendants**. To be a physical descendant of Abraham does not guarantee (contrary to the belief of the Pharisees [see Matt. 3:9; John 8:37–40]) that one will be a child of God—that is, saved (cf. Rom. 8:16–17, 21; Eph. 5:1; Phil. 2:15). Paul supports this by an appeal to Gen. 21:12 in verse 7b. The line of the covenant proceeds through Isaac, not Ishmael, even though the latter is as much a physical descendant of Abraham as the former.

Second, in verses 8–9 Paul contrasts **children by physical descent** and **children of the promise**, the latter a reference to physical descendants of Abraham whom God has sovereignly chosen to be the beneficiaries of the covenant promises. God had promised Abraham that he would be the father of a great nation (Gen. 12:3; 15:5). But as Abraham and Sarah grew older, they had long passed the age for bearing children. So Abraham decided to make things happen in the power of his flesh. He took Hagar, one of Sarah's handmaids, and had sexual relations with her. She conceived and gave birth to Ishmael. Abraham wanted Ishmael to be the child of promise, the one through whom the covenant blessings would be fulfilled. But God said, "Your wife Sarah will bear you a son, and you will call him Isaac. I will establish my covenant with him as an everlasting covenant for his descendants after him" (Gen. 17:19). God made it clear to Abraham that genetic or ethnic descent is no guarantee that one will inherit the covenant blessings. It is a matter of God's sovereign choice, not human effort or physical descent.

5. Moo, *Romans*, 568–69.

That not all ethnic Israelites are spiritual Israelites is proven again by the case of Jacob and Esau, twin brothers born to Isaac and Rebekah. Jacob was the object of God's electing love, whereas Esau was rejected. If **it was before the twins were born or had done anything good or bad** (v. 11) that God made this distinction between them, on what grounds was Jacob loved and Esau hated? It was **in order that God's purpose in election might stand: not by works but by him who calls** (vv. 11b–12a). Neither their birth nor their behavior factored into God's decision.

As the firstborn, Esau should have been the recipient of the blessing, yet God chose Jacob instead, based on nothing in either Jacob or Esau. Both were sinners, deserving of nothing from God but judgment. They were twins, conceived by **our father Isaac** (v. 10). Someone might object that although both Isaac and Ishmael had the same father, they had different mothers. To that, Paul would push back by saying, "Consider Jacob and Esau. They had the same father, Isaac, and the same mother, Rebekah." The point he's making is that the difference between them wasn't of their own doing or that of their parents. It was all of God.

In what sense can it be said by God, **Jacob I loved, but Esau I hated** (v. 13; cf. Mal. 1:2–3)? Here **hated** may be comparative in force. God loved Esau "less than" he loved Jacob (see Gen. 29:32–33; Deut. 21:15; Matt. 6:24; 10:37–38; Luke 14:26; John 12:25). Others argue that **hated** is privative in force, the point being that God did not love Esau at all, as he did Jacob. Another option is to understand God's love of Jacob to be equivalent to his choice of him, thus making God's hatred for Esau a reference to his decision not to bestow this privilege on him. Hence, "Jacob I chose, but Esau I rejected."

Or perhaps **hated** does have a positive force. Not only did God not savingly and redemptively love Esau, as he did Jacob, but he actively rejected him and manifested his displeasure and disfavor by means of retributive justice. It is not merely the absence of blessing that Esau suffers, but the presence of judgment (see Pss. 5:5; 11:5; Prov. 6:16; 8:13; Isa. 1:14; 61:8; Jer. 44:4; Hosea 9:15; Amos 5:21; Zech. 8:17; Mal. 2:16). John Murray reminds us, though, that we do not "predicate of this divine hate those unworthy features which belong to hate as it is exercised by us sinful men. In God's hate there is no malice, malignancy, vindictiveness, unholy rancor or bitterness. The kind of hate thus characterized is condemned in Scripture and it would be blasphemy to predicate the same of God."[6]

The principle in verses 6–13 that answers the problem of verses 1–5 is that God's promised blessings are enjoyed on the basis of God's sovereign choice and not on what a person is by birth or by works. The ultimate decision of who will experience God's mercy is never based on "human desire or effort" (9:16;

6. Murray, *Romans*, 2:22.

"human will or exertion" [ESV]). To demonstrate this principle, Paul uses two Old Testament texts (Gen. 25:23 and Mal. 1:2–3) that do not immediately pertain to personal salvation. But when that principle is then applied, it need not be restricted to God's choice of individuals and nations for earthly, historical roles.

There are other reasons gleaned from Rom. 9 itself that strongly suggest that Paul is talking about individual, not national, election.[7] As previously noted, the phrases **children of God** and **children of the promise** in Paul's writings always refer to those who are the redeemed of God (cf. Rom. 8:16, 21; Gal. 4:28; Phil. 2:15). Furthermore, when Paul refers to **works** (v. 12), he does so consistently to deny that they are the basis for justification (cf. Rom. 3:20, 27–28; 4:2, 6; 9:32; 11:6; Gal. 2:16; 3:2, 5, 10; Eph. 2:9; 2 Tim. 1:9; Titus 3:5). Note also the parallel between Rom. 9:11–12 and 2 Tim. 1:9. Both texts speak of God's "call" or "calling" (*kaleō, klēsis*) and insist that it is not based on "works" (*erga*). Both refer to God's saving "purpose" (*prothesis*) as originating in eternity past. It would seem that if 2 Tim. 1:9 has individual salvation in view, so too does Rom. 9.

But why did God orchestrate the world in this way? It was **in order that God's purpose in election might stand: not by works but by him who calls** (vv. 11b–12a) And the purpose of election was to lead to "the praise of his glorious grace" (Eph. 1:6). In Eph. 1:12 it is for "the praise of his glory" (see also Eph. 1:14).

We should also take note of Rom. 9:22–23, where Paul contrasts "objects of his wrath" (v. 22) with "objects of his mercy" (v. 23), the latter of whom "he prepared in advance for glory." "Destruction" (*apōleia* [v. 22]) and "glory" (*doxa* [v. 23]) are terms used by Paul to refer to eternal condemnation and eternal salvation (see Rom. 2:10; 8:18; Phil. 1:28; 3:19; 1 Thess. 2:12; 2 Thess. 2:3; 1 Tim. 6:9; 2 Tim. 2:10). One must also account for the fact that in the immediately subsequent context (Rom. 9:30–11:36) Paul clearly has Israel's salvation (or lack thereof) in view. It is unlikely that in 9:6b–29 he speaks of Israel's temporal or earthly destiny but then reverses course to discuss why Israel has failed to attain salvation.

Answering Objections (9:14–23)

The first objection to this reading of Paul is that it means that God is **unjust** (v. 14). Paul cites two proofs (**for** [vv. 15, 17]), from which he then derives two inferences (**therefore** [vv. 16, 18]).

7. What follows is largely drawn from Schreiner, "Does Romans 9 Teach Individual Election unto Salvation?" The case for corporate election, in contrast to Schreiner, has been made by Abasciano, "Corporate Election in Romans 9." See also Schreiner, "Corporate and Individual Election in Romans 9."

The charge of unrighteousness comes from Paul's assertion in verses 6–13 that when God determines who will receive mercy, he does not base his decision on any human distinctives that a person might claim either by birth or by effort. The objector evidently believes that a just and righteous God must elect people on the basis of moral distinctives for which they alone are responsible. To determine their eternal destiny independently of their deeds seems both irresponsible and unrighteous. Would this objection ever have been raised and dealt with by Paul at such great length had the issue in view been the historical or earthly status of individuals? The objection, Paul's vehement denial of unrighteousness in God, and his lengthy (vv. 14–23) explanation are intelligible only if eternal salvation and condemnation are at stake.

Paul illustrates his principle in verse 15 by citing God's word to Moses (Exod. 33:19): **I will have mercy on whom I have mercy, and I will have compassion on whom I have compassion**. But how does this statement prove that God is not unrighteous in electing unconditionally? Again, how does this apparent assertion of unconditional election prove unconditional election? The answer is in two parts. First, the declaration is an example of a Hebrew formula called *idem per idem* (see also Exod. 4:13; 16:23; 1 Sam. 23:13; 2 Sam. 15:20; 2 Kings 8:1). According to John Piper,

> By leaving the action unspecified the force of this idiom is to preserve the freedom of the subject to perform the action in whatever way he pleases. By simply repeating the action without adding any stipulations the *idem per idem* formula makes clear that the way the action is executed is determined by the will of the subject within the limits of prevailing circumstances. Therefore, when God says, "I will be gracious to whom I will be gracious and I will be merciful to whom I will be merciful," he is stressing that there are no stipulations outside his own counsel or will which determine the disposal of his mercy and grace.[8]

Second, Exod. 33:19b, from which this declaration comes, is an interpretation or explanation of the essence of God's name and glory (or goodness) referred to in Exod. 33:19a (cf. Exod. 34:6–7). The divine words **I will have mercy on whom I have mercy, and I will have compassion on whom I have compassion** are thus a display of God's glory and name, which consist primarily in his sovereignty in the dispensing of undeserved mercy and kindness.

The implied subject of the sentence in verse 16 (**it**) is God's bestowal of mercy (v. 15) or "God's purpose in election" (v. 11). Verse 16 is thus a heightened repetition of verse 11. The "works" in verse 12 are equivalent to the **human will or exertion** (ESV) of verse 16. God's will to have compassion is determined

8. Piper, *The Justification of God*, 62.

solely by God's will. Paul does not permit us to find its cause in anything other than God himself.

Paul illustrates the principle again by an appeal to God's hardening of Pharaoh's heart. Many contend that Pharaoh first freely hardened his own heart, and only then, as an act of judgment, did God harden his heart as well. This is based on the fact that in Exod. 8:15 and 8:32 it is said that Pharaoh hardened his own heart, but not until 9:12 does it say that God hardened it. But the hardening in 8:15 and 8:32 is simply the fulfillment of what God predicted he would do in Exod. 4:21: "The LORD said to Moses, 'When you return to Egypt, see that you perform before Pharaoh all the wonders I have given you the power to do. But I will harden his heart so that he will not let the people go.'" Pharaoh's resistance to God's command in Exod. 5:2 is clearly the work of God, as Exod. 5:22–23 declares. Again, in 7:13 Pharaoh's heart was hardened, "just as the LORD had said"—that is, in fulfillment of the prediction in 7:3–4 that God would harden his heart. Thus, those texts that say that Pharaoh's heart was hardened and those that say that Pharaoh hardened his own heart are simply fulfillments of God's declaration in 4:21 and 7:3 of what God would do.[9]

So, why then could not Paul's reference to Pharaoh's hardening pertain not to salvation or eternal destiny but to one's role or place in the historical process? Douglas Moo responds,

> First, structural and linguistic considerations show that v. 18 is closely related to vv. 22–23, where the "vessels of mercy, destined to glory" are contrasted with "vessels of wrath, prepared for destruction." As God's mercy leads to the enjoyment of glory, God's hardening brings wrath and destruction. Second, the word group "harden" is consistently used in Scripture to depict a spiritual condition that renders one unreceptive and disobedient to God and his word. Third, while the Greek word is a different one, most scholars recognize that Paul's references to Israel's "hardening" in Rom. 11:7 and 25 are parallel to the hardening here. Yet the hardening in Rom. 11 is a condition that excludes people from salvation. Fourth, it is even possible that the references to Pharaoh's hardening in Exodus carry implications for his own spiritual state and destiny.[10]

In verses 19–23 Paul once again anticipates the objection of a hypothetical adversary. In verse 18b he asserted that God may, in the pursuit of his eternal purpose, sovereignly harden the human heart. In the case of Pharaoh, God rendered him insensible to the divine command in order to provide for himself a platform or occasion on which he might display his power and mercy. When

9. God says that his purpose for hardening Pharaoh's heart is to "multiply my signs and wonders in Egypt" (Exod. 7:3; cf. 14:3–4).

10. Moo, *Romans*, 596–97.

God chooses either to soften the heart by his mercy or to harden it by his judgment, it is without regard to any human willing or working (v. 16). At first glance, the objection seems reasonable. If a person's hardness of heart is the work of a sovereign God, it is unrighteous and unfair for God to condemn the individual or to hold them accountable for their resistance to his commands. Whereas someone such as Pharaoh might resist God's will of precept (or command), in doing so he is in fact fulfilling God's will of purpose (or decree). Therefore, since no one can successfully resist the will of God's eternal and decretive purpose, it is wrong for God to find fault with their behavior. In other words, if God hardens the human heart, on what basis does he still hold the person morally accountable for their sin? One must ask if the question would even have been raised if the previous verses taught that the ultimate factor in human destiny was human choice.

The objection raised in verse 19 is not, however, a humble inquiry on the part of an inquisitive student of theology, as if he were simply asking, "*How* can these things be?" It is rather an indignant declaration and arrogant protest against God in which he insists, "These things *ought not* to be, and if they are, God is unrighteous!" Paul's emphatic question **Who are you, a human being . . . ?** in verse 20 assigns to the objector his proper place: As a mere human, you have no right to accuse God of unrighteousness. The objection is not a humble attempt to comprehend the mystery of God's sovereignty but rather a defiant refusal to believe it.

Paul uses a common biblical metaphor to illustrate his point. The relationship between Creator and creature may be compared to that between a potter and his clay (cf. Isa. 29:16; 45:9; 64:8; Jer. 18:6). The sole authority for determining what sort of vessels are to be made rests with the Creator/potter. He has the indisputable right to give full and artistic display to all his attributes and skills as a craftsman by making vessels as he sees fit, for either honorable use or dishonorable use. Consequently, the creature has no more of a right to protest how God dispenses with the creation than a piece of clay has the right to dictate instructions to the potter.

Also, it's important that we recognize the parallel between verse 21 and verses 22–23. So, when Paul speaks of making use of the same lump of clay, a reference to fallen humanity, one vessel for **special purposes** and another for **common use** (v. 21), he is talking about **objects of his** [God's] **wrath— prepared for destruction** (v. 22) and **objects of his mercy** prepared beforehand **for glory** (v. 23).

Paul portrays God as a potter who makes vessels from **the same lump of clay** (v. 21). It would seem that the image of the **same lump** of clay from which the different kinds of vessels are made is parallel to what Paul said in verses 10–13 about Jacob and Esau being born of the same mother and father (Rebecca and Isaac). John Stott draws this conclusion:

> If therefore God hardens some, he is not being unjust, for that is what their sin deserves. If, on the other hand, he has compassion on some, he is not being unjust, for he is dealing with them in mercy. The wonder is not that some are saved and others not, but that anybody is saved at all. For we deserve nothing at God's hand but judgment. If we receive what we deserve (which is judgment), or if we receive what we do not deserve (which is mercy), in neither case is God unjust. If therefore anybody is lost, the blame is theirs, but if anybody is saved, the credit is God's.[11]

God's ultimate design in his sovereign choices is stated in verses 22–23. The NIV renders the participle *thelōn* (**choosing**) in verse 22 as concessive: **although choosing to show his wrath and make his power known**. Others contend that it is causal—that is, *because* God wanted or wished to demonstrate his wrath and power. The latter is probably correct, indicating that God patiently endures the vessels of wrath because of his desire to accomplish three things: (1) he wants to demonstrate his wrath; (2) he wants to make his power known; (3) he wants to make known the riches of his glory on vessels of mercy.[12] The term of purpose (*hina*, **in order to** (ESV), with which verse 23 opens, clearly indicates that the third of these three goals is ultimate, the other two being subordinate.

What, then, does it mean to say that God **endured with much patience vessels of wrath** (ESV)? Apparently, God is patiently holding back immediate judgment so that the reprobate might continue to store up wrath for themselves and in this way make possible an even greater display of God's power and judgment. In dealing with Pharaoh, God endured his repeated refusal to let the people go in order that he might turn each occasion into an opportunity to display his power (Exod. 14:1–4, 14). Also, with a greater measure of sin comes a greater display of wrath, which in turn sheds an even greater light on the glory of mercy toward those who themselves deserve judgment no less than the others.

The **vessels of mercy** (ESV) in verse 23 are explicitly said to have been prepared beforehand by God for glory. In verse 22 the **vessels of wrath** (ESV) are said to be **prepared for destruction** (literally, "having been prepared for destruction"). In the NIV two different Greek verbs are both rendered by the English term **prepared**. In verse 22 it is *katartizō*, while in verse 23 *proetoimazō*

---

11. Stott, *Romans*, 269–70.
12. The translation "because" is also supported by comparing verse 22 with verse 17. In the latter text God is said to have raised up Pharaoh not in spite of his desire to demonstrate his power but precisely because of it.

is employed. Unlike verse 23, where God is clearly the subject of the verb **prepared**, in verse 22 we have a perfect passive participle, which raises this question: By whom or what were the objects of wrath prepared? Some contend that the voice of the Greek participle is middle, not passive; hence the vessels of wrath are conceived as having *prepared themselves* for destruction (ostensibly through their rebellion and unrepentant unbelief).[13] Other suggest that **prepared for destruction** is a descriptive phrase without implying any agent of the preparation. Then again, perhaps Paul deliberately expresses it this way to leave the issue shrouded in mystery. The more probable view is that God is the agent or cause by whom the vessels of wrath are prepared for destruction.

But why two different verbs, one active and the other passive? It is unlikely that Paul did this to suggest that whereas God is actively involved in preparing the elect for glory, he is passive and uninvolved in the preparation of the nonelect for judgment. Earlier, in verses 14, 18, and 21, God is active in both showing mercy to some and hardening others. But perhaps Paul wrote it this way to communicate that God's consigning of some to destruction in no way undermines their personal moral responsibility for the judgment they incur. The elect, prepared for glory, can take no credit for their salvation, while the nonelect, prepared for destruction, are alone responsible for the sins they commit and the wrath they endure.

God wants to demonstrate the reality of his wrath (v. 22a) so that all will understand that human sin, idolatry, and unbelief are the fault only of people and that they are deserving of his judgment. He wants all to stand in awe of his holy justice. Furthermore, God wants to make known the power he exerts when he judges those who are unrighteous and deserving of eternal judgment. Although the unbeliever ought to immediately suffer judgment, God patiently endures their ongoing idolatry and unbelief so that he might make known all the better and with even greater clarity the majesty of his undeserved mercy shed abroad on those whom he has chosen to inherit eternal life.

But his primary aim is to make known **the riches of his glory** in saving otherwise hell-deserving sinners (v. 23). The majesty of his saving grace and mercy is best seen in contrast with the judgment of the lost. If God mercifully saves some, even though they are as deserving of eternal death as all others, the majesty of his grace is magnified. None of us deserves to be chosen by God. It is altogether and entirely an act of God's mercy and grace. Nothing we have done exerted an influence on God to make the decision he made. We were **prepared**

---

13. The direct middle, in which the subject acts directly on himself (e.g., "Judas hung himself"), should be distinguished from the indirect middle, in which the subject acts on his own behalf ("for himself").

BIBLICAL BACKGROUND

Insights on Romans 9:21–22 from Greek Grammar

Daniel Wallace explains why the use of the direct middle is highly unlikely in Rom. 9:22:

> First, grammatically, the direct middle is quite rare and is used almost exclusively in certain idiomatic expressions, especially where the verb is used consistently with such a notion (as in the verbs for putting on clothes). This is decidedly not the case with [*katartizō*]: nowhere else in the NT does it occur as a direct middle. Second, in the perfect tense, the middle-passive form is always to be taken as a passive in the NT (Luke 6:40; 1 Cor 1:10; Heb 11:3)—a fact that, in the least, argues against an idiomatic use of this verb as a direct middle. Third, the lexical nuance of [*katartizō*], coupled with the perfect tense, suggests something of a "done deal." Although some commentators suggest that the verb means that the vessels are *ready* for destruction, both the lexical nuance of complete preparation and the grammatical nuance of the perfect tense are against this. Fourth, the context argues strongly for a passive and completed notion. In v 20 the vessel is shaped by God's will, not its own ("Will that which is molded say to its maker, 'Why have you made me this way?'"). In v 21, Paul asks a question with [*ouk*] (thus expecting a positive answer): Is not the destiny of the vessels (one for honor, one for dishonor) entirely predetermined by their Creator? Verse 22 is the answer to that question. To argue, then, that [*katērtismena*] is a direct middle seems to fly in the face of grammar (the normal use of the voice and tense), lexeme, and context.[a]

a. Wallace, *Greek Grammar beyond the Basics*, 418.

in advance for glory (v. 23), which is to say that it happened in eternity past, so that God would be magnified and praised for his sovereignty.

God's People (9:24–33)

These verses speak once again to what we have seen repeatedly in Romans: how God proceeds to save his elect people. The key is found in the words **call** and **called**. We see it in verse 24, where Paul declares that God has **called** people from among the Gentiles no less so than among the Jews. This **call** (v. 25) is the effective, effectual drawing of people to saving faith in Jesus (see Rom. 8:28: those "who are called according to his purpose"). This is the same calling that

Paul mentioned in 8:30, where he said that all those whom God foreknew he predestined, and all those whom he predestined he also "called." We know that this calling is the effectual call to salvation because Paul says that all those whom God called he also justified or declared righteous in Jesus.

The "objects of his mercy" whom God has chosen "for glory" (v. 23) include both Gentiles and Jews. Paul's intent is first to demonstrate from the Old Testament that Gentile salvation was long ago prophesied. To do this he cites Hosea 2:23 in verse 25 and Hosea 1:10 in verse 26. These two texts in Hosea were addressed to the ten apostate northern tribes of Israel before the Assyrian exile in 722–721 BC. They describe both the rebellious condition of Israel ("not my people" / "not my loved one") and her prophesied restoration ("my people" / "my loved one" / "children of the living God").

But if these passages in Hosea refer to the prophesied regathering and restoration of Israel, why does Paul apply them to the calling and salvation of **Gentiles**? Some argue that the rejection and the restoration of Israel have their parallel in the exclusion and eventual inclusion of the Gentiles in God's covenant blessings. In other words, Paul finds in the restoration of Israel to love and favor a *type* in terms of which the Gentiles will experience the same. Thus, the principle according to which God will regather Israel applies to the gathering in and salvation of Gentiles as well. In sum: the salvation of the Gentiles is analogous to, but not the fulfillment of, the salvation of the Jews. Others agree that the Old Testament texts in Hosea are a prophecy of the future regathering/salvation of Israel but that Paul applies both prophecies to the church. The latter, consisting of both Jews and Gentiles, has become the true people of God. That this is not so-called replacement theology will become evident when we examine Rom. 11.

In verses 27–29 Paul expands upon the truth articulated in 9:6: God's purpose has never been to save all ethnic Israelites, but only a **remnant**. Paul cites three texts to prove that this is not a new doctrine but something explicitly affirmed in the Old Testament: in verse 27 he cites Isa. 10:22, in verse 28 he cites Isa. 10:23, and in verse 29 he cites Isa. 1:9. That *only* a remnant is saved is indicative of the severity and extent of divine judgment (vv. 27–28); that *at least* a remnant is saved is indicative of the miracle of divine grace (v. 29). God will bring judgment to bear on the unfaithful in Israel and will execute the sentence on them required by his own nature and character as the just Judge of all the earth. But just as it might appear that this means the end of all Israel and the failure of God to fulfill his promises to them, we are told that he has spared a remnant. There is, as we saw in 9:6–7, a spiritually elect remnant of believers within the physically ethnic nation as a whole.

Gentiles are saved because by sovereign grace they attained righteousness in the proper manner: **by faith** (v. 30). Jews are lost because in arrogant pride they pursued righteousness in an improper manner: **as if it were based on works** (v. 32 ESV). This is not because the Mosaic law endorsed the idea that righteousness could or should be attained by works. Righteousness in the Old Testament, as in every age, is always a gracious gift of God received by faith alone. The reason for this ironic reversal is that in seeking after righteousness the Jews thought it would be the reward for their good works. The Gentiles, on the other hand, when they heard the gospel message, responded in simple, saving faith. Israel's problem was that instead of recognizing in Jesus the only hope for a righteousness that would avail with God, they saw him as an obstacle, **a stone that causes people to stumble and a rock that makes them fall** (v. 33). They **stumbled** (v. 32) when they refused to believe in him. Jesus and his work on the cross were viewed in this way because the salvation that God offers on the basis of the cross of Christ undermines our sense of self-righteousness. It is an offense to human pride.

The Wesleyan-Arminian Interpretation of Romans 9: Nations and Historical Prominence, Not Individuals and Personal Salvation

Given the controversial nature of Rom. 9, it behooves us to consider the Wesleyan-Arminian interpretation. The latter does not deny that Rom. 9:6–13 pertains to election, but insists that it is election to historical service, not eternal salvation. The former applies to all of ethnic Israel, whereas the latter applies to the believing remnant. Jack Cottrell explains, "The point of the Abrahamic covenant . . . was not the salvation of its recipients. Its point was rather that *through* Abraham and his (physical) seed the means by which all peoples could be saved would be brought into the world. This was a covenant of service; and the recipients of this covenant, i.e., ethnic Israel, were chosen to render this service and to experience its accompanying temporal privileges and rewards (vv. 4–5)."[14]

God thus called Isaac and Jacob into his service without regard for personal merit or faith, blessed and used them and their physical descendants, ethnic Israel (**God's children** and **children of the promise** [vv. 6–8]), for the purpose of bringing the Messiah into the world. God's choice of Isaac rather than Ishmael, and of Jacob rather than Esau, was truly unconditional. But it was an election to service and temporal privilege, not to salvation and eternal destiny.

Therefore, Isaac and Jacob are not examples of individuals elected to eternal life but rather are representative of the nation Israel collectively and its privileged status above all other nations of the earth. Or, if they are to be taken as

14. Cottrell, *Romans*, 2:66–67.

individuals, it is to honor and historical prominence, not eternal life, that they are predestined.

In support of this view, appeal is made to the fact that two of the Old Testament texts that Paul cites (Gen. 25:23; Mal. 1:1–5) refer to Jacob and Esau as heads of national entities and their respective historical destinies. God chose Jacob to be more prominent and privileged, the line through whom the promised seed would come, even though Esau was the elder of the two. But that has nothing to do with whether either or both of the men went to heaven. The name **Jacob** can refer not only to the individual but also to the nation (Israel) descended from him. Likewise, the name **Esau** can refer both to the person himself and the people (Edom) who are his descendants. Says C. E. B. Cranfield,

> It is important to stress that neither as they occur in Genesis nor as they are used by Paul do these words ["loved" and "hated" in 9:13] refer to the eternal destinies either of the two persons or of the individual members of the nations sprung from them; the reference is rather to the mutual relations of the two nations in history. What is here in question is not eschatological salvation or damnation, but the historical functions of those concerned and their relations to the development of salvation history.[15]

Thus, the **mercy** and **compassion** (v. 15) sovereignly displayed by God are nonsalvific and pertain to the bestowal of temporal blessing (such as those noted in vv. 4–5). Even Pharaoh stands parallel to Israel in this regard. Says Cottrell, "God has mercy on whom he wants to have mercy, i.e., he calls into his service whom he wants to call into his service; *but* some of these can serve his purposes only by being hardened. Thus it was with Pharaoh. God bestowed favor upon him by selecting him for a key role, but he could fill that role only by being hardened."[16]

The hardening of Pharaoh's heart had nothing to do with punishment for sin but was divinely providential hardening designed to accomplish through him a specific temporal purpose: "This particular hardening was not a natural consequence of Pharaoh's already rebellious heart, nor an act of divine retribution against him because of this rebellion. It did not cause him to be lost, nor did it somehow intensify his lostness. It simply brought him to a state of mind that resulted in his decision to forbid the Israelites to leave."[17] Cranfield says much the same thing: "[God] has mercy on some in the sense that He determines them for a positive role in relation to His purpose, to a conscious and voluntary

15. Cranfield, *Romans*, 2:479.
16. Cottrell, *Romans*, 2:102.
17. Cottrell, *Romans*, 2:105.

service: others He hardens in the sense that He determines them for a negative role in relation to His purpose, for an unconscious, involuntary service. . . . The assumption that Paul is here thinking of the ultimate destiny of the individual, of his final salvation or final ruin, is not justified by the text."[18]

Cottrell insists that the question of Paul's hypothetical critic in verse 19 is based on a flagrant misrepresentation of Paul's teaching. The critic has mistakenly assumed that what Paul said in verses 17–18 pertains to the salvation of Israelite individuals rather than to their historical privilege. Indeed, God does **still blame us** (v. 19) because individuals continue to live in unbelief. But God is perfectly free to use Israel to accomplish his historic purposes according to his sovereign choice. But this has nothing to do with whether or not any or all within that nation are individually redeemed.

The **lump of clay** (v. 21) from which God sovereignly makes vessels for either honorable or dishonorable use is the nation Israel, not the entire human race. Some Arminians contend that the **purposes** or **use** to which God puts them is their role in fulfilling his temporal goals, not their individual eternal destinies. Cranfield is representative when he says, "The conclusion to be drawn is that God must be acknowledged to be free—as God, as the One who has ultimate authority—to appoint men to various functions in the on-going course of salvation-history for the sake of the fulfillment of His over-all purpose."[19]

Cottrell rejects this, pointing out that "there is *no way* that the role of Israel—believing or unbelieving—can be described as dishonorable or even menial. The term *atimia*, however interpreted, simply does not fit the use God made of the nation of Israel. Theirs was indeed the most exalted and honorable role imaginable, apart from that of the Messiah himself."[20] He thus concludes that **special purposes** and **common use** do indeed refer to eternal destiny, but insists that these destinies are determined not by God himself but by the freewill decision of the individuals. The "distinction between the vessel of honor and the vessel of dishonor, though decreed by God, is ultimately the responsibility of the individuals placed within each group."[21]

As with so much else that has preceded in 9:1–18, Arminian commentators find in verses 20–21 a reference to national or corporate entities and not to individuals and their eternal destinies. For example, it is argued that the Old Testament texts quoted in verses 20–21 (Isa. 45:9–11; Jer. 18:1–6) deal with the nation Israel, not individuals. But it must be noted that Paul may be employing a common metaphor and need not apply it precisely the same way as does another

18. Cranfield, *Romans*, 2:488–89.
19. Cranfield, *Romans*, 2:492.
20. Cottrell, *Romans*, 2:119.
21. Cottrell, *Romans*, 2:120.

biblical author. Furthermore, it is more likely that the passage from which he derives the metaphor is Isa. 29:16, which does have reference to individuals.

Who, then, according to those in the Wesleyan-Arminian tradition, is the agent by whom these vessels of wrath are **prepared for destruction** (v. 22)? Cottrell insists that the voice of the participle *katērtismena* is middle; hence they prepared themselves for this end. That is, "they are responsible for their own destruction; by their sin and unbelief and refusal to repent, they sealed their own doom. Even if the agent of preparation were God himself, the lack of the prefix *pro-* ('in advance, beforehand'), unlike the verb in verse 23, would suggest that God prepared them for destruction only after they manifested their adamant unbelief. The more likely meaning, though, is that they prepared themselves."[22]

Some argue that Paul must be referring to national entities and not to individuals because no potter makes a vessel just to destroy it. But this ignores the obvious parallel between verse 21 and verse 22. The vessel made for **common use** in verse 21 is equivalent to **the objects of his wrath—prepared for destruction** in verse 22. Therefore, **common use** and **destruction** are synonymous. Also, to say that a potter does not make a vessel simply to destroy it is based on a misconception of destruction. By **destruction** Paul does not necessarily indicate extinction, but rather eternal condemnation. "To be destroyed in judgment" does not mean "cease to exist."

---

22. Cottrell, *Romans*, 2:126.

ROMANS 10

Saving Faith and the Lordship of Christ

The Negation of the Gospel's Purpose (10:1–8)

Paul's **heart's desire and prayer** for the salvation of his fellow Israelites (v. 1) must not be divorced from its context. He obviously felt no tension or inconsistency between affirming God's sovereignty in the salvation of sinners (8:28–32; 9:6–23) and praying fervently for the conversion of his brothers and sisters according to the flesh. It is not enough that Paul desires their salvation. This is more than a perfunctory statement of what pleases him. His yearning produces heartfelt, sincere action in which he intercedes for their conversion.

Paul concedes the presence of their religious zeal, something affirmed repeatedly in the New Testament (see Matt. 23:15; Acts 22:3; 26:9–11; Gal. 1:14; Phil. 3:4–9). But zeal in and of itself is morally neutral. Its ethical character is determined by the object on which it is focused. The **knowledge** (v. 2) that most Jews lacked concerned God's prescribed manner for attaining a righteousness that would avail in his presence. They pursued it as if it were granted on the basis of works (9:32) rather than by faith.

Obedience to the law of Moses was never intended to be a means whereby one might be reconciled to God. It was always and only a pointer to Christ, through faith in whom one may be saved. In what sense is Christ **the culmination of the law** (or **end** of the law [ESV; NASB])?[1] He is, of course, the fulfillment of the law (Matt. 5:17) in the sense that many Old Testament types, figures, institutions,

---

1. For more on this, see Meyer, *End of the Law*.

and rituals pointed to and were fulfilled in him. Christ is also the goal of the law (Gal. 3:23–26) in the sense that the law existed primarily to lead people to faith in the Messiah. Its purpose was not to save but rather to send the sinner to Christ. Christ is also the termination of the law (Rom. 6:14; 7:4) in the sense that the Mosaic law as a covenant has ended. God's people are no longer legally or morally bound to the stipulations of the old covenant.

To seek righteousness by means of the law requires that one obey **these things**—the dictates of the law (v. 5)—perfectly (see Gal. 3:10; 5:3). But clearly this is impossible. Some prefer to see no contrast between verse 5 and verse 6. The law-keeping in verse 5, so it is said, is "the obedience that comes from faith" (1:5). The **righteousness that is based on the law** (10:5 ESV) and **the righteousness that is by faith** (v. 6) are the same, insofar as those who have saving faith will obey the law. But this would run counter to the adverse relationship between working and believing so prevalent in 9:30–10:13 (and elsewhere in Paul's writings). In 9:32 the failure of most Israelites is that they "pursued it not by faith but as if it were by works." Likewise, they **sought to establish their own** righteousness (10:3) by obedience rather than by simple faith (for a similar emphasis, see Phil. 3:9). The law serves only to stimulate sin (Rom. 7:5–13), and faith alone secures a righteous standing before God.

Paul illustrates the nature of saving faith in verses 6–8 by citing Deut. 9:4 and 30:12–14. His point is that salvation is not a matter of searching high and low or of working to win God's favor. God has already made provision for us in Christ Jesus. When you seek after righteousness in the way that God has ordained, you do it by faith. You don't say in your heart that you will strive by your good deeds to ascend into heaven in order to bring Jesus down, nor will you resolve to descend into the abyss in order to raise Christ from the dead. Salvation is not a matter of searching high and low, or of working to gain God's approval. God has already done all that is necessary. Salvation is not a matter of performing some magnificent physical deed. It is already here, present and available. All one need do is believe.

The Nature of Saving Faith (10:9–13)

The precise focus of saving faith is the verbal declaration that **Jesus is Lord** and confident belief **that God raised him from the dead** (v. 9). Mere verbal profession must be the expression of what is true **in your heart** (v. 9). The faith that justifies proceeds from **your heart** (v. 10) and is given expression when **you profess your faith** (v. 10). Only then is a person **saved**.

The belief and declaration that **Jesus is Lord** is an essential element in the gospel message. The Greek word *kyrios* (**Lord**) is used more than six thousand times in the Septuagint to translate the name YHWH. Many of these Old Testament texts referring to YHWH are applied to Jesus in the New Testament.[2] Here, for example, its use in Joel 2:32 is applied to Jesus in verse 13. Confession that Jesus is Lord entails, at minimum, belief in and the declaration of his full and perfect deity. Jesus is YHWH incarnate. In Phil. 2:9 Paul describes the title *kyrios* as "the name that is above every name," which can only be the name of God himself. Thus, as C. E. B. Cranfield notes, "The confession that Jesus is Lord meant the acknowledgment that Jesus shares the name and the nature, the holiness, the authority, power, majesty and eternity of the one and only true God."[3]

But there is more in the confession of Jesus as Lord than simply acknowledging that he is God. This confession involves the acknowledgment of the rightful authority of Jesus Christ over the life of the believer. The believer has entered into a new relationship with Jesus in which they happily acknowledge that Jesus, because he is Lord, has absolute sovereignty and mastery of over their life. Moreover, mere confession is of no value apart from the commitment of the heart to cherish and trust and follow Jesus (see Matt. 7:21; John 6:40). If it is true that confession without commitment is of no value, it is also true that commitment without confession is spurious (see Matt. 10:32–33).

The sort of confession that Paul has in mind is not merely speaking the words **Jesus is Lord** with your mouth. Even Satan, hypocrites, and liars can utter such words. Paul is talking about a confession that comes from a heart that has been born again, a heart that embraces, trusts, and loves the lordship of Jesus. But why put stress on the resurrection? Because if Jesus is still dead in the grave, his death accomplished nothing of saving value. He may have provided an example of how to undergo unjust suffering, but that can't save anyone. Deliverance from divine wrath cannot be obtained simply by dying, if the one who has died is still dead. The bodily resurrection of Jesus was God the Father's confirmation and seal on the truth of what the death of Jesus accomplished.

The recipients of this salvation are stated in verses 11–13. Ethnicity is irrelevant, **as there is no difference between Jew and Gentile** (v. 12). Jew and Gentile alike (indeed, **anyone** [v. 11] and **everyone** [v. 13]) are together saved in the same way, by believing (v. 11) in Jesus as Lord and calling on his name (v. 13, a citation of Joel 2:32). In addition to salvation, Paul specifies two benefits that accrue to those who trust in Christ: God **richly blesses** them (v. 12), and they are assured that they **will not be put to shame** (v. 11 ESV, a citation of Isa. 28:16).

2. See Luke 1:76 and Mal. 3:1; Rev. 1:13–16 and Dan. 10:5–7; Heb. 1:8 and Ps. 45:6–7; John 12:37–41 and Isa. 6:1–12; 2 Cor. 3:16 and Exod. 34:29–35; 1 Pet. 2:3–4 and Ps. 34:8; Phil. 2:9–11 and Isa. 45:20–25; 1 Pet. 3:15 and Isa. 29:23; Rev. 1:17 and Isa. 41:4; 44:6; 48:12.
3. Cranfield, *Romans*, 2:529.

Shame is the fear of being exposed as naive and uninformed for believing in something that turns out in the end to be a fraud. Paul's point is that we never need worry or live in fear that the promises of God to believers will fail to come to pass. We have it guaranteed to us, based first on the integrity of God's character and second on the blood of Christ shed for us. To feel shame at being seen and known as having failed is terrifying. But as Jude says, God "is able to keep you from stumbling and to present you before his glorious presence without fault [i.e., without shame] and with great joy" (Jude 24).

But with what are believers richly blessed (v. 12)? Throughout Romans Paul has spoken of the riches that come to those who believe, things such as the forgiveness of sins, redemption, being foreknown and foreloved by God, being predestined to be conformed to the image of Jesus, being called, justified, and ultimately glorified and made like unto Jesus himself. The riches in view are justification and sanctification, the permanent indwelling of the Holy Spirit, and being adopted as the children of God who cry out, "Abba! Father!" (8:15). Later, in chapter 14, Paul will speak of the riches of the kingdom of God, which consist in "righteousness, peace and joy" in the Holy Spirit (14:17). The riches include the "promises" given to the patriarchs (15:8), "hope" in the power of the Spirit (15:13), and the assurance that our lowly, corrupt bodies will be resurrected and glorified. But all these are not the greatest of the treasures and wealth that God gives to those who believe. The most precious of all riches is God himself! We get to see God, to bask in the presence of his beauty. We will be forever satisfied and delighted with the splendor of God in all his beauty (Rev. 22:3–5).

The deity of Christ is especially highlighted in verse 13. To call **on the name of the Lord** is the language of prayer and supplication directed to God. As Cranfield notes, "The fact that Paul can think of prayer to the exalted Christ without the least repugnance is, in the light of the first and second commandments of the Decalogue, the decisive clarification of the significance which he attached to the title *kurios* as applied to Christ."[4] We must again emphasize the ease with which Paul applies to Jesus an Old Testament text that speaks of YHWH (cf. Joel 2:32). This reflects the confidence of his conviction concerning Christ's deity.

The Necessity of the Gospel's Proclamation (10:14–15)

Here the subject of the verbs, **they**, surely is the same as that of the third-person plural verbs in 9:32; 10:2, 3: the Jews. Paul labors to demonstrate that the people of Israel have had every opportunity to call upon the name of the Lord (vv. 12–13) and are therefore without excuse. To "call on the name of the Lord,"

---

4. Cranfield, *Romans*, 2:532.

however, occurs not in a vacuum but only in the context of gospel proclamation. Salvation is not possible apart from belief. But to believe, they must hear. But they cannot hear **without someone preaching to them** (v. 14). And in order to preach, one must be **sent** (v. 15). Paul's conclusion is to cite one portion of the larger affirmation of God found in Isa. 52:7: "How beautiful on the mountains are the feet of those who bring good news, who proclaim peace, who bring good tidings, who proclaim salvation, who say to Zion, 'Your God reigns!'" Again we see that God's sovereignty in saving sinners does not preclude, but is dependent

---

PENTECOSTAL INTEREST

Inclusivism and the Possibility of Salvation apart from Conscious Faith in Christ

Two Pentecostal scholars, Amos Yong and Veli-Matti Kärkkäinen, have articulated an inclusivist view of non-Christian religions and the possibility of salvation apart from personal, conscious faith in Jesus Christ that runs counter to Paul's perspective in Rom. 10. They together contend for the possibility of the Spirit's saving work in other religions. Kärkkäinen cites with approval Amos Yong's statement "that religions are neither accidents of history nor encroachments on divine providence but are, in various ways, instruments of the Holy Spirit working out the divine purposes in the world and that the unevangelized, if saved at all, are saved through the work of Christ by the Spirit (even if mediated through the religious beliefs and practices available to them)."[a] Kärkkäinen himself faults his fellow Pentecostals for having "succumbed to the standard conservative/fundamentalist view of limiting the Spirit's saving work to the church (except for the work of the Spirit preparing one to receive the gospel)."[b] While both men link salvation to the work of Christ, this salvation may be "mediated through the religious beliefs and practices available" in other non-Christian religions.[c]

Robert Menzies responds critically to this inclusivist approach and faults it on several accounts: (1) their failure to focus on the Bible as the sole source of our theology; (2) their proposal "is so out of step with the apostolic witness as recorded in the New Testament";[d] (3) "Yong's biblical analysis appears to overemphasize the universal dimensions of the Spirit's work on the one hand, and downplay the particular, Christ-centric nature of the Spirit's salvific work on the other";[e] (4) an inclusivist theology will seriously undermine our evangelistic church-planting efforts.[f] Menzies rightly contends that "the key point to note is that the measuring stick for determining whether an experience, action, or event is inspired by the Spirit is its relationship to Christ."[g] Only if any religious act "is performed out of a desire to exalt Christ do we know that it is a manifestation of the kingdom of God. An appeal to the general work of the Spirit in creation offers no escape, for this dimension of the Spirit's activity is not viewed as salvific by the New Testament authors. Only the operation of the Spirit that is bestowed by Christ is salvific."[h]

a. Yong, The Spirit Poured Out, 236.
b. Kärkkäinen, "Pentecostal Pneumatology," 170.
c. Yong, The Spirit Poured Out, 236.
d. Menzies, Christ-Centered, 132.
e. Menzies, Christ-Centered, 134.
f. Menzies, Christ-Centered, 137.
g. Menzies, Christ-Centered, 136.
h. Menzies, Christ-Centered, 136.

upon, the faithful proclamation of the gospel. Paul's language here appears to put to rest the question of whether salvation is obtainable by any means other than conscious, personal faith in Christ as Lord and Savior.

Israel's Responsibility (10:16–21)

Is the reason why few in Israel have **believed** the **message** (v. 16, quoting Isa. 53:1) due to the fact that they have never actually heard the good news? But they have indeed **heard through the word about Christ** (v. 17). To prove his point, Paul cites Ps. 19:4: **Their voice goes out through all the earth, and their words to the end of the world** (ESV). The psalmist is describing the universal display of God's existence and glory in the natural creation, and Paul finds in that verse a principle that applies to the proclamation of the truth to the Jewish people. Just as God makes himself known as the Creator in the natural world, he makes himself known as Savior through the preaching of the gospel.

But the language in verse 18 appears to be quite universal. What does Paul mean that the **voice** or message **has gone out . . . to the end of the world** (ESV)? He may have in mind the Jewish world and is saying that wherever there are Jewish people living, wherever Israelites may be found, they have had the gospel of Jesus Christ made known to them. However, it is more likely that by **all the earth** and **the end of the world** he has in view the inhabited regions of the then-known Roman Empire. The word for **world** (*oikoumenē*) is used in Luke 2:1 to describe the Roman Empire, not the entire globe. When we read verse 18 from within the mindset and quite limited perspective of someone living in the first century, we discover that what might first appear to us in the twenty-first century as universal and global language is in fact much more narrow in scope.

But there may be another reason why so many in Israel didn't believe the gospel. Maybe they didn't understand it. That is why they rejected Jesus. No, they most certainly did understand. Paul is not contradicting Rom. 10:2–3, where he affirmed Israel's ignorance. In one sense they know, in that the knowledge has been made accessible to them, and yet they do not *savingly* know, in that they have rejected it. This is similar to what Paul wrote in Rom. 1:21, where he described how people "knew God" but "neither glorified him as God nor gave thanks to him."

To make his point, in verses 19–20 Paul first quotes from the words of Moses, **I will make you envious by those who are not a nation; I will make you angry by a nation that has no understanding** (Deut. 32:21), and then from the words of Isaiah, **I was found by those who did not seek me; I revealed myself to those who did not ask for me** (Isa. 65:1). The **not a nation** that **has no understanding** is a reference to pagan, uncircumcised Gentiles who, unlike Israel, are responding to the truth of God's revelation. Paul hopes to stir up jealousy among the Jewish people and open their eyes to the gospel. The point in verse 20, yet again, is that Gentiles who had not previously sought after God are now finding salvation in Jesus Christ. The purpose is that this will awaken the people of Israel to the salvation that they were supposed to embrace as God's covenant people. Sadly, though, verse 21 sums up their response. Paul takes his words from Isa. 65:2: **All day long I have held out my hands to a disobedient and obstinate people**.

Paul's assessment of Israel's willful unbelief and culpability may give the impression that he believed that God had finally cast aside his old-covenant people, that his saving work among the Jews had ended. To this concern Paul turns his attention in Rom. 11.

ROMANS 11

God's Purpose for Israel

The Principle of the Remnant (11:1–10)

Is there a distinctive future for ethnic Israel in which the vast majority of Jewish people will be saved, somehow in connection with the second coming of Christ to earth? The designation FR (future restoration), together with "futurist," will be used with reference to those who embrace this view. Others insist that God is going to save the elect in Israel progressively, down through history, in the same way he saves elect Gentiles, as each individual comes to faith in Christ. The designation HR (historical remnant), as well as "historicist," will be used of those who hold to this view. They believe that the salvation of ethnic Israelites will occur repeatedly, progressively, incrementally through the many centuries that span the gap between Christ's first coming and his second coming.[1] The evidence both for and against each of these views will be examined.

God's appeal to a "disobedient and obstinate people" at the close of chapter 10 (10:21) invariably raises this question: **Has God rejected his people?** (11:1 ESV). **By no means!** says Paul. This he proves by citing two examples, the first being himself and his own salvation. Paul is an example of the remnant within the nation as a whole, an individual who is both an ethnic and an elect Israelite. God never chose in saving grace all the physical descendants of Abraham, Isaac, and Jacob, but only a remnant, of which Paul is a current, living constituent member.

---

1. The best defense of this view is by Robertson, "Distinctive Future for Ethnic Israel." This essay has been slightly revised and updated in Robertson, *The Israel of God*, 167–92

Precisely who are **his people** (vv. 1, 2), **whom he foreknew**, the people **he did not reject** (v. 2)? The answer depends on the meaning of the verb **foreknew**. On the one hand, it would seem that if Paul cites his own salvation as proof that God has not rejected his people, then surely the people whom he foreknew are the remnant according to the election of grace. However, both John Murray and C. E. B. Cranfield, among others, insist that the people whom God foreknew and has not rejected are the nation as a whole, ethnic and elect Israel alike. They appeal to Rom. 10:21, where ethnic Israel as a national body is in view. They argue that since Rom. 11:1 follows immediately upon 10:21, the "people" referred to in the former must be the same as the "people" in the latter. This view may be correct, but it faces two obstacles.

First, the title "people of God" may be understood in one of two ways. Certainly, ethnic Israel as a whole was God's "people" in that he blessed them with all the theocratic privileges described in Rom. 9:4–5. It is to the nation, the theocratic entity, composed of Abraham's physical descendants, that the divine appeal noted in 10:21 is issued. But if ethnic Israelites are God's "people," why do they not believe? Because, says Paul, there is a "people" within the "people." There is an elect Israel within ethnic Israel (cf. Rom. 9:6). Israelite unbelief in 10:21 must be explained on the same terms as Israelite unbelief in 9:1–5. God never intended to save all ethnic Israelites—that is, all his theocratic "people"— but only elect Israel, the remnant. Simply put, Rom. 9:6 and 11:1–2 are making the same point.

The second reason why the "people" in 11:1–2 are more likely the remnant and not ethnic Israel as a whole is that God **foreknew** them. If the people in 11:1–2 are all ethnic Israelites, then God's foreknowledge of them must be something less than salvific in nature. This is clear, for all concede that not every ethnic Jew has been or will be saved. But in view of Paul's reference to divine foreknowledge in Rom. 8:29, the burden of proof is on those who argue that foreknowledge in 11:2 is *not* salvific. The people whom God foreknew are the elect remnant (cf. 11:5) precisely because they were foreknown—that is, fore-loved or fore-chosen. Otherwise, we are forced to conclude that all the people whom God foreknew in Rom. 8:29 are to be called, justified, and glorified, whereas the majority of people whom God foreknew in Rom. 11:2 are to be given a spirit of stupor, eyes that see not and ears that hear not (11:8).

Paul's second proof that God has not rejected his people is the salvation of Elijah and seven thousand others **who have not bowed the knee to Baal** (v. 4 [the story is told in 1 Kings 18:20–19:18]).[2] Some contend that the salvation of

2. The number "seven" in Scripture often signifies wholeness, completeness, or perfection. It may well be that there were seven thousand men but an even greater number of women and children as well.

a remnant of Jews throughout redemptive history, whether in Elijah's day or in Paul's, is a token or pledge that ethnic Israel has not been cast off and that God will yet save all the nation Israel as a nation.

However, the appeal to the remnant in Rom. 9–11 is to demonstrate or prove that God never intended to save the nation as a whole. Paul's point is to show how God is faithful to his word despite extensive unfaithfulness in ethnic Israel. The proof is the remnant. The remnant, of which Paul is a part, is cited *not* to prove that God *will* save the nation but to explain why he *didn't*—namely, in order that his sovereign and distinguishing purpose according to the election of grace might be manifest.

Thus, when Paul responds to his own question in verse 1, he does not appeal to some distinctive future for the ethnic nation as a whole. Instead, he points to God's saving activity **at the present time** (*en tō nyn kairō* [v. 5]) and to the principle of the remnant, as illustrated in the experience of Elijah and the seven thousand in Israel's past. In every case, as we've seen all through Romans and see again here in verse 5, "the contrast between grace (cf. 3:24; 4:16) and works reflects the earlier contrast between faith (dependence on God) and works (3:27–28; 9:32), as well as the irrelevance of works to chosenness (9:11)."[3]

Verses 7–10 reiterate in slightly different terms the truth of what Paul earlier asserted in 9:16–21. The people of Israel **failed to obtain** (v. 7 ESV) what they were seeking because, as stated in 9:31–32, they pursued it "as if it were by works" rather than by faith. The **elect** remnant **among them** attained the righteousness of God, but the rest (the **others**) were **hardened** (v. 7), as seen in the words of Moses from Deut. 29:4 (v. 8). Likewise, David, in Ps. 69:22–23 (cited in vv. 9–10), speaks yet again of the hardening that came upon the majority in Israel. Thus, we see that the gospel of Jesus Christ has revealed two groups within national Israel: a *remnant* who, through sovereign electing grace, have embraced the Messiah, and *the rest* (v. 7) who were justly hardened in their unbelief.

By **their table** (v. 9) Paul likely has in view the good things, the blessings, the physical pleasures that "the others" of verse 7 enjoy, the abundant food and drink that God has provided. All these became a stumbling block and a trap, as their devotion and delight shifted from God himself to the blessings he provides. The phrase **their backs be bent forever** (v. 10) again refers to God's judgment of them for their spiritual rebellion and idolatry. The image is of someone carrying such a heavy load or burden that they are bent over double, straining under the weight, so greatly weighed down that their religious efforts serve only to crush them beneath the weight of demands they cannot hope to fulfill.

---

3. Keener, *Romans*, 131.

The Pattern of the Restoration (11:11–16)

Paul labors to make four major points in verses 11–16. First, his words are directed primarily to Gentiles in the church at Rome (observe the repeated use of the second-person plural in what follows) who were boasting over their status as God's people, to the exclusion of the Jews (see esp. vv. 18, 25). Yes, Israel has stumbled, but not **in order that they might fall** (v. 11 ESV). Whereas the nation as a whole has rejected Christ and thus failed to attain to the righteousness that is available only in him (cf. 9:31–33), this does not mean that Israel has fallen into irretrievable spiritual ruin. In fact, God has used it (and will use it) to set in motion a process that will eventually lead once again to Israel's blessing. This is confirmed in verse 16. Paul appeals to Num. 15:17–21, where Israel was commanded to offer to the Lord a loaf from the first batch of dough. In this way the entire batch was consecrated or made holy. This suggests that God's ongoing work of salvation among Jewish people, such as in the case of Paul, is a pledge or guarantee that God will continue to save a remnant throughout history (the HR view).

Second, because of Israel's rejection of the gospel, the blessings of salvation have come to the Gentiles (v. 11; see esp. Acts 13:46–47; 18:5–6; also Matt. 21:33–43).

Third, the salvation of the Gentiles in turn makes the Jews jealous (v. 11). They see the Gentiles getting saved; they witness their joy, peace, and the blessings of salvation and, by God's grace, realize what they are missing. As a result, they yearn to experience it also. The Holy Spirit uses this envy to save the Jews.

Fourth, Paul concludes that if the Gentiles were blessed when Israel rejected the gospel, how much more Gentiles will be blessed when Israel accepts it. Many have concluded from verses 12–15 that Paul is describing what will happen at the time of the second coming of Jesus at the end of the age (the FR view). The **full inclusion** (v. 12) of Israel and their **acceptance** (v. 15), so say advocates of the FR position, are references to a mass, national salvation of Jews in the future.

Others point out that in verses 13–14 Paul has in view the salvation of individual Jewish men and women in the era in which he lived and ministered, extending through the era in which we live, leading up to the second coming of Christ at the close of history (HR). By means of his ministry in the first century ("at the present time" [11:5]) Jewish people are being saved. Thus, Paul envisions his own ministry of gospel proclamation as contributing to the **full inclusion** (v. 12) and **acceptance** (v. 15) of Israel. Those who embrace the HR perspective ask how this could be true if the full inclusion or acceptance of Israel refers to a singular, national, mass salvation of the Jews at the end of the age.

It seems more likely that when Paul refers to the **full inclusion** and **acceptance** of Israel, he is describing the sum total of all Israel's remnants throughout history. The remnant of true believers in the days of Elijah, as well as Paul, who identifies himself as a member of the "remnant chosen by grace" (11:5), together with all Jewish people who come to faith in Jesus through the course of history—constitute the **full inclusion** and **acceptance** of Israel. This is the essence of the HR interpretation.

We know that because of Israel's failure (their rejection of Jesus) the gospel came to the Gentiles (see Acts 13:44–47; 14:1–3; 18:4–7; 19:8–10; 28:23–28). This is what Paul means when he refers in verse 12 to Israel's **transgression** and **loss** leading to the **riches** of the Gentiles. But if the Gentiles were blessed through Israel's unbelief, how much more they will be blessed through Israel's belief! In other words, if failure brought blessing, how much more will fullness do so. This **full inclusion**, or "fullness" (*plērōma*), of Israel most likely refers to the full number of ethnic Israelites who will, by God's electing love, come to faith (HR).

Thus, if God's rejection or casting away of Israel has led to the extension of salvation to the Gentiles, imagine what God's acceptance of Israel will mean. It will mean nothing less than **life from the dead** (v. 15). Some defenders of the futurist view (FR), such as John Murray, say that this phrase is metaphorical and refers to unprecedented blessing, such as the spiritual quickening or salvation of the whole world. But most futurists, as we'll see shortly, understand this phrase as a reference to the bodily resurrection of all believers.

The FR view finds its most persuasive support in verses 12–15. Verses 12 and 15 appear to be asserting the same truth: if the transgression, defeat, and consequent rejection of the majority of Israelites have resulted in such glorious salvific blessing for the Gentiles, how much greater must the Gentile blessing be that will result from Israel's **full inclusion** or **acceptance**. If God did great things for the Gentile world when Israel sinned (in rejecting the Messiah), how much more he will do for them when Israel is saved.

The central question here is the meaning of the word *plērōma* ("fullness" or **full inclusion**) in verse 12 and the word *proslēmpsis* (**acceptance**) in verse 15. The futurist insists that these terms must be the antithesis of Israel's **transgression**, **loss** (v. 12), and **rejection** (v. 15). Since these latter terms point to the national failure of Israel, Israel's restoration must be on a scale commensurate with it.

The futurist believes that verse 15 reiterates the assertion of verse 12. As a result of their transgression and failure (v. 12), Israel has been rejected or cast away (v. 15). Israel's fulfillment, which brings increased riches to the Gentiles (v. 12), is therefore equivalent to their acceptance, which yields a virtual life from the dead (v. 15). Since the rejection (v. 15a) that Israel experienced was national, their acceptance (v. 15b) must also be national. Finally, unlike other futurists, Murray believes that the **life from the dead** that results from Israel's acceptance into national favor is salvation for the Gentiles, not bodily resurrection. He therefore envisions a worldwide conversion consequent upon the restoration of the nation Israel.

In response, it is true that verses 11–15 describe a sequence in which Jews reject their Messiah, after which Gentiles believe, thereby provoking the Jews to jealousy and faith. This conversion of the Jews in turn leads to an even greater blessing for the world. Could it be that Paul envisions this fulfillment as occurring in the present era of gospel proclamation (HR)? Palmer Robertson is an articulate proponent of HR. He explains,

> Both in the case of the Gentiles and the Jews, the full cycle of movement from a state of disobedience to a state of mercy occurs in the present age. From this perspective, the receiving of Israel would refer to the ingrafting of believing Jews throughout the present era, which would reach its consummation at the point in time at which their "fullness" would be realized. The parallel experience of the Gentile world offers no support to the idea that Israel's period of "falling" and "casting away" coincides with the present gospel age, while their "receiving" and "fullness" is reserved for a subsequent era.[4]

The historicist contends, in the light of verse 14, that Paul has in view individual Jewish salvation in the present era, parallel to what the Gentiles now experience, and not some national conversion at the end of the age. There Paul speaks of his hope that by *his* ministry he might move to jealousy his compatriots and save some of them. This saving of **some** (v. 14), says Robertson,

> ought not to be regarded as the deliverance of some pitiful minutia of Judaism hardly worthy to be compared with the "fullness" to be effected at the end of time. Much to the contrary, this saving of "some" should be viewed as conjoining integrally with one of the major themes of Romans 11. As Paul says, there remains at the present time a "remnant" according to the election of grace (v. 5). It is not that "some" which the apostle hopes to save is equivalent in number to the "remnant" which he discusses throughout the passage. But the saving of "some" and the maintaining of a "remnant" are interrelated ideas. Paul's hope that "some" would be saved through his current ministry is based on the principle that a "remnant" would remain throughout the ages.[5]

Paul said in verse 11b that Gentile salvation is designed to provoke Jews to jealousy. As an apostle to the Gentiles, he is striving to achieve this very effect

4. Robertson, "Distinctive Future for Ethnic Israel," 214–15.
5. Robertson, "Distinctive Future for Ethnic Israel," 215.

among his compatriots in order that they might be saved. This activity by Paul, in *his* day, is directly related to the **acceptance** of the Jews in verse 15. "The 'for if' (*ei gar*) of verse fifteen connects the 'receiving' [or **acceptance**] of the Jews with the present ministry of the apostle Paul in the gospel era. By his present ministry among the Gentiles, the apostle hopes to move the Jews to jealousy, and thereby to save some from among Israel. Their 'saving' as described in verse 14 corresponds to their 'reception' in verse 15. In each case Paul describes the hoped-for consequence of his current ministry."[6] Likewise, in verse 31, it is God's saving activity among individual Jews like Paul "now," in the present age, by which Israel's fullness is eventually to be attained (HR).

The futurist view (FR) must explain how Paul's ministry in the first century can contribute to Israel's **full inclusion** (v. 12) and **acceptance** (v. 15) if the latter pertains to only one generation of Jewish people living at the time of Christ's second coming at the close of human history.

But if this is true, how can Paul's ministry to the generation of ethnic Jews in the first century sustain any meaningful relationship to it? Or, to put it yet another way, if Israel's **full inclusion** refers to their national conversion at the end of the age, how is it that Paul at the beginning of the age is contributing to it? Paul appears to say that his ministry, in the early stages of this present age, is designed to contribute to, or perhaps even hasten, the **full inclusion** and **acceptance** of Israel.

The historical view (HR) believes that it is more in keeping with the biblical text that the **full inclusion** of Israel is simply the sum total of all Israel's remnants throughout history, to which Paul contributes by saving some in his day. Thus, the fulfillment or acceptance of Israel should be viewed from the perspective of what God has been doing throughout history and is doing now among the Jews, not what many think God will do only at the end of the age. There is, therefore, no need to posit some future time in conjunction with the second coming in which the remnant principle will be replaced by a fullness principle.

There is yet another problem with the futurist view that must be addressed. Verses 12–15 assert that the fullness of Israel yields increased blessing for the Gentiles, what Paul in verse 15 refers to as **life from the dead**. Murray takes this to mean that after and as a result of Israel's mass conversion there will occur a spiritual vivification or quickening of the Gentile world. But how can this be if the **full number** of the Gentiles will *already* have come in—that is, if the salvation of all elect Gentiles will have antedated the coming of Israel's fullness? According to Murray's interpretation of verses 25–26, all elect Gentiles will have

6. Robertson, "Distinctive Future for Ethnic Israel," 211.

been saved before Israel is restored. For the sake of argument, let us assume that is correct. How then can Israel's restoration yield not only additional but unprecedented Gentile salvation? One answer may be that it is not salvation but some other form of blessing (but what kind? when? how?). Murray will attempt to deal with this by offering a different interpretation of Gentile "fullness" in verse 25 (more on this below).

According to the historical view, it is during the progressive realization of Israel's fullness in the present age, as elect Jews are being saved, that there accrues to the Gentile world even greater and more widespread opportunity for salvation than resulted from Israel's initial unbelief. As Jews are saved, the salvific blessings of the gospel are dispensed throughout and upon the Gentile world with greater and more decisive results than in the first century, when, in consequence of Israel's rejection of Messiah, the kingdom of God was taken from them and given to a nation bearing the fruit thereof.

Here we must look ahead to briefly note one element in Paul's discussion in verses 16–24. **The part of the dough offered as firstfruits** and **the root** (v. 16) likely refer to Abraham and the patriarchs. Their initial consecration to God is indicative of God's purpose to save ethnic Jews, be they ever so few, throughout history (cf. v. 28 [HR]). But why is it simply assumed that this restoration will be national and in mass at the end of the age only (FR)? Paul clearly draws a parallel between the experience of Israelite believers and Gentile believers. Consider, for example, the statement at the close of his argument in verses 30–31: "Just as you [Gentiles] who were at one time disobedient to God have now received mercy as a result of their [Israel's] disobedience, so they too have now become disobedient in order that they too may now receive mercy as a result of God's mercy to you." Through Paul's ministry and that of others, Gentiles are being grafted into the olive tree *when they believe*. As individual Gentiles come to faith (v. 20), says Paul, they receive all the blessings of redemption. Why should we think that it is any different for Jews, especially when Paul says in verses 30–31 that it is the same? As Gentiles are saved through Paul's ministry, the Jews are provoked to jealousy and saving faith. It is then, when they believe, that they are grafted back into the olive tree from which they had been broken off (v. 17).

Those who insist on a mass, future restoration of ethnic Jews (FR) point to the phrase **life from the dead** in verse 15b to support their position. There Paul says that if the rejection of the Jews has made possible the **reconciliation** of the Gentile world, then what will Jewish **acceptance** mean but **life from the dead**? Most futurists argue that this refers to the final, bodily resurrection at the end of the age. Therefore, the **acceptance** of the Jews that makes it possible must likewise have in view an eschatological, end-of-the-age restoration.

But it is doubtful that **life from the dead** refers to the final, bodily resurrection of all believers, and this for two reasons. First, we must take note of the relationship between verse 15 and verses 13–14. As stated before, Paul is emphasizing his current, first-century ministry. He has in mind what he is doing *then*, not what God will or will not do in the eschaton. The aim of all his efforts, according to verse 14, is to **save some of them**—that is, Jews, his brothers and sisters according to the flesh. Verse 15 is directly related to verse 14 by **for if** (*ei gar*). In other words, verse 15 provides the grounds for verse 14, or perhaps is an expanded explanation of the meaning of verse 14. But the point is that Paul is describing in verse 15 what he means by **save** (v. 14) when he speaks of the Jews being saved through his first-century ministry. If the relationship of verse 15 to verse 14 is to be maintained, it must be that **life from the dead** (v. 15b) is descriptive of salvation (v. 14b), not bodily resurrection. It may even be that Paul is alluding in these verses to the parable of the prodigal that he would have heard from Luke, later to be incorporated in Luke 15. When the prodigal returned home, the father declared, "For this son of mine was dead and is alive again; he was lost and is found" (Luke 15:24). The point is that his "faith" is a coming to spiritual life again after spiritual death.

Romans 11:15, therefore, is not to be read as parallel to 11:12. In verse 12 there is a clear "much more" argument (or **how much greater**), typical of Paul. But not so in verse 15. In verse 15 Paul is providing an explanation for the salvation of individual Jews that he mentioned in verse 14. The point of verse 12 is that if the unbelief of Jews entails riches for the Gentiles, the belief of the Jews will bless Gentiles even more. What that blessing may prove to be is hard to say. Paul never defines it. But this isn't his argument in verse 15. Whereas in verse 15a he does speak of the **reconciliation** that came to Gentiles because of Jewish unbelief, in verse 15b he speaks of the **life** that comes to the Jews because of their belief, a **life** that in verse 14b he referred to as their (Jewish) salvation. When we see verse 15 in its proper grammatical relation to verses 13–14 (**for if** [v. 15a]), it is clear that Paul envisions his own efforts, by God's grace, as contributing to the **life from the dead** that comes with God's **acceptance** of the Jews when they believe.

Second, if **life from the dead** means the final, physical, bodily resurrection for all believers, both Jew and Gentile, Paul would be saying that the resurrection is in some sense dependent upon or caused by a corporate or mass restoration of ethnic Jews. If the **acceptance** in verse 15 is a reference to an end-of-the-age mass salvation among ethnic Jews (FR), Paul would be saying that everyone's bodily resurrection is suspended upon it, or can't occur without it, or is in some sense the result of it. We must ask whether the New Testament teaches that the final resurrection of believers is causally related to the salvation of national

Israel. We read most often in the New Testament that the bodily resurrection of believers is tied to or grounded in the bodily resurrection of Jesus Christ. It is because of his atoning death and resurrection that we are to be likewise raised in a glorified body (see esp. Rom. 8:11; 1 Cor. 15:20–23; 1 Thess. 4:13–18; 1 John 3:1–3). We will be bodily raised because of Christ's resurrection (he is the firstfruits) and at his return.

The precise wording that Paul employs does not settle the argument. Whereas it is true that **life from the dead** language typically refers to bodily resurrection in the New Testament, we must consider Rom. 6:13, where it explicitly refers to regeneration or spiritual life from the dead. We must also take into account that numerous times in the New Testament the new birth and salvation are portrayed as a coming to life out of death (for one clear example, see Eph. 2:1–10).

The One Olive Tree (11:17–24)

In order to make his point concerning the salvation of both Jews and Gentiles, Paul employs an illustration taken from the world of agriculture or, better still, horticulture. He does it by describing God's elect people of all ethnicities as an olive tree. There is only one olive tree, not two. The olive tree symbolizes the people of God, both Jewish and Gentile believers. In that one olive tree there are **natural** branches (v. 21), a reference to ethnic Jews, and unnatural branches, or what Paul calls **a wild olive shoot** (v. 17), a reference to ethnic Gentiles.

When Israel as a whole rejected the Lord Jesus as Messiah, God broke off the natural branches. He rejected those who rejected his Son. God then took Gentiles who did believe in Jesus and grafted them into the olive tree. Now, both ethnic Jews who believe in Jesus and ethnic Gentiles who believe in Jesus are together one people in the one olive tree, together sharing in **the nourishing sap from the olive root** (v. 17) (much the same thing is said by Paul in Eph. 2:11–13, 17–19).

Contrary to what is known as "replacement theology," no believing Gentile has replaced any believing Jew. Rather, believing Gentiles have now been included or grafted into the one olive tree. There in that tree, a symbol of God's elect people, we now see both natural branches, Jewish believers, and unnatural branches, Gentile believers, together sharing equally in the blessings of the covenant and its promises.

Paul then warns Gentile believers not to be arrogant. That many Jewish people were broken off because of their unbelief is no reason for believing Gentiles to boast. Believing Gentiles are graciously nourished and supported by the root of the olive tree, a reference either to the covenants that God made with Abraham, Isaac, Jacob, and David, or to the patriarchs themselves. Many of the natural branches, like Paul himself, are still a part of the olive tree. They are the "remnant" (11:5) that Paul has been describing. Thus, if Gentiles turn their back on the Messiah, they will likewise be cut off. Not all of them, of course, for there will always be a believing remnant.

The good news is that God is prepared to graft Jews back into the olive tree if they believe (vv. 23–24). Does this happen throughout the course of church history, over the past two thousand years, each time individual Jews come to faith in Jesus as Messiah (HR), or does it only or primarily happen at the end of history in conjunction with the second coming of Jesus (FR)? I believe it is the former.

Does verse 21 imply that genuine believers can lose their salvation? Some say yes. Those who believe in the preservation of the saints take one of three views. It may be that Paul is echoing a theme found elsewhere in his letters and throughout the New Testament: ultimate salvation is dependent on perseverance in faith (cf. Rom. 8:13; Col. 1:23; Heb. 3:6, 14; 1 Pet. 1:5; 1 John 2:19), a faith that God graciously preserves and sustains within us. Others have suggested that Paul's discussion is about Gentiles as a class, considered collectively, and Israel as a class, considered collectively. In other words, just as "Israel" was **broken off** (v. 20) because of unbelief, so also "Gentiles" may be if they do not believe. On this view, those who were **broken off** were not born-again believers but were Jews who, by virtue of their ethnicity, were members of the covenant community of Israel. Their **unbelief** (v. 20) was their rejection of Jesus as Messiah. Thus they were members of the olive tree but did not experience saving faith. The breaking off of such branches was the corporate rejection of Israel. Could it be, then, that the threatened breaking off of Gentile branches should likewise be viewed as a corporate judgment?

Douglas Moo has another, far more probable, explanation:

> While the olive tree represents the true, spiritual people of God, those who are said to belong to this tree are not only those who, through their faith, are actually part of the tree but also those who only appear to belong to that tree. This is evident from the fact that Paul speaks of unbelieving Jews as having been "cut off" from the tree (v. 17). In reality, these Jews had never been part of the tree at all; yet to preserve the metaphor he is using, Paul presents them as if they had been. In the same way, then, those Gentiles within the church at Rome—and elsewhere—who appear to be part of God's people, yet do not continue in faith, may never have been part of that tree at all.[7]

7. Moo, *Romans*, 707.

Moo's point is that there are both genuine, spiritual attachments to the olive tree and unreal, counterfeit attachments. It is precisely the failure to **continue in his** [God's] **kindness** (v. 22) that demonstrates one's attachment to be merely external and nonsalvific. The future tense **will be cut off** (v. 22) likely points to the day of final judgment, much in the way Jesus referred to this in Matt. 7:22–23. Thus, the first and third views may be combined. Those who have truly believed *will* continue in God's kindness (see Heb. 3:6, 14). Those who do not continue in God's kindness show thereby that they were only superficially, but not savingly, part of the tree (on this, see esp. 1 John 2:19). Failure to persevere does not mean that one who was truly saved becomes truly lost. Rather, perseverance is itself the proof that one was truly saved. If one does not persevere, one has always been lost and never saved.[8]

The Salvation of All Israel (11:25–27)

We begin with Paul's declaration in verse 25 that **a partial hardening** (ESV) has happened to Israel. This refers not to the degree or time but to the *extent* of the experience in view. Paul is not saying that those hardened are only partially hardened, as if to suggest that their hardening is not as intensive as it could have been. Neither is Paul saying, at least in this phrase, that Israel's hardening is temporary, as if he meant to assert that "for a while" hardening has happened to Israel. His point is simply that *not all* Israelites in this present age have been hardened. Although a part of Israel is hardened (the precise numerical proportions are not in view here), there have been, are, and always will be some ethnic Israelites who are saved. In summary, Paul is simply repeating in different words what he said in Rom. 11:7.

He then says that this hardening has happened to Israel **until the full number of the Gentiles has come in** (v. 25b). The key to understanding Paul are two Greek words translated as **until** (*achri hou*). The futurist view (FR) insists that this refers to a point of consummation that brings the hardening of Israel to an end. The hardening of Israel has a terminus, an event or occurrence at which time the hardening will cease and salvation ensue. "Paul's meaning," says C. E. B. Cranfield, "is not that Israel is in part hardened during the time in which the fullness of the Gentiles is coming in, but that the hardening will last until the fullness of the Gentiles comes in. The entry of the fullness of the Gentiles will

8. Yet another perspective is the one defended by Schreiner and Caneday, *The Race Set before Us*. They argue that such conditional statements and associated warnings ("He will not spare you either," "You also will be cut off") as we find in verses 21–22 are designed to motivate true believers to persevere ("continue") in faith. Those who are truly born again will continue in faith because they respond to the warnings of what might happen should they not.

be the event which will mark the end of Israel's hardening."[9] The point of this interpretation is that Paul envisions a time after which a change will occur in the spiritual status of Israel: their experience of hardening will terminate with the coming of Gentile fullness. The state of affairs subsequent thereto, says the futurist, can only be that of Israel's national salvation (FR).

Advocates of the historical view (HR) argue that the word **until** need not imply a time after which the hardening of Israel will cease. The **hardening** of which Paul speaks is simply the historical or temporal manifestation of God's eternal decree of reprobation, the converse of which is election. In other words, the futurist view would imply that the principle of reprobation, operative throughout redemptive history (even in Israel [cf. 9:6–13]), will at some future time cease to be. This is theologically problematic.

Furthermore, *achri hou* (**until**) need not require the reversal of circumstances that had prevailed prior to reaching that point. The force of the word is to carry actions or conditions to their ultimate point, as, for example, when Paul declares that he persecuted Christians "to [*achri*] their death" (Acts 22:4). Or again, in the days of Noah people were eating and drinking, marrying and giving in marriage, "until [*achri*] the day when Noah entered the ark" (Matt. 24:38 ESV). That is, their actions continued up to the time their end came. Thus, according to Palmer Robertson, "The phrase implies not a new beginning after a termination point in time, but instead the continuation of a prevailing circumstance for Israel until the end of time."[10]

Ben Merkle argues in similar fashion, insisting that "what is important is not what will take place *after* the event is completed, but *that* the event is eschatologically fulfilled."[11] He then cites the use of this terminology in 1 Cor. 11:26, where Paul states that the church is to partake of the Lord's Supper and by doing so proclaims the Lord's death "until" (*achri hou*) he comes. Paul's purpose "is not to stress that one day the church will not celebrate the Lord's Supper. Instead, his point is that this celebration will continue 'until' the end of time."[12] We find much the same in 1 Cor. 15:25, where Paul declares that Christ must reign "until" (*achri hou*) he has put all enemies under his feet, the last of which is death itself. "The intended stress is not that a time will come when Christ will no longer reign, but that he must continue to reign until the last enemy is conquered at the final judgment."[13]

We must also consider the meaning of **the fullness of the Gentiles** (v. 25 ESV). This surely refers to the full number of the elect from among the

---

9. Cranfield, *Romans*, 2:575.
10. Robertson, "Distinctive Future for Ethnic Israel," 220.
11. Merkle, "Future of Ethnic Israel," 715.
12. Merkle, "Future of Ethnic Israel," 715.
13. Merkle, "Future of Ethnic Israel," 716.

Gentiles, the salvation of whom is realized progressively throughout the present age, at the end of which the total number thereof will have come in. John Murray interprets verse 12 to mean that after the fullness of Israel has come in—that is, after the final end-of-the-age mass salvation of Israel as a nation has occurred—even greater salvific blessing will accrue to the Gentiles. "Thus there awaits the Gentiles," says Murray, "in their distinctive identity as such, gospel blessing far surpassing anything experienced during the period of Israel's apostasy, and this unprecedented enrichment will be occasioned by the conversion of Israel on a scale commensurate with that of their earlier disobedience."[14] But if the fullness of the Gentiles (v. 25) refers to the total number of elect to be saved, then the salvation of all Israel (which awaits and follows the coming in of Gentile fullness) would terminate any further expansion among the Gentiles of the kind of blessing that verse 12 suggests. In other words, if all elect Gentiles are to be saved before Israel is restored (and according to the futurist view, that is what verses 25–26 assert), how can Israel's restoration yield subsequent, additional, indeed unprecedented, Gentile salvation?

The only escape from this difficulty is to interpret the fullness of the Gentiles as something other than the full number of elect Gentiles to be saved. According to Murray's interpretation of verses 12–15, he must somehow make room for unprecedented Gentile salvation after Israel's final, national restoration. But verses 25–26 will not permit this. Murray obviously recognizes this and proceeds to say that Gentile fullness denotes "unprecedented blessing" for them but does not exclude even greater blessing to follow. The "greater blessing" to follow the final restoration of national Israel is, of course, the conversion of the world in accordance with Murray's postmillennial eschatology.

However, not only does this strain the sense of the term "fullness," or **full number** (*plērōma*), but also Paul's statement that at the end of the age this fullness will have **come in** or will have reached its culmination is emptied of significance if in fact beyond that point there is yet more Gentile "fullness" to come. If, according to Murray, Israel's national salvation must await the coming in of Gentile fullness, how can Gentile fullness extend beyond the salvation of Israel? Or again, if Gentile fullness does not terminate with Israel's salvation, as Murray is forced to say, why must Israel's salvation await it?

Murray rightly insists that the fullness or fulfillment of Israel in verse 12 and the fullness of the Gentiles in verse 25 are similar, if not identical, in significance. Therefore, since Israel's fullness entails a mass, national salvation at the end of the age (so says Murray), it is only natural to assume that the coming in

14. Murray, *Romans*, 2:79.

of Gentile fullness implies the same for them. Thus, Murray's view entails the following end-of-the-age scenario:

mass salvation of Gentiles
↓
mass salvation of Israel
↓
yet another mass salvation of Gentiles

But it is more likely that the coming in of Gentile fullness is what Paul earlier described in verses 16–24 under the imagery of unnatural branches being grafted into the olive tree as they come to faith in Christ, a process ongoing in the church age from Paul's day to the present (HR). If so, then on Murray's view the fullness of the Gentiles comes in a manner radically different from the way in which Israel's fullness comes in. Gentile fullness would be a progressive, throughout-history occurrence, whereas Israelite fullness would be an instantaneous, at-the-end-of-history occurrence. But this would violate the point of verses 16–24 and verses 30–31, which is that both Gentile and Jew are now (from Paul's perspective) and into the future being saved, and are together and in parallel fashion being grafted into the one olive tree.

This brings us to the crucial phrase **and in this way all Israel will be saved** (v. 26). There are two important questions to be addressed. First, who or what constitutes **all Israel**, and second, what does Paul mean by the words **and in this way**? As for the first question, there appear to be five possible answers. **All Israel** may refer to (1) all ethnic descendants of Abraham of every age; or, (2) all ethnic descendants of Abraham living in the future when Christ returns; or, (3) the mass or majority of the ethnic descendants of Abraham living in the future when Christ returns; or, (4) both elect Jews and elect Gentiles who together make up the church of Jesus Christ, the true "Israel of God"; or, (5) all elect Israelites within the ethnic community of Israel (cf. Rom. 9:6).

View 1 is a form of ethnic universalism. But since Scripture nowhere endorses the notion of a postmortem opportunity to be saved, and since Paul has already denied in Rom. 9:6–13 that all ethnic Israelites will be saved, this interpretation must be rejected. View 2, argues John Murray, is contrary to the analogy drawn in Rom. 11 between Israel's national apostasy and their national restoration. "The apostasy of Israel, their trespass, loss, casting away, and hardening were not universal. There was always a remnant, not all branches were broken off, their hardening was in part. Likewise restoration and salvation need not include every Israelite. 'All Israel' can refer to the mass, the people as a whole in accord with the pattern followed in the chapter throughout."[15]

View 3 is widely held today. The belief is that Paul is describing an end-of-the-age salvation of the nation as a whole, though not necessarily including every single member of that nation or every single ethnic Jew. But if a time is coming when the principle of hardening is to be withdrawn from Israel, would not every single Israelite alive at that time be saved?

View 4 suggests that a way to avoid all such problems is to take **all Israel** as a reference to the church, elect Jews and Gentiles who are together the Israel of God (cf. Gal. 6:16). The problem with this interpretation is that the term **Israel** appears ten other times in Rom. 9–11 and always refers to ethnic Jews (cf. 9:4, 6 [2x], 27, 31; 10:19, 21; 11:1, 2, 7). Also, what becomes of Paul's statement in verse 25, immediately preceding verse 26, that **Israel** is experiencing partial hardening? If **Israel** in verse 25, a clear reference to ethnic Jews, is not carried over to verse 26 with the same denotation, Paul's argument does not make sense.

Regardless of which view one holds, Israel in verse 26 is not the precise equivalent of Israel in verse 25. According to the futurist view, Israel in verse 25 refers to the ethnic nation as a whole during the inter-advent period, whereas Israel in verse 26 is restricted to one generation of ethnic Jews living at the time of the parousia. The historical view differs only with regard to the use of Israel in verse 26, in which case it refers to all *elect* ethnic Jews in the present age. On the historical view, therefore, the distinction between Israel in verse 25 and Israel in verse 26 is the same as the one Paul makes in Rom. 9:6. Nevertheless, the important point that unites both views is their insistence that Israel in verses 25–26 is exclusive of ethnic Gentiles.

View 5 is that **all Israel** means the total number of elect ethnic Jews, the sum total of all Israel's remnants throughout the present, inter-advent age (HR). **All Israel** thus parallels the fullness of the Gentiles (v. 25). "And if 'All Israel' indicates, as it does, that not a single elect Israelite will be lacking 'when the roll is called up yonder,' then 'the fullness of the Gentiles' similarly shows that when the attendance is checked every elect Gentile will answer 'Present.'"[16]

Several objections have been raised against this interpretation by advocates of the futurist view. Often one hears that Paul must be referring to a future restoration of Jews in verses 25–26, for he has used the future tense repeatedly in this chapter whenever describing salvation. But surely this is no reason for

15. Murray, *Romans*, 2:98. For the idea of Israel "as a whole" but not necessarily all, see 1 Sam. 7:5; 25:1; 1 Kings 12:1; 2 Chron. 12:1; Dan. 9:11.
16. Hendriksen, *Romans*, 381.

accepting the futurist view, for how else could Paul possibly have spoken? If someone in the first century is writing about the salvation of others that has yet to occur, it is only normal to employ the future tense. If Paul is describing in his day the manner in which all elect Israelites will come to faith up to the end of the age, how else *could* he have stated it if not with the future tense?

Another objection is that if all Paul meant to say is that all elect Israel will be saved, the climactic element in verse 26 is lost. Of course all the elect of Israel will be saved! How utterly prosaic! But this objection fails to realize what that so-called climactic element in verse 26 really is. Paul is not simply asserting *that* all elect Israel will be saved; he is describing the mysterious *manner* in which it will occur. That is, it is not so much the *fact* as it is the *fashion* in which they will be saved. It is by means of nothing less than the incredible scenario of Jewish unbelief → Gentile salvation → Jewish jealousy and salvation → Gentile blessing. This is the way in which all elect Israel will eventually and progressively come to saving faith (HR). Furthermore, in a context in which the question has been raised whether any Israelites will be saved (cf. 11:1–5), it is even less prosaic—indeed, it is profoundly important.

Second, what is the force of the words **and in this way** (*kai houtōs*), or "and thus"? Although not impossible, it is highly unlikely that the words should be translated as "and then," with a temporal or sequential force. If that were Paul's intent, he probably would have used *kai tote* or *eita* or *epeita*. One simply cannot use the phrase "and thus" to prove that Israel's salvation is temporally subsequent to the coming in of Gentile fullness.[17] The most common meaning of *kai houtōs* ("and thus") is "in this way," "in such a manner," or "in accordance with this pattern." In other words, Paul is telling us not *when* all Israel will be saved but *how*. All Israel will be saved in the way Paul has described in the first twenty-four verses of Rom. 11. Robertson explains:

> First the promises as well as the Messiah were given to Israel. Then, somehow in God's mysterious plan, Israel rejected its Messiah and was cut off from its position of distinctive privilege. As a result, the coming of Israel's Messiah was announced to the Gentiles. The nations then obtained by faith what Israel could not find by seeking in the strength of their own flesh. Frustrated over seeing the blessings of their messianic kingdom heaped on the Gentiles, Israel is moved to jealousy. Consequently they too repent, believe, and share in the promises originally made to them. "And in this manner" ([*kai houtōs*]), by such a fantastic process which shall continue throughout the entire present age "up

---

17. At best, no more than 4 of the 205 instances in which this phrase appears in the New Testament may reasonably be taken in the sense of "and then," "thereafter," "and consequently," or some such idea (cf. John 4:6; Acts 17:33; 20:11; 28:14).

to" ([*achri hou*]) the point that the full number of the Gentiles is brought in, all Israel shall be saved.[18]

But what about the Old Testament confirmation of this truth that Paul cites in verses 26–27? In these verses Paul combines Isa. 59:20, 21, and Jer. 31:33–34 (and possibly alludes to Isa. 27:9 and Ps. 14:7). Although many have simply assumed that this is a reference to the second coming of Christ, it seems more likely that Paul has in view the work of Messiah at his first advent. The future tense in the passage (**The deliverer will come . . . , he will banish . . .** [ESV]) is future from the perspective of the Old Testament prophet who is speaking and not necessarily from the perspective of Paul in the first century. It was by virtue of Christ's atoning death and resurrection that the new covenant has been inaugurated and the foundation laid for the removal of ungodliness from Jacob (i.e., from elect Israel). The forgiveness of sins is available to both ethnic Gentiles and Jews because of what Jesus did at his first coming when he ratified the new covenant in his blood (see esp. Matt. 26:28; Heb. 8:6–13; 9:15; 10:11–18). It is therefore by means of what the deliverer, Jesus, accomplished at his first advent that all elect Gentiles (**the full number of the Gentiles**) and all elect Israelites (**all Israel**) will be saved.

The Irrevocable Calling of God (11:28–32)

The enmity of the Jews (**enemies** [v. 28]) is not subjective; that is to say, it is not their enmity against God but God's enmity against them because of their unbelief. We know this from the contrast drawn between, on the one hand, being **enemies** of God and, on the other hand, being **loved** (or "beloved"). To be an enemy of God is to be the object of his wrath; to be beloved is to be the object of his love and grace.

But who are **they** in verse 28 of whom these things are said? Surely, they are "all Israel" (v. 26), those whom God intends to save by taking away their ungodliness and forgiving their sins (vv. 26–27). Consequently, the **enemies** of God and the **loved** of God are the same people, the elect of ethnic Israel. Their rejection of the Messiah, as a result of which the gospel comes to the Gentiles, incurs divine wrath and enmity. Hence, they are God's enemies. But when they are in turn saved, being provoked to jealousy and faith by Gentile blessing, they enter a new relationship with God, that of being beloved because of election (cf. Rom. 5:6–11).

In saying that they are beloved **for the sake of their forefathers** (v. 28 ESV), Paul does not mean that their election is a reward for any supposed merit or

18. Robertson, "Distinctive Future for Ethnic Israel," 222.

Contrasting the Interpretations of the Historical Remnant and Future Restoration Views

Romans 11 is a challenging chapter for the interpreter of Scripture. The following is a summation of seven primary differences on important texts as articulated by the two perspectives. By way of brief reminder, the historical remnant (HR) view argues that Paul is describing the way in which both elect Gentiles and elect Israelites are being saved throughout the course of the present church age, which will culminate in the return of Christ. The future restoration (FR) view contends that Paul's focus is on the final, mass salvation of the majority of Jewish men and women in conjunction with the second coming of Christ.

1. The HR interpretation of "his people" (v. 1) is that these are the elect of God in ethnic Israel whom God will save throughout the course of church history. The FR interpretation of "his people" (v. 1) is that this refers to the nation of Israel as a whole, who will be saved when Christ returns at the close of the present age.
2. The HR interpretation of the words "full inclusion" and "acceptance" (vv. 12, 15) is that Paul has in view the sum total of Israel's elect remnant who come to saving faith in Christ throughout church history. The FR view is that these words refer to the mass salvation of the majority of Israelites who are alive at the time of the return of Christ.
3. "Life from the dead" (v. 15), according to HR, refers to the spiritual salvation of elect Gentiles throughout the course of the present church age. Advocates of the FR view insist that "life from the dead" most likely has in view the final, bodily resurrection at the end of history.
4. The word "until" (v. 25), according to the HR view, points to the fact that the hardening of Israel will continue in the present church age up until the time that all elect Gentiles are saved. The FR interpretation argues that "until" (v. 25) points to the time at the close of history when all elect Gentiles will have been saved, at which time all elect Israelites will be saved.
5. "And in this way all Israel will be saved" (v. 26), so contends the HR view, refers to the manner in which elect Israelites are being saved throughout the course of the present church age. The FR view believes that this salvation of all Isael will be an end-time

mass ingathering of elect Israelites in conjunction with the second coming of Christ.

6. The HR interpretation believes that "all Israel" (v. 26) refers to all the elect in Israel who are being saved in the present church age. The FR perspective insists that "all Israel" (v. 26) refers to the vast majority of ethnic Israelites who are saved in conjunction with the second coming of Christ at the close of history.

7. According to those who embrace the HR view, in verses 26b–27 the phrase "the deliverer will come from Zion" has in view Christ's first coming. The future tense ("will come") is from the perspective of the Old Testament author whose words are being cited. The advocates of the FR view believe that the future tense ("will come") refers to the parousia of Christ at the close of history when the Lord saves the majority within ethnic Israel.

innate goodness in Abraham, Isaac, and Jacob (cf. Rom. 9:6–13). Rather, Paul is referring to the divine promise given to Abraham of an elect remnant from among his physical seed, in fulfillment of which **all** [elect] **Israel** is being saved. Therefore, they are beloved because God promised a saved remnant to the fathers in the Abrahamic covenant, and to his word God is ever faithful. The **gifts** and **call** of God, therefore, are not nonsalvific theocratic privileges given to all ethnic Jews regardless of their relation to the Messiah. They refer to the products of God's special, saving, electing grace such as faith, hope, love, and peace—that is, those spiritual blessings that accompany the salvation of those whom God has called to himself.

The word **for** (ESV) with which verse 30 begins (inexplicably omitted by the NIV) indicates that what follows confirms and illustrates the assertion of verses 28–29. This is significant because in verses 30–31 Paul explicitly declares that the salvation of elect Israel, their experience of being beloved of God in fulfill-ment of the divine and irrevocable promise given to the fathers, is being realized **now**! Note well in verses 30–31 the threefold **now** (*nyn*), which emphasizes that the salvation to which Paul has just referred is being realized in the gospel era, the **now** of gospel proclamation (HR). The irrevocable gifts and calling of God (v. 29) that account for the ultimate realization of all Israel's salvation as God's beloved are being experienced **now**,[19] in the present church age. This salvation, this removal of ungodliness from Jacob, this forgiveness of sins, this restoration

---

19. There is some measure of dispute about whether the third use of "now" (*nyn*) in verse 31b is part of the original text. I concur with Douglas Moo that it probably is to be included, and for

of all Israel is not said to be restricted to the end of the age, in some way associated with the second advent of Christ (FR), but is presently being realized as a result of Christ's first advent (HR).

Three Declarations, Three Rhetorical Questions, Three Doxological Assertions (11:33–36)

Paul begins this concluding paragraph with three declarations (v. 33). First, he declares that God's riches and wisdom and knowledge are infinitely deep. **Riches** likely refers to the infinite resources of God from which flow all divine blessings, especially the saving kindness expressed in the grace he shows to undeserving sinners (see 11:12). Not only are God's riches infinite and unending; so too is his **wisdom**. God is never at a loss for a way to accomplish a purpose, a means to achieve an end, a pathway to reach a destination, an instrument to fulfill a goal. **Wisdom** may be a reference to the plan of salvation by which both Jews and Gentiles are one in Christ, a plan just delineated in Rom. 9–11. Moreover, his **knowledge** is without limit. Paul isn't speaking here of our knowledge of God, as if to say that we will never exhaust all there is to know about God. That surely is true, but the knowledge of God here is God's knowledge, the extent and depth and dimensions of what he, as God, knows (see Ps. 147:5).

Second, God's **judgments** are infinitely unsearchable. His ways and means of carrying out his eternal purpose are ultimately inscrutable, infinitely beyond the capacity of human minds to decipher or comprehend. Therefore, we cannot judge him or call him to account or question his activities. The word **judgments** (*krimata*) refers to his determination of guilt and innocence and whether, when, and how to respond: With immediate judgment? With long-suffering and patience? With saving mercy? All these determinations are beyond our ability to decipher or ultimately comprehend.

Third, God's ways or **paths** are infinitely inscrutable. The word **paths** (*hodoi*) refers to conduct, a way of life, decisions a person makes. This encompasses why a person thinks the way they do, feels, reasons, discriminates, decides, acts, chooses, and determines what means are best to achieve the greatest ends. God's decisions regarding what to cause, what to permit, and what to prevent are beyond our capacity to grasp.

Paul continues by asking three rhetorical questions (vv. 34–35). First, who has ever figured out God's mind (see Isa. 55:8–9)? The answer is, of course, no one. Second, who has ever told God what to do? God does not need advice on

---

these reasons: it has "strong early attestation, fits neatly into Paul's balanced sentence, and is—at least superficially—the 'most difficult'" (Moo, *Romans*, 711n2).

how to behave or counsel to extricate himself from difficult and ticklish situations. God never faces a conundrum for which he doesn't have the perfect solution. God never lacks sufficient wisdom to know how best to govern his universe (see Isa. 40:13–14).

In his third rhetorical question Paul asks, Who has ever made God a debtor? If he is infinitely rich and owns everything, having made it all, what can humans possibly give him that they didn't first receive from him? No one gives to God as if they originate or create things that he otherwise does not or would not have. Our "giving" does not increase his inventory of goods and services and products and resources (cf. 1 Chron. 29:11). Since God owns it all and therefore can't be given anything that isn't already his, you can't put God in your debt. You can't do anything that would result in God owing you anything.

Paul then concludes with three doxological assertions (v. 36). For **from** [*ex*] **him and through** [*di'*] **him and for** [*eis*] **him are all things**. That is to say, he is the source, the means, and the goal of all things. Everything that exists came **from him** and continues to exist **through him** as he exerts the power to sustain and preserve it in existence, and everything ultimately is designed **for him**—that is, to bring him honor and praise and majesty (cf. Acts 17:24–25). What is there left for Paul to say? Only this: **To him be the glory forever! Amen.**

Renewal and Relationships in the Body of Christ

Our Renewal (12:1–2)

The word **therefore** (*oun*) with which verse 1 opens alerts us to the spiritually organic relationship between Christian doctrine and Christian duty. From the lofty theological heights of Rom. 1–11, Paul now descends into the rigorous realities of daily Christian living (cf. Eph. 1–3 and 4–6). This move from Rom. 1–11 to 12–16 is a move from exposition to exhortation, from theological principles to ethical practices. Christian obedience is always theologically motivated: we do what we do only because God did what he did.

The **mercy** (v. 1) of God, on the basis of which Paul issues his exhortation, is God's saving deeds described in Rom. 1–11: election, justification, adoption, sanctification, calling, glorification, and more. If there is a notable difference between God's grace and his mercy, it is that grace contemplates sinners as guilty, while mercy views them as wretched. Grace is God's attitude of kindness when what we deserve is death, while mercy is divine pity for those who are utterly helpless and hopeless. Later, in 15:8–9a, Paul will declare that our all-consuming purpose in life is to glorify God for his mercy.

The spirit in which Paul issues his appeal is revealed in the words he uses: **urge** and **brothers and sisters** (v. 1). Paul is not so much pleading or beseeching as he is claiming in Christ's name an obedience that we are obliged to render. But there is also tenderness in the appeal, for Paul speaks as a Christian brother to other Christian **brothers and sisters**. This is a family affair. Paul is no less responsible than we to heed the call to holiness.

For the word **offer**, see Rom. 6:13, 16, 19. Here the term has the sense of presenting or offering up a sacrifice (cf. Lev. 1:3–17). But no such sacrifice is required in the new covenant, as Christ has presented or offered himself for us. Our sacrificial offering today is a response to the once-for-all sacrifice of Christ on the cross. Clearly, Paul intends **bodies** in a comprehensive or holistic sense that includes the totality of who we are. To **offer** our **bodies** unto God means that we consecrate and dedicate everything we are—body, soul, spirit, mind, heart, will, emotions—in such a way that God is seen to be glorious and great (cf. 1 Cor. 6:19–20; Phil. 1:20).

This offering is a **living sacrifice**,[1] one that does not die or have a temporary shelf life. The presentation of our bodies to God is comprehensive and perpetual. There is no time limit. Paul may also have in mind what he said in 6:11, where he spoke of believers as "alive to God in Christ Jesus." It is also to be a **holy** sacrifice, by which he means that we are set apart for God, consecrated exclusively for him and his glory. This must be a sacrifice that is **pleasing** to God, one that is consistent with revealed truth and brings him pleasure.

The word **worship** (*latreia*) was used earlier in Rom. 9:4 to speak of the activities and sacrifices offered up in the temple during the time of the old covenant. The NIV translates the one word *logikēn* as **true and proper** (from which we derive our English term "logical"). It may be that Paul is saying that our worship is reasonable, wholehearted. Some have suggested that it means "appropriate," "rational," perhaps even "fitting the circumstances," worship that makes sense in view of the way God has treated us so mercifully in Christ Jesus. Our worship is never to be mechanical, merely external, or automatic, or purely an act of ritual. It is genuine and flows from within our hearts and spirits. At the same time, the ESV rendering of this term as **spiritual** risks losing sight of the fact that as believer priests we are to dedicate the whole of who we are, body and soul, and not just our subjective, internal affections.

There is a twofold responsibility that is ours. First, we are to resist and push back against any tendency to conform to this world. The term translated as **world** more literally means "age," a reference to the world or society or culture in which we live that is dominated by sin, unbelief, idolatry, and immorality (cf. 2 Cor. 4:4). The contrast is between this present, temporary, corrupt, satanically shaped "age" in which we live and the beauty and righteousness of the "age" to come.

---

1. "Rather than the sacrifice of the dead carcasses ('bodies') of animals," says Gordon Fee, "one now gives oneself wholly back to God in the form of a 'living sacrifice' (hence 'bodies'), as those 'alive' from the dead (6:11, 13)" (*God's Empowering Presence*, 599).

But the believer must **be transformed by the renewing of** their **mind** (v. 2), what Paul referred to earlier as being "conformed to the image of [God's] Son" (8:29). This is no superficial resemblance, but rather an inward renewal that affects all aspects of life. The word translated as **transformed** is used in the New Testament in only three other texts: Matt. 17:2 and Mark 9:2, where Jesus is said to have been "transfigured" in the presence of his disciples; and 2 Cor. 3:18, where Paul describes Christians as being "transformed" into the image of Jesus Christ. Here Paul uses it to refer to the reconfiguration of our thought processes, a metamorphosis, if you will, in what we know to be true and what we value as of greatest importance.

In describing this transformation, Paul uses the Greek present tense, most likely to emphasize the ongoing, continuous experience of being changed. The verb is also passive, pointing to the fact that we are to be transformed, undoubtedly by the work of the Holy Spirit. Furthermore, the verb is imperative, a command. God isn't giving us a choice either to be transformed or not. Not to experience this transformation is, therefore, a sin. Finally, Paul does not want us to think of merely substituting one outward fashion for another. What he calls for is a deep, internal metamorphosis that is expressed in a distinct and decidedly Christlike outward lifestyle.

The transformation in view is one that is primarily in one's **mind** (v. 2; cf. Eph. 4:23). The need for renewal is that our minds are fallen, and apart from God's grace we use them to disbelieve God and to defy him. We are born into this world with a bent or mental disposition to oppose God and to view virtually anything in this world as of greater value than the Creator himself (see esp. Eph. 4:17–19). This word for **renewing** appears elsewhere only in Titus 3:5, where Paul refers to "the washing of rebirth and renewal by the Holy Spirit." We can experience this only when the Spirit sovereignly reshapes and fashions our thoughts and values and beliefs. And he does this primarily through the instruction of Scripture.

Paul is not saying in verse 2 that we should labor to determine if God's will is good or bad. It is always **good, pleasing and perfect**. He means that we learn of the goodness and the acceptable nature of this perfect will by experience (i.e., we **test** and **approve** it). God's **will** here is not the sovereign, secret will of God. God does not intend for us to know most of his sovereign will ahead of time (cf. Deut. 29:29). This is a reference to what he has revealed to us in Scripture: its commands and prohibitions. But there is also God's **will** for our lives when we face complex moral challenges and decisions to which Scripture does not explicitly speak. To have a mind renewed by the Holy Spirit and in tune with the truth of Scripture and its principles and values enables us to discern how God wants us to act in any and all circumstances.

Our Responsibility (12:3–8)

In what way should our minds be renewed? The question is fitting, given the connective term **for** (*gar*) that opens verse 3. Paul is likely providing us with specific ways in which our transformed lives are expressed. Paul focuses on one in particular in verse 3, specifically pride. To counter this tendency that all of us find in our hearts, Paul refers to "thinking" four times in verse 3. Here is a more literal rendering of the verse: "I say to everyone among you not to *think* of himself more highly than he ought to *think*, but to *think* with a view to sober *thinking*." **Think** in these four instances refers less to intellectual analysis and more to moral evaluation, specifically the way we assess ourselves in relation to others. We defeat pride by thinking deeply about the fact that who we are and what gifts we possess are both an expression of God's grace to us, an assertion Paul makes based on **the grace given** to him. He speaks of God having **distributed** a **measure** (*metron*) (ESV) of faith to all, suggesting that whereas all have been given **faith**, some receive more than others. The faith that God has given is itself subject to growth and increase (see 2 Thess. 1:3). If sinful pride is a threat to unity in the church, so too is false humility. If we can think too highly of ourselves, we can also underestimate and undervalue what we can and ought to do. Paul is not telling us not to think about ourselves at all; rather, he is telling us not to think beyond or below what God has imparted to us. Rather, we are to think soberly and honestly with sound judgment.

The church is a living, functioning, mutually interdependent **body** (see 1 Cor. 10:16–17; 12:12–27; Eph. 4:4, 12, 16; Col. 2:19; 3:15) in which **each member belongs to all the others** (v. 5). We cannot function as God intended apart from the mutual interplay of each member in the body. This unity is complemented by an obvious diversity insofar as **we have different gifts, according to the grace given to each of us** (v. 6). Spiritual gifts cannot be attributed to the moral excellence or performance or worth of human beings; rather, they are the product of the grace of God. This is made clear by noting the words Paul uses: the word **gifts** in verse 6 is *charismata*,[2] from which we get our word "charismatic." And the word for **grace** in verse 6 is *charin*. The point is that spiritual gifts, or *charismata*, are an expression of divine *charis*, or grace. Even Paul's apostolic calling and gift are an expression of God's grace and not a result of his personal accomplishments (see v. 3a).[3] The primary purpose of spiritual gifts is to edify others (cf. 1 Cor.

2. Of the seventeen occurrences of *charisma* in the New Testament, sixteen are in Paul (the other being 1 Pet. 4:10).
3. There is no reason to conclude that one receives at the moment of conversion all the gifts one will ever receive (see 1 Cor. 12:31; 14:1, 12, 13, 39; 1 Tim. 4:14; 2 Tim. 1:6).

12:7; 13:4–5; 14:12, 26), and yet we will invariably be edified and strengthened in the exercise of whatever gifts God has given to us (cf. 1 Cor. 14:4).

Prophecy (v. 6 ESV) is a gift designed to characterize the ministry of the church throughout the course of the present church age (see Acts 2:17–18; for texts indicating that the "last days" refer to the entire church age, see 2 Tim. 3:1;

Spiritual Gifts?

The viewpoint expressed by Gordon Fee in his book *God's Empowering Presence: The Holy Spirit in the Letters of Paul* should be noted. Fee questions whether *charismata* in Rom. 12:6–8 refers primarily to what we know as spiritual gifts. He explains,

> It is not at all plain that Paul intended everything that he calls [*charismata*] in 12:6b–8 to be understood as special gifts *of the Spirit*, at least in the same way that he expressly equates this term with the Spirit's manifestations in 1 Corinthians 12. The list in vv. 6b–8 is so heterogeneous and covers such a broad range of behavior, it seems far more likely that for Paul the emphasis lies on the "grace of God" here being worked out among them in concrete ways, rather than on the empowering of the Spirit for such behavior or on "Spirit gifting" as such. Thus the list includes items such as prophecy, teaching, and exhorting/encouraging, which in 1 Corinthians 12 come under the purview of Spirit [*charismata*], as well as various forms of serving others within the believing community (service, contributing to the needs of others, giving aid, and showing mercy), which are never elsewhere in Paul attributed directly to the Spirit as *his* gifts. These latter items move away from the idea of "gifts" per se, at least in terms of Spirit manifestations, to proper ethical behavior, in which the fruit of love finds concrete expression in their midst. That these are indeed the outworking of the Spirit in Pauline theology need not be doubted. What is doubtful is that our translation "gifts *of the Spirit*" is an adequate understanding of Pauline usage. While both enumerations are called [*charismata*], only that in 1 Cor 12:8–10 is tied specifically by Paul himself to the activities of the Spirit in the community.[a]

In other words, according to Fee, "these are concrete expressions of the grace of God at work in the life of individuals for the sake of others; but for him they would not be 'Spiritual gifts,' but *gifts of God* which are *effectively brought into the life of the community by the Spirit*."[b]

a. Fee, *God's Empowering Presence*, 34–35.
b. Fee, *God's Empowering Presence*, 607.

Heb. 1:1–2; 9:26; James 5:3; 1 Pet. 1:20; 1 John 2:18; cf. also 1 Cor. 10:11; 1 Tim. 4:1). Prophecy is the speaking forth in human words something that the Holy Spirit has spontaneously revealed or brought to mind (1 Cor. 14:29–30). Prophecy is not based on personal insight, intuition, or illumination. Prophecy is the human report of a divine revelation. This is what distinguishes prophecy from teaching. Teaching is always based on a text of Scripture. Prophecy is always based on a spontaneous revelation. Prophecy is to be exercised **in proportion to our faith** (v. 6 ESV). The possessive pronoun **our** is not in the Greek text. More literally, Paul refers to "the faith." But the NIV and ESV are correct in identifying this **faith** as the personal faith of the prophet. Thus, there will always be greater and lesser degrees of prophetic ability and consequently greater and lesser degrees of prophetic accuracy (which, it seems reasonable to assume, may increase or decrease, depending on the circumstances of the person's life, over time). Thus, the prophet is to speak in proportion to the confidence and assurance they have that what they say is truly of God. They are not to speak beyond what God has revealed. They must be careful never to speak on their own authority or from their own resources.

Others have argued that "the faith" (*hē pistis*) in verse 6 refers to those objective truths embodied in the gospel tradition. Thomas Gillespie appeals to three other Pauline texts in which he believes that *pistis* with the definite article points to the content of faith (although Rom. 10:8 is questionable). He concludes, "Together Galatians 1:23, Romans 10:8, and Philippians 1:27 suggest that when Paul uses *hē pistis* to denote the content of Christian belief, he has in mind the substance and structure of the gospel. This means that in Romans 12:6b prophecy is (1) drawn into the orbit of gospel proclamation, and (2) subjected to the standard provided by the content of this message."[4] However, if this were Paul's meaning, it would be an exceptionally rare usage of *pistis*.

Elsewhere, Paul expresses his desire that all would prophesy (1 Cor. 14:5) because "the one who prophesies edifies the church" (1 Cor. 14:4). In two other texts he seems to envision the possibility that any Christian might speak prophetically (1 Cor. 14:24, 31). But again, we shouldn't conclude from this that everyone will. Paul is drawing a distinction between, on the one hand, "prophets" who consistently display a facility and accuracy in this gift and, on the other, those who merely on occasion "prophesy." Thus, not all will be "prophets" (cf. 1 Cor. 12:29; Eph. 4:11), but it would appear that all may prophesy.

Serving (v. 7) is the translation of the common term for "ministry" (*diakonia*), which could conceivably be a reference to any or all manner of giving of oneself for the benefit of others. Some believe that it has reference to

4. Gillespie, *The First Theologians*, 61.

The Spiritual Gift of Prophecy

Prophetic ministry was a prominent feature in the early church and remains a vibrant expression of spiritual life in the contemporary charismatic world. Prophets, such as Agabus (Acts 11:28), were present in Antioch (Acts 13:1), Tyre (Acts 21:3-4), Caesarea (Acts 21:8-9), Rome (Rom. 12:6), Corinth (1 Cor. 12:7-11; 14:1-40), Ephesus (Eph. 2:20; Acts 19:1-7; 1 Tim. 1:18), and Thessalonica (1 Thess. 5:19-22).

Prophecy is a spiritual gift exercised by women, no less so than by men (see Acts 2:17-18; 21:9; 1 Cor. 11:5), and is primarily intended to strengthen, encourage, and comfort other believers (1 Cor. 14:3). Unlike prophecy in the old covenant (see Deut. 13:2; 18:20-22), prophecy in the new covenant is to be carefully "weighed" (1 Cor. 14:29), "tested" (1 Thess. 5:21a), or judged to determine what is "good" and "evil" (1 Thess. 5:21b-22), and it is always subordinate in authority to that of the apostles (1 Cor. 14:37-38).

Paul exhorts all Christians to "eagerly desire" prophecy (1 Cor. 14:1) insofar as this spiritual gift "edifies the church" (1 Cor. 14:4). The Spirit uses prophecy to bring conviction of sin to unbelievers by exposing "the secrets of their hearts" (1 Cor. 14:24-25). Paul warns against treating prophecies "with contempt" (1 Thess. 5:20), as all can learn from prophetic utterances (1 Cor. 14:31). Prophecy may also serve as the means by which other gifts of the Spirit are imparted (1 Tim. 4:14), can provide direction for ministry (Acts 13:1-3), on occasion is the way in which the Spirit warns believers of impending danger (Acts 21:4, 10-14), and is one of many means by which the believer is empowered to wage war against the world, the flesh, and the devil (1 Tim. 1:18-19).

In the corporate gathering of the church, at most "two or three prophets should speak and the others should weigh carefully what is said" (1 Cor. 14:29). The prophetic gift is not ecstatic, nor do those prophesying lose control of their speech (1 Cor. 14:32). Prophecy, like all spiritual gifts and ministry in the corporate assembly, reflects God's desire for peace (1 Cor. 14:33) and must be submissive to apostolic authority (1 Cor. 14:36-38).

Contrary to the belief of contemporary cessationists, there is nothing in the teaching of the New Testament or in the nature of the prophetic gift to suggest that this gift was restricted to the early church and subsequently ceased to be bestowed by the Holy Spirit. It is designed by God to characterize the experience of the church throughout the course of the church age (Acts 2:17-18).

Helen Collins identifies five characteristics of the gift of prophecy as described in 1 Cor. 14 and Rom. 12. First, "prophecy is *comprehensible*" in that Paul sees prophecy as "rational, intelligible, spoken utterance." Second, "prophecy is *inspired*" insofar as in 1 Cor. 14:30 "Paul implies that prophecy can be given spontaneously and unexpectedly." Third, "prophecy is *specific*" in that it "relates in a particular way to the context and to gathered listeners, to function for them as encouragement, consolation, or building up (1 Cor. 14:3)." Fourth, "prophecy is *revelation*." "In this way, prophecy as a sign of God's presence [1 Cor. 14:22] particularly enacts and reinforces a sense of expectancy." Finally, "prophecy is *corporately affirmed* . . . through the discernment of the church in validating and confirming it to be such." Thus, "while all the gifts fuel a sense of expectancy by their very possibility, the gift of prophecy particularly embodies this, because it concerns God's direct address to God's people. Through prophecy, there is always an innovative word, a new direction, a fresh guidance from God for here and now, that is ever dynamic and new, reinforcing the anticipation of a genuine two-way relationship of speaking and listening."[a]

a. Collins, *Charismatic Christianity*, 26–29.

providing financial or material assistance to those in dire need. Paul may have in mind the office of deacon. Peter likely has in view this same gift when he speaks of serving "with the strength God provides" (1 Pet. 4:11). Those with the gift of serving see a need, a weakness, a person in crisis, or a task that calls for immediate action and instantly feel an impulse from the Spirit to step in and devote their energies to helping bring resolution. They typically stay out of the limelight on purpose, preferring to labor anonymously for the sake of those in the body of Christ.

Teaching (v. 7), as over against prophecy, entails the explanation of tradition that is already written, most likely the Old Testament Scriptures and the words and works of Jesus. It may also include whatever New Testament Scripture was already penned and had been recognized as inspired (see 2 Pet. 3:15–16). Paul encouraged Timothy to devote himself to other faithful men "who will also be qualified to teach others" (2 Tim. 2:2; cf. 2 Tim. 3:10; Titus 2:1). All elders must be "able to teach" (1 Tim. 3:2; cf. Titus 1:9). Women, as well as men, may receive and utilize this gift (Titus 2:3). Those with this gift are capable of understanding and articulating biblical truth and defending it against the inroads of theological error. A teacher will love to study and is, in most cases, reasonably articulate, at least to the degree that others can follow their instruction and are persuaded of the truth they communicate.

The gift of **encouragement** (v. 8) is often linked with teaching (1 Tim. 4:13), but here Paul probably emphasizes the application of truths communicated in teaching or the passionate urging and encouraging of people to live out what they know to be true. The Greek word used here, *paraklēsis*, may even include the idea of appeal, in which truths that are taught are communicated in such a way that a person is called into action and encouraged to apply biblical doctrine in practical ways.

As for **giving**, it is to be done **generously** (*haplotēs*), although the Greek word used here can also mean "simplicity." If the latter is in view, Paul would have in mind a person who is careful that their motivation is single and spiritual, altogether for the glory of God and the good of the person(s) to whom their giving is directed, as well as devoid of any desire to gain influence or secure power in the church or put people in their debt (see Matt. 6:2–4). On the other hand, generosity is in view when the word is used in 2 Cor. 8:2; 9:11, 13.

The one who is to **lead** exercises administrative oversight (see 1 Thess. 5:12; 1 Tim. 3:4, 5, 12; 5:17). This should be carried out with diligence, not laziness. Since Paul does not specify over whom or what one would lead, we should not restrict this gift to those who are elders or pastors. Although elders in the local church assuredly lead (see 1 Thess. 5:12; 1 Tim. 5:17), one need not be an elder in order to possess and faithfully and fruitfully exercise this gift.

The gift of **mercy** finds expression in any number of contexts but probably has in view ministry to the sick or those who are discouraged and depressed, perhaps even suffering economic hardship. Those with this gift typically are deeply compassionate and empathize with those who are suffering. Paul encourages them to fulfill this ministry with **cheerfulness** (*hilarotēs*) (ESV), a word closely related to the one he employs in 2 Cor. 9:7 (*hilaros*, "cheerful") to emphasize the proper attitude in financial stewardship. One must display mercy joyfully, not begrudgingly or reluctantly, as if one were discharging a debt or acting solely from a sense of moral duty.

Our Relationships (12:9–16)

Here Paul describes how Christians are to love one another, together with numerous other Christian duties that we should embrace because of the mercy shown to us in Jesus (12:1). Loving one another—together with godly, Christ-exalting living in general—is an expression of what it means to present our bodies as living sacrifices to God. He mentions no fewer than nineteen expressions of true love and "proper worship" (v. 1). In other words, what we read in verses 9–16 are precisely the ways in which our worship is "holy and pleasing to God" (v. 1). There is no outline to follow and no discernible reason why Paul lists these in the order that he does.

(1) **Love must be sincere** (v. 9a).[5] There is no verb in the Greek text. It simply reads, "sincere love." The word **sincere** or **genuine** (ESV) translates the Greek word *anypokritos* (*an* [alpha privative] + *hypokrisis* [from which we get our word "hypocrisy"]). It literally means "lacking or devoid of hypocrisy." The noun *hypokritēs* was used of an actor who played a part on the stage. Since actors in the ancient world often wore masks, the word came to suggest someone who wears a mask to hide their true feelings and thoughts, all the while putting on an outward show. Thus "hypocrisy" referred to someone who acts like or pretends to be something or someone that in reality they are not.

(2) **Hate what is evil** (v. 9b). Paul follows his command concerning "love" with an exhortation to **hate**. If one loves what is good and true, he will **hate** or abhor what is evil and false.

(3) **Cling to what is good** (v. 9c). If we are to abhor what is evil, we are also expected to **cling** to what is good. Biblical love discriminates between what is evil and what is good. Love must fasten itself on the things worth loving.

(4) **Love one another with brotherly affection** (v. 10a ESV). Here the word **affection** translates the Greek term *philadelphia*. This word referred to family affection, the passion one has for one's own kin, one's own flesh and blood. Paul's point is that our love for other Christians in the body of Christ is to be more passionate and sacrificial than even the love we have for our own unbelieving, physical family members.

(5) **Honor one another above yourselves** (v. 10b; cf. Phil. 2:3). If there is to be a competitive spirit in the local church, let it be seen in the race to show honor to others more than they show it to you. Display to them by your words and deeds that they are worthy of your service, devotion, and praise.

(6) **Never be lacking in zeal** (v. 11a) and (7) **Keep your spiritual fervor** (11b; **be fervent in spirit** [ESV]) are similar in force and should be paired. The verb translated as "fervent" literally means "boil" or "seethe" (cf. Acts 18:25). Both the NIV and the ESV believe that this is a reference to our human spirit and that the point is that it isn't enough to discharge one's duty without feeling passionately for the things God approves. It is more likely that the word **spirit** here is a reference to the Holy Spirit, especially given the parallel reference to the **Lord** at the end of the verse. Paul's point is that we must be diligent and fervent

5. The sheer magnitude of the frequency of the terminology of love in the New Testament alone bears witness to its importance. The verb *agapaō*, "love," appears 130 times; the noun *agapē*, "love," 116 times; the adjective *agapētos*, "beloved," 62 times. That comes to more than 300 instances in which true, biblical love in some form or other is mentioned in the New Testament. Of these, 132 are in the letters of Paul.

to allow the Holy Spirit to set us on fire. We must remove all obstacles that keep the Spirit in check, and we must avail ourselves of every means possible so that he might work powerfully in and through us. Labor and pray and strive so that the Spirit might burn constantly in your heart and life.

(8) We should be **serving the Lord** (v. 11c). In doing so, we must never think that God needs something from us, as if he were deficient in some way and we supply him with what he lacks (see esp. Acts 17:24–25). Thus, as Peter says, "If anyone serves, they should do so with the strength God provides" (1 Pet. 4:11; see also Rom. 15:18; Col. 1:28–29). Serving the Lord must always flow out of and be in complete dependence upon God and his grace and strength and the power of the Holy Spirit.

(9) **Be joyful in hope** (v. 12a). Biblical hope is a robust confidence in the certainty of God's promises. It is a lively and vigorous knowing that God will never fail to do what he has promised. In Rom. 5:2 Paul said that "we boast in the hope of the glory of God." The focus of our hope, the aim of our hearts, is that when the end comes, we will see and enjoy and be enthralled forever in the glory of God. The dative case of **hope** is ambiguous. Is it by means of hope or because of hope that we rejoice? Probably the latter.

(10) We are to be **patient in affliction** (v. 12b). Tribulation and trial are as much a part of daily Christian living as are loving one another and serving the Lord. We mustn't bristle or become bitter when hardships come, but rather display patience, confident that God is working all things together for our good (Rom. 8:28). As Paul said in 5:3–4, we can do more than merely patiently endure afflictions; we can also "glory in our sufferings, because we know that suffering produces perseverance; perseverance, character; and character, hope."

(11) We are to be **faithful in prayer** (v. 12c). The word **faithful** or **constant** (ESV) is the opposite of "random, occasional, sporadic, intermittent." Prayer must be a regular and consistent practice of the Christian life. The word **faithful** is often translated as **devoted** (ESV) when prayer is the focus (see Acts 1:14; 2:42; 6:4; Col. 4:2).

(12) **Share with the Lord's people who are in need** (v. 13a) or, literally, **contribute to the needs of the saints** (ESV). The word translated as **share** or **contribute** is the verbal form of the word typically rendered as "fellowship" or "communion." There is more to being a generous giver than merely contributing money. We are to be intimately joined with the saints in their need. We are to be fellowshipers or communers with those in need. Enter into the depth of their poverty and identify with them in such a way that your giving is joyful and generous.

(13) **Practice hospitality** (v. 13b). Literally, "pursue" (*diōkontes*) it. Go hard after it. Make whatever sacrifices are needed to make it happen. Paul's point is

that we are not merely to be hospitable when circumstances make it unavoidable. The idea here is of the energetic pursuit of opportunities to be hospitable.

(14) **Bless those who persecute you; bless and do not curse** (v. 14). See Matt. 5:44 and Luke 6:27–28. **You** is likely a scribal addition to the text, but the force of the exhortation is the same in either case. The command to **bless** is a present active imperative, which might be rendered as "*be continually blessing those who persecute you.*"

(15) **Rejoice with those who rejoice** (v. 15a), and (16) **mourn with those who mourn** (v. 15b). Experience proves that it is actually easier to weep and mourn with those who are hurting than it is to rejoice with those who rejoice. When we witness others flourish, grow, and succeed, our response is too often one of resentment or envy. We struggle to rejoice with those who rejoice because we are greedy and prideful. But both of these exhortations can be misunderstood and misapplied. We are not supposed to rejoice with those whose success came as a result of sin, nor should we commiserate with those whose suffering is the consequence of rebellion, idolatry, or immorality.

(17) **Live in harmony with one another** (v. 16a). Literally, "Think the same as one another" (see Rom. 15:5; 2 Cor. 13:11; Phil. 2:2; 4:2). This exhortation, like the previous two, is not unconditional or universal in its application. We can't live in harmony or be of the same mind with those who deny the resurrection of Jesus from the dead, or who persist in unrepentant theft or chronic adultery. But when it comes to those who by God's grace strive to live godly lives and embrace the truth of Scripture, we must make every effort to be unified and supportive and mutually encouraging.

(18) **Do not be proud, but be willing to associate with people of low position** (v. 16b). The latter phrase may be rendered as "lowly things," a reference to tasks, chores, or responsibilities in the church that bring us little if any recognition. The translation **people of low position** would refer to fellowshiping with the downcast, the disheartened, the socially outcast, the less educated, the less wealthy, those who have little opportunity to return the favor. In any case, arrogance has no place in the life of the Christian or in the church corporately. In fact, pride is the greatest enemy and obstacle to obeying all of these commands. The antidote to haughtiness or pride is found in 1 Cor. 4:7, where Paul asked the people in that local church, "For who makes you different from anyone else? What do you have that you did not receive? And if you did receive it, why do you boast as though you did not?"

(19) **Never be wise in your own sight** (v. 16c ESV). Nothing is so contrary to the previous eighteen exhortations as a self-inflated opinion of oneself. If there are to be no social aristocrats in the church, neither are there to be intellectual snobs.

Our Response to Evil (12:17–21)

In Rom. 12:17–21 Paul describes one particular characteristic of human nature that we all share, at least to some degree: the impulse to exact revenge on our enemies, the desire to get even. Many fail to recognize that Paul is here concerned solely with our private, individual relations with one another. He is not addressing the responsibility of the state or the police or the military or our courts of law. We must keep in our minds the differing responsibilities of the private and the public spheres of authority. The Bible often tells the individual to do something that it would never tell the state to do. Conversely, the state has rights and prerogatives and an authority that are expressly forbidden to the individual (see Rom. 13:1–7). In summary, we must be careful that we do not apply the principles of Rom. 12:17–21 to the government, or the principles of Rom. 13:1–7 to the individual. Each has its own sphere of authority, its own unique responsibilities. There are six exhortations that follow.

First, **Do not repay anyone evil for evil** (v. 17a [see virtually identical terminology in 1 Thess. 5:15; see also 1 Cor. 4:12–13; 1 Pet. 3:9; Prov. 20:22; 24:29]). The word for **evil** (*kakos*) refers to anything morally reprehensible. At first glance this may appear to be contrary to the *lex talionis* in Lev. 24:17–20. The point of this law was to ensure that punishment was proportionate to the offense. The penalty must fit the crime. The phrase "eye for an eye" was itself simply a formula. Rarely if ever was it literally applied. It meant only that compensation had to be appropriate to the loss incurred (see Num. 35:16–34). Furthermore, this particular law fell within the domain of public civil justice. It was not a law endorsing personal revenge. The intent of the law of retaliation was to undermine the personal vendetta. It was an instrument of the court, a means of satisfying the legal demands and penal sanctions of the state.

Second, **Be careful to do what is right in the eyes of everyone** (v. 17b). Christians are to take thought for and seek after in the sight of all people those things that the Bible says are good, even if others don't recognize them to be good. When Paul refers to what is **right** (*kalos*, which stands in obvious contrast with *kakos*, **evil**, in the first half of v. 17), he means the principles of God's Word. We are to be diligent to preserve our reputation and image in the sight of unbelievers as we stand firmly for the truths of Scripture, whether they recognize and agree with those truths or not.

Third, **If it is possible, as far as it depends on you, live at peace with everyone** (v. 18). The Word of God is both idealistic and realistic. Its idealism is seen in the exhortation to **live at peace with everyone**. Its realism is seen when Paul adds the phrase **if it is possible**. The latter does not refer to an inability arising from our weakness. The impossibility here is not subjective, in ourselves, but objective, in others. There are at least two instances in which we may not be able to be at peace with all people. The first is when the spirit or temperament of the other person makes it impossible. Sometimes it simply isn't possible to be at peace with them because *they* refuse to be at peace with us. This is the force of the phrase **as far as it depends on you**. We can exercise restraint. We can control ourselves. We can do things that make for peace. So, if disharmony is to exist, be sure that it isn't *your* fault. The second factor that may make living peaceably with others impossible is when peace comes only at the expense of purity or truth. Where biblical truth is at stake, peace must be sacrificed. We are never permitted to be at peace with sin or falsehood.

Fourth, **Do not take revenge, my dear friends, but leave room for God's wrath, for it is written: "It is mine to avenge; I will repay," says the Lord** (v. 19 [the latter phrase is a reference to Deut. 32:35]). This exhortation is almost identical to the one in verse 17 but with the added command to **leave room for God's wrath**. The word **God's** is not in the original Greek text. This has led some to think that the wrath in view is ours. But the very point of the prohibition is that we are not to show anger or wrath in retaliation against our adversary. Some say that the **wrath** in view is the judicial wrath of the state as described in Rom. 13:1–7. But the second half of verse 19 would seem to indicate that the wrath is indeed **God's** wrath. Paul's point is that we should not seek to exact revenge or impose justice on our enemies, even if we are in the right and they are in the wrong, because God will see to it that justice is served. Permit him to exact his judgment and retribution as he sees fit and at the appropriate time.

Paul is not saying there will be no justice. He couldn't have been clearer in verse 19 when he says that God **will repay**. Either your adversary will repent in this life and trust Christ to be forgiven for the wrongs done against you and others, or your enemies' debt will be paid in hell. All wrongs will be punished. All sins will be judged. Either they are judged and punished in the person of your substitute, Jesus Christ, on the cross, or they are judged and punished in hell in the person who commits them (see Deut. 32:43; Isa. 59:17; Nah. 1:2).

Fifth, it isn't enough merely to refrain from retaliation or to control the impulse to get even. The Christian must take steps to do good to those who seek their harm. Says Paul, **On the contrary** [a rendering of the single connective term *alla*]: **If your enemy is hungry, feed him; if he is thirsty, give him something to drink. In doing this, you will heap burning coals on his head** (v. 20), a clear reference to Prov. 25:21–22. Some believe that the **burning coals** are a reference to divine wrath and judgment (see Pss. 11:6; 140:10). In other words, we are to act kindly to enemies, for in doing so we increase their guilt and magnify the punishment that they will ultimately endure at the hands of

God. Or perhaps Paul is simply describing the inevitable result of our kind deeds. But that seems to run counter to verse 21.

Perhaps the **burning coals** are a symbol of the irritation and aggravation that our enemy will experience when they see us respond to their evil with good? We might like to think so, but it seems unlikely. After all, isn't that just a roundabout way of getting even? Paul is likely describing the burning sense of shame and remorse that our enemy feels when they see how their evil has been met with kindness. Or the burning coals might be a metaphor for the melting down of their anger by the power of our mercy. There was an ancient Egyptian ritual in which a person gave public evidence of his repentance by carrying a pan of burning charcoal on his head. Could this be what Paul means? Whatever the case, Paul's point seems to be that the best way to handle an enemy is to transform them into a friend. When Jesus addressed himself to the problem of anger, he let it be known that suppressing your enmity was a bare minimum. It isn't enough just to control the outward display of your feelings, all the while permitting the spirit of alienation and animosity to fester secretly and out of sight in your soul (see Matt. 5:21–24, 44; Luke 6:27–31).

Sixth, in the form of antithetic parallelism, Paul tells us, **Do not be overcome by evil, but overcome evil with good** (v. 21). This is a short summation of everything he's said in verses 17–20. To be overcome by evil is to allow your enemy to get your goat. It is to allow them to cripple your joy in Jesus and your commitment to do good. It is to give them the power to induce worry, resentment, anger, and depression in you rather than the joy and peace of knowing that you are eternally forgiven in Christ. In telling us not to be overcome by evil, Paul means that we must guard our hearts lest we be enticed into retaliation and revenge. We are overcome by evil whenever we allow ourselves to justify ignoring the commands of verses 17–21 by reminding ourselves of how much harm an individual has caused us. It is to let the pain of their persecution triumph over the peace and freedom and joy of knowing that we are fully and eternally forgiven.

The Christian and Government

Obeying the Law of the Land (13:1–7)

It is possible that Paul takes up the theme of the authority of the state and our responsibility to submit to it because of his comment in Rom. 12:2 that we should not be conformed to this present age. Some might have drawn the unwarranted conclusion from that text that Christians should always stand in an adversarial relationship with the state. Peter likely faced the same challenge. Some might appeal to the fact that Christians are aliens and exiles on earth (1 Pet. 2:11) to justify their disobedience to the governing authorities. Yes, we are citizens of heaven (Phil. 3:20) and, consequently, must always put on display the counter-cultural nature of our lives. But we must be careful not to provoke unnecessary conflict between the earthly, secular state and the Christian church.

Paul makes several important assertions. First, **There is no authority except that which God has established. The authorities that exist have been established by God** (v. 1). Paul essentially repeats this point in verses 4 and 6. Earlier, in Rom. 9:17, Paul said that God "raised up" Pharaoh and invested him with power in Egypt, even though Pharaoh was evil and oppressive. Jeroboam was one of the most wicked kings of Israel, and 1 Kings 12:15 explains how he came to power: "This turn of events was from the LORD." Daniel was speaking to the wicked Babylonian king Nebuchadnezzar when he said that God "deposes kings and raises up others" (Dan. 2:21). Again, Daniel described Nebuchadnezzar as "the king of kings" to whom God had given "dominion and power and might and glory" (Dan. 2:37). He later rebuked Nebuchadnezzar for his failure to recognize that "the Most High is sovereign over all kingdoms on earth and gives them to anyone he wishes" (Dan. 4:25). When Jesus stood before Pontius

Pilate, he said, "You would have no power over me if it were not given to you from above" (John 19:11).

This is why even unbelieving pagans in power are called **God's servants** (Rom. 13:4, 6). This term describes a function, not a personal relationship to God. God referred to the pagan king Cyrus as "his anointed," raised up to serve a specific purpose (Isa. 45:1). Clearly, then, neither the state nor governmental authority per se is evil. But the possibility still exists for a government or a ruler to do evil things. This does not mean that God himself is personally responsible for the evil that such wicked rulers commit. They alone will be held accountable for the way in which they have wielded the authority given to them by God.

Second, because all governmental authority comes from God, all Christians are to live in subjection to it. **Let everyone be subject to the governing authorities** (v. 1). Again, in verse 5, **It is necessary to submit to the authorities** (cf. 1 Pet. 2:13–14). This language raises important questions: What is our responsibility when the state or government rewards those who do evil and punishes those who do good? What happens when the state does precisely the opposite of the purpose for which God raises it up? Paul doesn't explicitly answer those questions, but other texts in both the Old and New Testaments will demonstrate that our submission or subjection to civil authority is not necessarily absolute and unqualified, as if there were no circumstances that might yield exceptions.

Third, because all governmental authority comes from God, to resist it is to resist him (v. 2). Insofar as the state is God's minister, having been appointed by God, a crime against the state is a sin against God. And this sort of sin, depending on its severity, incurs God's judgment. In verse 4 Paul refers to this judgment as an expression of God's **wrath** (v. 4b). But there may be exceptions to that principle, as in those cases where one must commit a crime in order to obey God (see Acts 4:18–20; 5:27–29). The avoidance of God's judgment is only one reason why we should obey the government. It is also **for the sake of conscience** (v. 5 ESV). We have a responsibility to obey God irrespective of the consequences of our behavior. Our obedience is a matter of principle and not mere pragmatism.

Fourth, the purpose of government is twofold: to promote and praise what is good, and to prohibit and punish whatever is evil (vv. 3–4). The primary purpose of civil government is public morality, justice, and the punishment of the offender. It is not the purpose of the state to promote the gospel. That is the purpose of the church. However, it is the purpose of the state to provide a legal and moral atmosphere in which the church can do its work (see 1 Tim. 2:1–2).

In Rom. 12:17–21 Paul argued that we as individuals in our interpersonal relationships with other individuals are forbidden from avenging ourselves (v. 19a). But now, in 13:4, Paul describes the civil authority as **God's servants,**

Ethical and Social Justice: Capital Punishment?

Many Christians believe the death penalty to be manifestly unjust and cruel regardless of the crime committed. Supporters of capital punishment typically appeal to Gen. 9:5–6, Exod. 21:12, and Acts 25:11, where the apostle Paul appears to acknowledge that some crimes are worthy of death, and that if he were guilty of such, he would offer no protest to suffering the maximum penalty. In order to carry out the function of the state expressed in Rom. 13:3–4, God has invested the governing authority with the power to inflict punishment. The word "sword" in verse 4 is *machaira*, which is often used of the instrument that people use to kill others (see Luke 21:24; Acts 12:2; 16:27; Heb. 11:37; Rev. 13:10; and esp. Rom. 8:35). The Septuagint also uses this word in the same way in Deut. 13:15; 20:13. The sword is not merely a sign or symbol of the state's authority to enforce its laws, but is also a power to execute.

agents of wrath to bring punishment on the wrongdoer. Clearly, then, what we are forbidden from doing as individuals, God has ordained and authorized the government to do. Confirmation is found in the fact that the verb *ekdikeō* ("avenge") in 12:19 is directly related to the noun *ekdikos* ("avenger") in 13:4.

Fifth, it is the right of government to levy taxes and the obligation of its citizens to pay them (vv. 6–7). **This** (v. 6a) to which the government gives its attention is the collection of taxes. And they do so as **God's servants**. The word translated as **taxes** in verse 7 refers to what is levied on persons and property. The word translated as **revenue** refers to levies on imported and exported goods. But observe that it isn't enough for us merely to pay our taxes. We must also show the respect and honor due to those men and women for fulfilling their God-ordained responsibilities. The **respect** and **honor** here refer primarily to the attitude we should have toward those who serve as servants of God in collecting legitimate taxes.

Neither Paul nor any other biblical author endorses a particular form of government. Paul lived under a Roman dictator and knew nothing of democracy. Irrespective of the precise form of government, are Christians ever free to publicly criticize their elected officials? Yes, as we see in Prov. 16:12; Isa. 10:1–2. Daniel twice rebuked the kings of Babylon (Dan. 4:27; 5:22–23). John the Baptist referred to King Herod as a "fox" (Luke 13:32) and rebuked him for carrying on an adulterous affair with his brother's wife (Mark 6:18).

Neither the authority given to the state nor the obligation of the Christian to obey it is absolute and unqualified. Although Nero was in power when Paul wrote Romans (AD 56), the first five years of his reign were known for their enlightenment, justice, and equity. Under what conditions should a Christian disobey the governing authorities? It would appear that when the state prohibits us from doing what the Bible commands, or commands us to do what the Bible forbids, we are justified in disobeying. Consider the example of the Israelite midwives in Exod. 1:17, 20–21, as well as the way in which Shadrach, Meshach, and Abednego defied Nebuchadnezzar's order that all bow down before the golden image erected in his honor (Dan. 3:16–18). Daniel himself disobeyed the decree of King Darius that forbade praying to any other god (Dan. 6:10). And Peter and John defied the command that they not speak to anyone in the name of Jesus (Acts 4:19–20). Their response was unambiguous: "We must obey God rather than human beings!" (Acts 5:29).

The Law of Love (13:8–10)

The NIV rendering of verse 8a, **Let no debt remain outstanding**, is, more literally, **Owe no one anything** (ESV). Does this text, together with others, rule out all borrowing, whether in the form of a mortgage for a house, a loan for a car, or a neighbor's lawn mower? No, but there are texts that put borrowing in a bad light (see Deut. 28:12; Prov. 22:7). Clearly, it is good to be in a position where you do not have to borrow. But does that mean that *all* borrowing is unwise or unbiblical? If we were to take Rom. 13:8 as absolute and unqualified, it would put us in conflict with texts that instruct us on how to lend (see esp. Pss. 37:26; 112:5; Matt 5:42; cf. Exod. 22:25; Deut. 28:12; 23:19). After all, if you lend, you become complicit in someone's borrowing.

Romans 13:7 appears to say that it is right to "owe" taxes, revenue, respect, and so on, provided that we "pay" what is owed. If you incur a debt, pay it. The biblical warnings about the dangers of debt describe what *may* happen but not necessarily what *must* happen. Proverbs 22:7 is warning us to avoid the kind of poverty that forces us into dependence on the rich. Does borrowing put you at any undue risk? Is the asset that you borrow to buy always there to be sold to repay the loan? There are also several texts that condone and regulate lending and borrowing. In the parable of the talents, the master rebukes the servant who squandered his one talent: "You should have put my money on deposit with the bankers, so that when I returned I would have received it back with interest"

(Matt. 25:27). If it were wrong to invest money with banks that pay interest and make loans to earn the money to pay the interest, it is unlikely that Jesus would have employed this illustration. In Deut. 15:7–8 Moses commands those who are wealthy to "freely lend them [impoverished fellow Israelites] whatever they need" (see Deut. 24:10; Exod. 22:14; 2 Kings 4:3).

The debt of love can never be fully discharged (Rom. 13:8). Love is a perpetual debt that all of us owe. In fact, love is the way that obedience to God's law is **fulfilled**. Paul confirms this by citing the sixth, seventh, eighth, and tenth commandments from the law of Moses. If you truly love your brother or sister in Christ, you will never violate any of these commands, or any of the others as well, because **love does no harm to a neighbor** (v. 10).

The command **Love your neighbor as yourself** (v. 9 [cf. Matt. 22:36–40]) has been misunderstood. Jesus does not command us to love ourselves, for this is something we do instinctively. The point of Paul (quoting Jesus) is that the believer should take note of the energy, zeal, and passion that one has for the welfare and happiness of one's own soul and let that be the measure of how much one loves others. Paul's command is to love your neighbor as much as, to the same degree that, you do, in fact, love yourself. Neither Jesus nor Paul is calling for self-love. They both simply assume that it already exists. Self-love is not sinful. Selfishness is. To be selfish is to love oneself without any regard for others, seeing them only as a means to obtain something for oneself. But when we love someone with the same energy with which we love ourselves, it is good and godly.

But how is love a debt? The answer is found in the fact that God first loved us in Christ Jesus. We have received grace from him instead of judgment, forgiveness of sins instead of punishment. We are indebted to others, to love them, not because they have done something for us but because Jesus has. The apostle John puts it this way: "Jesus Christ laid down his life for us. And we ought [we are indebted] to lay down our lives for our brothers and sisters" (1 John 3:16). Again, "Since God so loved us, we also ought [we are indebted] to love one another" (1 John 4:11).

The Urgency of the Time (13:11–14)

The opening words of verse 11, translated by the ESV as **besides this**, are a bit misleading. I prefer the more literal translation, "and this." We probably should include the exhortation "do," such as we find in the NIV: **and do this**. The word **this** directs our attention back to all that Paul has said beginning in 12:1. His point is that since we are aware of the **time**, we should put into practice all that he has just said, especially in the way we are to love one another.

But what are **the present time** and **the hour** that have come? Clearly, it is a **time** for waking up from spiritual slumber. He says in verse 12 that **the night is far gone; the day is at hand** (ESV). Paul uses the imagery of night and day to describe the two ages. The present age is, as it were, the night, during which works of darkness are committed. The future age, the age when the kingdom of God will come in its consummate and final expression, when all sin and sickness and death will be forever banished, is, as it were, the daytime. What makes this so instructive is that the New Testament consistently describes the future age as having broken into the present. The glorious consummation yet to come has already reached back into the present time. Thus, we live in the overlap between this present dark age, the night, and the future age of glory and light, the day. As one commentator has put it, "The Christian lives between the time when sin and darkness reign and the time when the light of Christ rules completely. If we are sleepy and complacent, it is time to wake up, lest we relapse in the life of darkness (Rom. 1:21)."[1]

This means that **our salvation is nearer now than when we first believed** (v. 11). By **salvation** Paul has in view the day when Christ returns and we experience final resurrection and the glorification of our bodies. Paul's point is that with each passing day we are coming ever closer to that moment when Christ will return and we will be transformed to be made like him (Phil. 3:20–21). So, **wake up from your slumber**. Resist the temptation to be conformed to the beliefs, values, and behavior of this present dark age (cf. Rom. 12:1–2). **Put aside the deeds of darkness and put on the armor of light** (v. 12). Walk in the light of the day that has dawned with the coming of Christ and his defeat of the powers of this present age. When Paul says in verse 12 that **the night is far gone** (ESV), he means "that the reign of evil has almost expired and is in its last gasp."[2] In saying that **the day is at hand** (ESV), he means that the light of the kingdom of God has broken into our world with the coming of Jesus Christ. In light of this truth believers should live accordingly and stop walking in the darkness of dead works (cf. 1 Thess. 5:4–8). Moral licentiousness and laxity are fitting for those who live in the night—that is, who live under the power and influence of evil. That sort of spiritual laziness is altogether inappropriate for Christians because we are children of the day and children of the light.

But it's not enough to wake up. We must also get dressed! **Put on the Lord Jesus Christ** (v. 14a ESV) as if he were a garment in which you are attired and covered and enshrouded (cf. Gal. 3:27). Christians must **behave decently, as in the daytime, not in carousing and drunkenness, not in sexual immorality**

---

1. Doriani, *Romans*, 474.
2. Schreiner, *Romans*, 678.

Spiritual Warfare: Adorning Ourselves with the "Armor of Light"

The urgent need for us all to "put on the armor [hoplon] of light" (Rom. 13:12b) is reminiscent of Paul's appeal in Ephesians that we "put on the full armor [panoplia] of God," so that we can take our "stand against the devil's schemes" (Eph. 6:11). Although the Greek words for "armor" are different in these two texts, they are lexically related and convey much the same idea. The imagery of armor may have come from the apostle Paul's observation of the Roman soldier to whom he was chained (Eph. 6:20; cf. Acts 28:16; Phil. 1:13). Others think that the imagery of a soldier fully arrayed in battle armor is taken from Isaiah (Isa. 11:4–5; 49:2; 59:17), who describes the armor of God and his Messiah. These texts portray the Lord of Hosts as a warrior dressed for battle as he prepares to fight on behalf of his people. Thus the "full armor" or the "armor of light" that Paul tells us to put on or with which we are to adorn ourselves is in fact God's own armor. And Paul's invitation is that we take it up and wear it even as God has worn it on our behalf. In other words, it is the armor of God not simply because he gives it but because he wears it.

The "armor of light" isn't something with which we are born. We must put it on. Also, once put on, the armor should never be taken off, even if we think hostilities have subsided. The armor is designed both to equip us to "behave decently" (Rom. 13:13) and to enable us to take our "stand against the devil's schemes" (Eph. 6:11; cf. vv. 13–14). The "deeds of darkness" (Rom. 13:12) flourish in "this dark world" (Eph. 6:12) and must be resisted by our clothing ourselves with Jesus Christ (Rom. 13:14) and the many spiritual resources that he supplies: truth and righteousness (Eph. 6:14), the gospel of peace (Eph. 6:15), faith and the assurance of salvation (Eph. 6:16–17), and the word of God (Eph. 6:17). Only in this way will we not "think about how to gratify the desires of the flesh" (Rom. 13:14).

In both Rom. 13 and Eph. 6 Paul is encouraging us that we are not helpless victims of Satan's power and purposes for this earth. By means of the "armor of light" God has graciously provided for us everything we need to resist and overcome Satan and his demons. In fact, when we employ God's resources and power, we are assured of victory over all Satan's schemes (Eph. 6:11).

and debauchery, not in dissension and jealousy (v. 13; cf. 1 Cor. 6:9–10; Gal. 5:19–21). Only in this way will you not **gratify the desires of the flesh** (i.e., make **no provision for the flesh** [ESV]) (v. 14b). Paul means that we must give no space or place in our lives to those images that awaken lust or those thoughts that give strength to sinful desires. Instead, we are to reflect and ruminate on being declared righteous by faith alone in Christ alone. Immerse your thoughts in the redemption and forgiveness that are yours in Jesus.

We must not overlook the order in which Paul places these commandments. Many fail to live in holiness because they think that they must first make no provision for the flesh if they are to be clothed with Christ. That approach breeds legalism and a religious spirit and is always destined to fail. It leads to self-righteousness, arrogance, and pride. The only way to fulfill the second command is by obeying the first: you put on Christ so that you will make no provision for the flesh. Walking in close, tight, intimate fellowship and communion with Jesus is the only way you will find strength to say no to every temptation to gratify your sinful desires. Paul knew that it was hopeless to try to resist fleshly urges apart from the strength that comes by clothing oneself in Jesus. It is from the place of strength and joy and hope that Jesus supplies us as we adorn ourselves with him so that we can then find victory over the flesh and its desires.

Christian Liberty and Love

Identifying the Weak and the Strong (14:1–3)

The person weak in faith is a vegetarian—**eats only vegetables** (v. 2; cf. v. 21). Vegetarianism for health reasons is not weakness. Paul is talking about persons who abstain from all meat because they believe that to eat meat is to fall or lapse in one's relationship with and commitment to Christ. Eating meat, they argue, is morally and spiritually dangerous. Also, the person weak in faith regards some days, probably Sabbaths, as "more sacred" (v. 5) than other days. Finally, the person whose faith is weak does not "drink wine" (or any other form of intoxicating beverage) (vv. 17, 21).

The weak believer, then, is the one who entertains scruples on secondary matters. This person has misgivings about the moral and spiritual propriety of such practices. The weak brother or sister is the one who has not sufficiently understood the freedom that Paul speaks of in 1 Tim. 4:4–5: "For everything God created is good, and nothing is to be rejected if it is received with thanksgiving, because it is consecrated by the word of God and prayer" (1 Tim. 4:4–5; see also Rom. 14:14; 1 Cor. 10:25–26). Weakness in faith, therefore, is a failure to understand the implications of the gospel in the area of practical freedom. The weak believer has failed to grasp the truth of 1 Cor. 8:8: "Food does not bring us near to God; we are no worse if we do not eat, and no better if we do" (cf. Mark 7:14–15).

The **weak** also fear that by partaking of certain foods and drink or participating in certain practices they will be spiritually infected in some way, and that partaking will weaken them in their walk and expose them to even greater evils. They likely believe that there is spiritual value or moral virtue in abstinence per se, that to deny oneself is inherently good and to indulge is inherently bad. Weak believers are more timid than others in the way they think God has called them to live. They are more inclined to yield to pressure from other believers and are frightened of being held in contempt by them.

But weakness is not synonymous with excess. The weak believer, so some have thought, is the one who can't restrain themselves or control their urges and desires and is given to overindulgence in matters such as eating and drinking. But "the weak of Romans 14," explains John Murray, "are not those given to excess. They are the opposite; they are total abstainers from certain articles of food."[1] Those who have a weakness that leads to excess or overindulgence are dealt with in completely other terms. Paul refers to such behavior as sin. Drunkards, for example, certainly have a weakness, one that Paul condemns (1 Cor. 6:10). But here in Rom. 14 he tells us to **accept** or welcome the one who is weak (v. 1). Weakness in Rom. 14 is not uncontrolled overindulgence but overly scrupulous abstinence.

Abstinence per se is not weakness. The decisive factor is one's motive for abstention. We also know from verses 5–6 that the weak are not legalists. Paul would never say that a legalist honors the Lord or by means of such legalism "gives thanks to God" (v. 6). Does a person abstain because they think it makes them more holy or closer to God than others? And do they seek to impose this practice on others and hold them in contempt if they don't comply? If so, they are legalists. So, whereas it is certainly possible for a weak Christian to fall into legalism, that is not primarily what Paul has in mind in Rom. 14.

The weak in Rome may well have been Jewish Christians who believed that they were still under obligation to observe the dietary laws of the old covenant and were required to observe the feasts and holy days described in Leviticus, such as the Sabbath. Support for this is found in Paul's use of the term *koinos* (v. 14), which means "unclean" (or "common"). This term "had become a semi-technical way of describing food prohibited under the Mosaic law (Mark 7:2, 5; Acts 10:14)."[2]

The strong are those who correctly perceive the truth of 1 Tim. 4:4–5 and Rom. 14:14a. Paul was strong (cf. 15:1). The strong are those who, by reason of their knowledge of God and grace, enjoy the full range of Christian liberty without being condemned in their conscience.

Paul encourages the strong in faith to **accept the one whose faith is weak** (v. 1). This refers both to recognition of the weak believer by the Christian community as a member of the body of Christ and to loving reception of them into the routines of Christian fellowship. Be sure that the weaker brother or sister is

---

1. Murray, *Romans*, 260.
2. Moo, *Romans*, 829–30.

not made to feel inferior or unwanted or odd. Though their scruples are held in error, it is not through callous disputes or being held in **contempt** (v. 3) that their weakness will be turned into strength.

Paul is also careful never to concede to the position of the weak as the correct one. He refuses to reduce the strong to the level of the weak, although he will call on the strong believers to curtail their liberty out of love. The weak, however, ought to grow strong. The way to make them strong is not to offend them but to love them. Moreover, the strong must not **treat with contempt** the weak (v. 3a). The tendency of the strong is to despise the weak as those not worthy of being taken seriously. But Paul rebukes the smile of disdainful contempt. To the weak, Paul says that they must not **judge** the strong (v. 3b). If the strong smile disdainfully and in a patronizing way at the weak, the weak frown with disapproval at the strong. The strong believe that the weak are legalistic and Pharisaical; the weak believe that the strong are dangerously loose and unprincipled. Both are to refrain from such judgments.

But how do we know that Paul is dealing with secondary issues—that is, those that play no part in our acceptance by God? First, according to verse 3, **God has accepted them**. If God does not make eating and drinking a condition for acceptance, neither should other Christians. Second, Paul's plea for tolerance also indicates that he is addressing matters not relevant to justification. He pleads for mutual acceptance. If anyone in the church at Rome had insisted that a particular custom must be observed in order for one to be saved, Paul would have severely denounced them, as he does in Gal. 1:6–10; 3:1–3; Col. 2:20, 23. Paul's tolerance and sympathetic gentleness in Rom. 14 are "strong support for the view that the weak were not abstaining from meat and observing days with the intention of earning thereby a status of righteousness before God . . . , but because they felt sincerely, albeit mistakenly, that it was only along this particular path that they could obediently express their response of faith to God's grace in Christ."[3]

Third, Paul's counsel in verse 5b that each "should be fully convinced in their own mind" indicates that he is addressing issues on which God has not spoken. He calls on each believer to evaluate, think, reason, and make up their own mind as to how they should behave. If one's eternal status before God were at stake, Paul would never have issued such advice.

Paul's Counsel to the Weak (14:4–12)

Beginning with verse 4 through verse 12, Paul speaks directly to the weak believer. Beginning in verse 13 and extending through verse 23, he will address the

3. Cranfield, *Romans*, 2:696.

strong. First, Paul tells the weak that they should not judge the strong because "God has accepted them" (v. 3b). It is wrong to pass judgment on the strong for the simple reason that God hasn't. If God has received the strong into fellowship, so too must the weak.

Second, the Christian has but one **master**, the Lord Jesus Christ (v. 4a). The conscience of a Christian is bound to none but Christ. In matters on which the Bible does not speak, we are answerable to none but God. For the weak to judge the strong on a matter of conscience is intrusive. Christ's **servants stand or fall** to him alone (v. 4). This standing or falling does not refer to the final judgment, as if one's salvation were in view. Rather, it refers to one's daily Christian walk,

BIBLICAL BACKGROUND

Are Romans 14 and 1 Corinthians 8–10 Addressing the Same Issue?

Some believe that Paul is addressing the same issue in both Rom. 14 and 1 Cor. 8–10. In Corinth, much of the meat being sold for consumption by the public had come from animals sacrificed or consecrated to pagan idols. Two groups emerged in the church in regard to the propriety of buying and eating such meat. One group, probably the majority, knew that "an idol is nothing at all in the world" (1 Cor. 8:4) and that the meat was neither better nor worse for its association with the pagan deity. Hence, they entertained no scruples about eating the meat. The other group, not possessing such knowledge, believed that to eat the meat was to participate in idolatry. They believed that the meat had somehow become infected by its association with pagan idolatry. Paul aligns himself with those who believed that the Christian was at liberty to eat meat of this sort. But he also knows that such knowledge is not preeminent—love is. And if their eating would motivate a weaker believer to eat in violation of their conscience, they should forgo their liberty and refrain.

Whereas the principles to which Paul appeals in resolving both problems appear to be similar, if not identical, the circumstances evoking the problem differ in three respects: (1) in Rom. 14 there is no mention of food or drink offered to idols; (2) the observance of days as special is in Rom. 14 but not in 1 Cor. 8–10; (3) the weakness in Rom. 14 involves a vegetarian diet—that is, a scrupulous attitude toward *all* meat—whereas in 1 Cor. 8–10 there is no reason to doubt that the weak would have eaten meat not offered to idols.

from which the weak brother or sister is sure that the strong brother or sister will stray because of their practice. Paul is confident that notwithstanding the dangers that the exercise of liberty may bring, it will in the final analysis prove to be a triumphant success. The strong will stand, **for the Lord is able to make them stand** (v. 4).

Third, the reason why neither party should judge the other is that both aim to serve and glorify God. Whether they eat or abstain, each **does so to the Lord** (v. 6). The purpose of both the strong and the weak in all they do is to **give thanks to God** (v. 6). Whether we live or die, we live or die **for the Lord** (vv. 7–8). Whether you hold one day of the week as being more holy than another or view them as equal, you do so to honor the Lord (v. 6). Whether you eat meat or not, whether you drink wine in moderation or not, you do so in gratitude to the Lord.

Fourth, **each** (v. 12), both the strong and the weak, **will give an account** of themselves **to God**, not to one another. The emphasis in verse 12 is on the word **each** (*hekastos*). How dare any Christian presume to exercise a judgment that is the prerogative of Christ alone? The certainty of judgment is seen in the way God grounds it in Paul's life (**As surely as I live** [v. 11a]). That **all** will **stand** before God and **every knee will bow** and **every tongue** confess points to the universality of judgment (vv. 10b–11; cf. Isa. 45:23). No one is exempt. **God's judgment seat** (v. 10), his *bēma* (as is true of "the judgment seat of Christ" [2 Cor. 5:10]), determines not entrance into the kingdom but rather the rewards that each will receive for Christ-exalting service (see 2 Cor. 5:8–10).

Paul's Counsel to the Strong (14:13–23)

Paul's point is that the liberty of the strong must be qualified by **love** (v. 15). But is the exhortation in verse 13a to **stop passing judgment on one another** directed to the strong or the weak, or both? Some say it is the weak Paul is addressing because in verses 1–12 judging was the fault of the weak (cf. vv. 3, 4, 10). But probably it is the strong Paul has in mind, and for three reasons: (1) in verses 10–12 both the strong and weak are rebuked for presuming to judge one another; (2) the antithesis of judging is being careful not to put a **stumbling block or obstacle** in a brother's or sister's path (v. 13b), something only the strong can do in relating to the weak; (3) verses 14–15 are intelligible only if it is the strong who are being addressed.

So, why does Paul place so much of the burden on the strong by asking them to curtail their liberty out of love, rather than ask the weak to change their convictions about what is permissible for a Christian to do? The reason is that the weak are bound by their conscience; there is no flexibility or freedom for them to adjust their behavior, for in doing so they would be violating what they sincerely believe is God's will. The strong, on the other hand, are at liberty in their conscience either to partake or to abstain. They know that it is of secondary importance, whereas the weak regard it as of primary moral significance. The former, therefore, are at greater liberty to bend than are the latter.

The **obstacle** and **stumbling block** refer, respectively, to something against which the foot strikes and a trap or snare in which the foot may be caught. Here the terms are used metaphorically and are synonymous. They refer to anything that becomes an occasion for falling into sin. Paul does not mean that the strong deliberately seduce the weak. He is speaking of the strong who, in the exercise of their liberty, fail to take into account the moral scruples of their weaker brothers and sisters and thus create an occasion for the latter to fall into sin.

Verse 14 reiterates 1 Tim. 4:4–5. Paul **is convinced** and **fully persuaded in the Lord Jesus, that nothing is unclean in itself** (v. 14; cf. Mark 7:19). This conviction has penetrated into his conscience and set him free from all perplexity. This is not merely Paul's preference but rather is a theological reality that admits of no exceptions. The weak argue that certain foods and drinks are intrinsically or inherently unclean and therefore are defiling to the believer. Paul's response is no, **nothing is unclean in itself** (see Mark 7:14–23; Acts 10:15, 28).

The key is the distinction in verse 14 between, on the one hand, what is objectively true and, on the other hand, one's subjective perception of that truth. Objectively, nothing is unclean **in itself**. But it may become unclean if one **regards** (v. 14) or believes it to be so (see 1 Cor. 8:4, 7). The knowledge of or faith in the objective cleanness of all food is not something that all possess. The strong understand this truth. The weak do not. Paul's point, then, is this: if partaking of what you correctly know to be clean causes your brother or sister to stumble because *to them* it is unclean, you are not walking according to love.

When the strong exercise their liberty without regard for the scruples of the weak, their **brother or sister is distressed** (v. 15a). Worse still, they may **destroy someone for whom Christ died** (v. 15b; cf. v. 20). This is more than the pain or annoyance that the weak believer feels on seeing a strong believer partake of food or drink that the weak believer sees as unclean and forbidden. Rather, Paul envisions a situation in which a strong Christian, in the exercise of their liberty, causes a weak Christian to sin. The weak believer sins when they are influenced by the strong believer's behavior to act contrary to their conscience. Paul envisions the grievous vexation of conscience that afflicts a believer when they violate what for them is the moral will of God. Paul's advice to the strong is simple: when the exercise of your legitimate liberty emboldens the weak to violate their conscience, you must, in love, defer to their interests and refrain from what would otherwise be permissible for you to do.

Paul's appeal to the death of Christ is powerful. Since Christ was willing to lay down his very life for your salvation, how can you possibly refuse to forgo a comparatively insignificant liberty for the sake of your fellow believer? It is the contrast between, on the one hand, the extreme and glorious sacrifice that Jesus made in dying for the weak person and, on the other hand, the strong believer's selfish insistence on exercising their freedom regardless of the spiritual interests of the weak brother or sister.

Some argue that the verb **destroy** refers to eternal death. But there are several reasons why this cannot be true. First, "Are we really to believe that a Christian brother's single act against his own conscience—which in any case is not his fault but the fault of the strong who have misled him, and which is therefore an unintentional mistake, not a deliberate disobedience—merits eternal condemnation? No, hell is reserved only for the stubborn, the impenitent, those who willfully persist in wrongdoing."[4] Second, Paul has already affirmed in unequivocal terms the security of the believer (Rom. 8:28–39; cf. John 10:28). If nothing in all creation can separate one from the love of Christ, then surely another believer's callous disregard for a weak brother's or sister's religious scruples cannot do so. Third, this cannot refer to eternal destruction because Jesus said that God alone destroys body and soul in hell (Matt. 10:28). Fourth, the context provides a perfectly reasonable explanation of Paul's words. He envisions serious damage both to the conscience of weak believers (cf. v. 15) and to their growth as disciples of Jesus. Judith Gundry-Volf identifies two forms of damage incurred by the weak: "a subjective form consisting in grief and deep self-deprecation, and an objective form consisting in concrete sin, resultant guilt and possible incapacitation to behave consistently with one's beliefs."[5] She adds, "None of Paul's descriptions of the negative consequences born by the weak when they follow the example of the strong—stumbling, sinning, sorrow, defiling and wounding of the conscience [cf. 1 Cor. 8:7], self-condemnation— necessarily entails loss of salvation or complete dissolution of a relationship to God."[6]

The destruction in view, therefore, presents an obstacle to one's sanctification, not to one's justification. That does not diminish the severity of abusing our liberty. Freedom is a **good** thing, but we must be diligent lest what we know **is good be spoken of as evil** (v. 16). The translation **be spoken of as evil** is the permissive passive of the verb that means "blaspheme" (*blasphēmeō*).

4. Stott, *Romans*, 365–66.
5. Gundry-Volf, *Paul and Perseverance*, 95.
6. Gundry-Volf, *Paul and Perseverance*, 95.

Christian liberty in secondary issues is a wonderful blessing to those who know Christ. At the same time, however, let us never reduce the kingdom to issues of eating and drinking. The kingdom is far more than that. The word **for** (*gar*) points

Is Sunday the Christian Sabbath?

How does Paul's statement in Rom. 14:5 impact our understanding of whether Sunday is the Christian Sabbath? Jesus responds to the accusation of the Pharisees that he and his disciples had profaned the Sabbath when they plucked heads of grain to satisfy their hunger (Matt. 12:1–2) by declaring that he is "Lord of the Sabbath" (12:8). In essence, Jesus is saying to them, "I am the fulfillment of all that David and the temple and the Sabbath typified. I bring to you a rest and satisfaction that not even the Old Testament Sabbath could provide."

The Sabbath was instituted by God as a sign of the old covenant with Israel (see Exod. 31:12–13, 16–17). However, as Paul makes clear in Col. 2:16–17, Jesus is the fulfillment of all that the Old Testament prophesied, prefigured, and foreshadowed. The physical rest provided by the Old Testament Sabbath finds its fulfillment in the spiritual rest provided by Jesus. We cease from our labors not by resting physically one day in seven but by resting spiritually every day and forever in Christ by faith alone. To experience God's Sabbath rest, therefore, is to cease from those works of righteousness by which we were seeking to be justified. The New Testament fulfillment of the Old Testament Sabbath is not one day in seven of physical rest but an eternity of spiritual rest through faith in the work of Christ.

Of course, God does not intend for us to work seven days a week. Our bodies and spirits need to experience renewal and refreshment by resting. But resting on Sunday is not the same thing as the Old Testament observance of the Sabbath day. Some Christians have chosen to treat Sunday as if it were a Sabbath, as if it were special, and that's entirely permissible. But you must not tell anyone that it is wrong if they treat "every day alike" (Rom. 14:5).

For Christians who are trusting in the work of Jesus Christ rather than in their own efforts, for those resting by faith in Jesus, every day is the Sabbath! Every day is a celebration of the fact that we don't have to do any spiritual or physical works to gain acceptance by God. We are accepted by him through faith in the works of Jesus Christ.

to verse 17 as support for the advice given in verses 15–16. The kingdom is primarily about **righteousness** and **peace** (between the strong and the weak) and **joy in the Holy Spirit** (v. 17). The **righteousness** here probably is ethical, daily right living in the community of faith. The essential character of God's kingdom, which attests to its presence in the hearts of believing men and women, is the absence of a demand that we always be granted our freedom, regardless of how it may affect others. The kingdom is not about eating or drinking. Nor is the kingdom about not eating and not drinking. When matters of food and drink and observing some days as more holy than others become our chief concern rather than righteousness and peace and joy in the Spirit, it points to how far removed we are from the interests of God's kingdom.

Paul concludes that **anyone who serves Christ in this way is pleasing to God and receives human approval** (v. 18), and that we should strive **to do what leads to peace and to mutual edification** (v. 19). God is pleased with the person who thinks more highly of the spiritual welfare and building up of their weak brother or sister than they do of their own liberty in such matters.

Once again, in verse 20, Paul affirms the principle that everything **is clean**. As noted earlier, he probably has in mind the dietary restrictions of the old covenant (cf. Mark 7:19; Acts 10:15). **But it is wrong for a person to eat anything that causes someone else to stumble** (v. 20). Christian liberty is a good thing. It simply isn't the best thing. If your exercise of freedom entices a weak believer to violate his or her conscience, you are not acting in love. Verse 21 is an authoritative declaration designed to summarize the principle outlined in verses 13–20. The unselfish action of the strong brother or sister who, although possessing liberty, forgoes such out of loving deference to their weaker brother or sister is better than eating and drinking.

Perhaps some were abstaining from wine (v. 21) because wine is potentially intoxicating, and they had seen the disastrous consequences when people got drunk. But we must remember that not even the strong Christian is permitted to drink to excess. Perhaps like the meat discussed in 1 Cor. 8–10, it was associated with idolatrous practices. It may have been used as a libation in animal sacrifices. Or perhaps they opposed drinking wine for purely ascetic reasons. That is to say, they believed that self-denial per se was essential to holiness.

Another question raised by verse 21 is whether a Christian should take a vow of total abstinence to be observed throughout one's life. Certainly, he or she is free to do so. But this is not what Paul is recommending. First, Paul himself did not take this approach (see 1 Cor. 10:23–33). The exercise of liberty is dependent on the immediate circumstances (see 1 Cor. 9:19–23). Paul's behavior on matters nonessential to salvation was dependent on those to whom he ministered and their attitude toward the issue at hand (see 1 Tim. 5:23). Second, it would be inconsistent with his emphasis on liberty in verses 1–12. To endorse liberty so strongly, only to universally and unconditionally wipe out every possibility of its exercise, is inconceivable. Third, it is completely impractical. If we permanently forsook everything that was offensive to others, it is doubtful we could survive long in this world.

In verse 22 Paul urges the strong not to flaunt their freedom or to parade it around as if it were a badge of Christian maturity. They are not to overtly display and trumpet their rights and liberties to the detriment of the weak. The word **faith** (v. 23) does not refer to saving faith in Jesus or even confident faith in the promises of God. It refers specifically to the firm persuasion and confidence in one's conscience that all things truly are clean in themselves, and the consequent sense of freedom in Christ to enjoy such things with gratitude and to the glory of God.

When Paul says you are to keep this **between yourself and God** (v. 22), he means two things. First, keep it private; don't be ostentatious or make a public point of the fact that you are above the scruples of the weak. But, second, neither should you renounce your freedom. Keep it. It is good. Be thankful for it. Certainly, you should never apologize for it. Christian liberty is a precious gift, but it does not have to be expressed outwardly to be enjoyed.[7]

The word **doubts** in verse 23a implies that a weak brother or sister has qualms and misgivings about the moral propriety of eating or drinking or whatever the decision may be with which they are faced. Their conscience lacks confidence. They do not feel free to partake. They do not have the faith that all things are clean. Paul thus envisions a situation in which this weak brother or sister, perhaps in order to escape the disdain or rejection of a strong believer, eats or drinks contrary to their scruples. Their own misguided, but sincere, conscience says, "Do *not* eat. Do *not* drink." But under the influence of the example of a stronger brother or sister, they violate the dictates of their conscience and engage in what, to them, is wrong. In such a case, says Paul, both they and the strong brother or sister whose unloving example they followed have sinned.

If you are not sure whether eating meat or drinking wine is wrong and you think it might be, but you go ahead and eat or drink it anyway in spite of your scruples, then you are **condemned** (v. 23)—that is, guilty of sin. To be **condemned** here, once again, like the reference to destruction back in verses 15 and

7. Ironically, those who feel the freedom to eat meat and to drink wine can themselves fall into legalism. They can hold to the truth of Christian liberty so tenaciously that they ignore the welfare of their weaker brothers and sisters. They insist at all times and under every circumstance to have the right and freedom to eat and drink whatever they want. In effect, they have become slaves to their own freedom. They are in bondage to their own liberty. If you believe that you must always exercise your freedom, even to disregarding your fellow believer, not only are you not walking in love, but also you are enslaved to your own liberty.

20, does not mean eternal destruction in hell or the loss of salvation. It means being condemned in your conscience. You will suffer the pain and distress of guilt for having lived not from faith but from doubt and fear and hesitation. But it also likely includes incurring God's disapproval. He won't altogether reject this person, but he is not pleased with their choices.

The second half of verse 23 has been greatly misunderstood. We need to be careful that we do not extend the application of this principle beyond how Paul makes use of it in this context. His point here is that a Christian sins when he or she does what their conscience forbids. Paul isn't talking about doubts in general, as if to say that if you ever struggle to believe a promise God has made or a truth revealed in Scripture that you are sinning. We should hope and pray and study so as to grow out of our doubts and into a more confident embrace of all that God has revealed. But in this context the reference is to **doubts** about whether it is appropriate to engage in certain secondary activities, such as eating meat and drinking wine and observing certain days as more holy than others.

APPLICATION

Liberty and Legalism in the Present Day

There is much in Rom. 14 by way of practical application to the challenges of Christian living in our own day, specifically when it comes to the threat of legalism. Paul wants us to enjoy the freedom we have in Christ, but not as an opportunity to indulge the flesh (Gal. 5:13). Freedom from the conscience of other people is vitally important if we are to walk in the joy that Christ died to obtain for us.

Most Christians at some point in their lives have been the victims of legalism. They live in constant dread of engaging in some practice that another Christian regards as unholy, in spite of the fact that the Bible is silent on the subject. They are terrified of incurring the disdain and rejection of those whose respect they covet. Worse still, they fear God's rejection for violating religious traditions or cultural norms that have no basis in Scripture but are prized by the legalist. They have been duped into believing that the slightest misstep or mistake will bring down God's disapproval and disgust.

Legalism may be defined as the tendency to regard as divine law things or actions that God has neither forbidden nor required in Scripture, together with the inclination to judge others for their failure to abide by what the legalist considers to be God's will for all people. In Paul's day it found expression in particular beliefs about eating meat or only vegetables (Rom. 14:2–3), whether a believer could drink wine (Rom. 14:21), and whether particular days of the week or year were more holy than others (Rom. 14:5–6). In our day we face contentious debates about the use of alcohol in moderation; whether to attend movies and, if permitted, which ones, if any, are off limits to Christians; styles of dress; the purchase of life insurance; whether women should wear makeup; homeschooling versus public education for our children; watching or participating in athletic events on Sunday; tattoos; and the use of the internet for entertainment.

One characteristic feature in virtually all forms of legalism is the tendency to search out what is bad or wrong in others in order to judge them as less than spiritual, rather than to identify what is good and right so that they might be encouraged. What often drives the legalistic spirit is the belief that one's approval by God is determined by the degree to which one abides by those rules that one believes are essential to holiness and godly living. At the same time, some embrace legalism from a genuine concern for the spiritual welfare of another Christian. They fear that others will surely "fall" (Rom. 14:4) from their relationship with Christ if they indulge themselves in those nonbiblical standards that the legalist mistakenly believes are essential to a God-glorifying life.

In making contemporary application of Rom. 14 we need to be reminded that the Christian is not "free" to do what the Bible clearly prohibits. If the Scriptures do not explicitly forbid some practice, you may well be at liberty to indulge or pursue it, but you are not free to insist that others abide by your personal decision in the matter. God's desire is that we experience joy and freedom in our Christian lives, and that we make use of our liberty to bless and encourage others in the use of theirs. Above all else, the apostle Paul was adamant in his words to the Romans and to us as well that preeminent over the exercise of liberty is the consistent demonstration of love (Rom. 14:15; Gal. 5:13). God wants us to enjoy our freedom in Christ, but never to be enslaved to it!

The Importance
of Christian Unity

Unity between the Strong and the Weak (15:1–7)

In order to track with Paul's argument in this chapter, the interpreter should begin not with verse 1 but with verse 7. The goal of the apostle's argument is that the believers in Rome, both Jew and Gentile, should **accept one another . . . in order to bring praise to God** (or, more literally, "for the glory of God") (v. 7). We see this in the opening word of verse 7, translated **then** in the NIV, but more accurately rendered in the ESV as **therefore** (*dio*). From this we see that verse 7 is the aim of the argument in verses 1–6. Being hospitable to one another and thereby fostering unity in the body of Christ is Paul's focus (as was also the case in 12:13; see also 1 Tim. 3:2; Titus 1:8; Heb. 13:2; 1 Pet. 4:9).

The more natural break between chapters 14 and 15 would be after 15:13. Paul's focus in chapter 15:1–13 remains the relationship between the strong (most likely Gentile Christians) and the weak (Jewish Christians) in the body of Christ (although Paul, a Jew, sees himself as **strong**). We see this in 15:1, where Paul, who identifies himself with the strong, writes, **We who are strong ought to bear with the failings of the weak and not to please ourselves**. By the **failings of the weak,** Paul is talking not about moral failure or physical weakness but about their inability to understand the freedom they have with regard to secondary issues such as what to eat and drink and whether certain days are more holy than others.

The responsibility of the **strong** is to **bear with** the weak, by which he means that the former should be willing and able to forgo the exercise of their liberty for the sake of the weaker brother or sister. He's not telling the strong that they should adopt the scruples of the weak, as if the weak are ultimately correct in their conclusions and the strong are in error. If anything, Paul wants the weak to become strong. He never tells the strong to embrace for themselves the failings of the weak. Thus, to **bear with** the weak doesn't mean that the strong are simply to tolerate the weak or put up with them, as if he were endorsing an attitude of mere resignation or condescending acquiescence. Rather, Paul is calling on the strong to lovingly uphold and carry along the weak so that they will be encouraged and strengthened, and hopefully will grow strong.

The aim of the strong is not to satisfy their own desires by the unfettered expression of liberty but rather to **please** the weak **for their good, to build them up** (v. 2). In making a decision on whether to exercise one's liberty, the first consideration of the strong should be the **good** of the weak so that they may be edified. Paul believes that the strong hold the key to Christian unity. If the strong should dogmatically insist on holding their ground and demanding that others tolerate their exercise of liberty, the gulf between the two groups will only widen and disunity will prevail. The initiative, therefore, rests with those who are strong.

If the strong should object to this responsibility (the verb translated as **ought**, *opheilō*, in v. 1 strongly suggests that this is a moral obligation), Paul directs their attention to the example of Jesus. The words **for even** (*kai gar*) with which verse 3 begins suggest something explicit and unavoidable. Paul is providing the reason why the strong should happily embrace this call. It is because that is precisely what Jesus did when he entered this world and suffered in our place (cf. Phil. 2:6–8). Whatever inconveniences or sacrifices the strong must endure in order to please their weaker brothers and sisters, it can never compare with the inconvenience, pain, and reproach that Jesus endured for us, to reconcile us to God. Here Paul quotes Ps. 69:9, where David describes how the insults and reproach that were directed primarily at God have fallen on him. Paul takes that obviously messianic psalm and applies it to Jesus. For us, Jesus willingly became the target of all human hatred of God. How, then, can the strong be so ungrateful and self-centered as to refuse to show toward their fellow believers a love that is by comparison so much less demanding?

Somewhat surprisingly, Paul does not appeal to anything in the life of Jesus to make his point, but instead cites the words of David in Ps. 69, probably to highlight for his readers the power and influence of the Old Testament Scriptures (which he emphasizes in v. 5). By **everything that was written in the past** (v. 4a) he obviously means the books of the Old Testament, which are there to instruct us. The Old Testament, as inspired Scripture (see 2 Tim. 3:16–17), is the source or means through which God imparts **endurance** and **encouragement** (*dia*, "through" or "on account of," appears before both terms) (v. 4b). Contrary to those who would insist that we can easily ignore the Old Testament, Paul points to it as one of the primary ways that **hope** is instilled in the hearts of believers.

The ultimate aim of pleasing others and finding mutual encouragement in the Scriptures is that in spiritual unity (**with one voice** [v. 6 ESV]) all believers, both Jew and Gentile, might glorify God the Father. Again, the purpose of unity in the body is **to bring praise to God** (v. 7; cf. Rom. 12:16; 2 Cor. 13:11; Eph. 4:2–3; Phil. 2:2; 4:2). That God, by his grace and mercy in Christ Jesus and the power of the inspired biblical text, can unify otherwise hostile parties in one body serves to draw attention to his greatness and glory. When Christians are seen pleasing others and forgoing their own liberty for others' sake, people can only conclude that something else is more important to them than their own promotion—namely, God's glory.

Unity in Praise among the People of God (15:8–13)

In Rom. 15:8 Paul declares that Jesus came to serve his own brothers and sisters, the people of Israel, **the Jews** (the Greek word is *peritomē*, "the circumcision"). All that Jesus did was to remind them that God would be faithful to the promises he made to Abraham, Isaac, and Jacob, the patriarchs of the nation (the phrase **on behalf of God's truth** likely refers to the validity and ultimate fulfillment of the covenant promises [cf. 2 Cor. 1:20; Gal. 4:4–5]). But Christ no less came to serve believing Gentiles, to enable them **to glorify God for his mercy** (v. 9). Paul cites three parts of the Old Testament. He twice appeals to the Psalms in verses 9b and 11, specifically Pss. 18:49 and 117:1. He quotes from Deut. 32:43 in verse 10, and then again from the Septuagint version of the prophet Isaiah in verse 12 (Isa. 11:10). Thus, the Writings, the Law, and the Prophets are all called to bear witness to God's saving purpose among the Gentiles. Paul's aim is to reinforce the truth, especially among Jewish believers, that Gentiles who trust in Jesus, no less so than Jews who trust in Jesus, are saved and counted among the covenant people of God. Whether they are identified as strong or weak, as Jew or Gentile, together they are one people, called to celebrate and sing to and glorify God.

The purpose of God in saving Gentiles (the same can be said of God's purpose in saving Jews) is worship! Consider the repetition of language: **glorify God** (v. 9a), **praise** and **sing** (v. 9b), **rejoice** (v. 10), **praise** and **extol** (v. 11), and **hope** (v. 12). These verbs make clear that the ultimate purpose of Christ's saving mercy is theocentric, to focus upon and draw attention to the majesty and glory of God.

Having made his point that all Christians, regardless of ethnicity, are together one people who with one voice glorify and sing to the one God of heaven and earth, Paul turns to pray for them (v. 13). He prays for an abiding **joy**, that deep, durable delight in the splendor of God. He also prays for **peace**, a tranquility of soul and spirit that has the power to overcome whatever turmoil and tragedy we've yet to face. All of this is with a view to the impartation of **hope** (cf. Eph. 1:12; Col. 1:27; 1 Thess. 1:3; Titus 2:13) from him who is **the God of hope** (hope thus finds its source not in human resolve but in God's grace).

All this occurs only **as you trust in him** (or perhaps, as/when you believe), indicating that these experiences do not fall haphazardly from heaven but are imparted in response to trust, faith, and belief in who God is and what he has done for us in Christ. The God of hope is not a miser with his mercy but rather aims for us to **overflow** or abound in hope. This is possible only **by the power of the Holy Spirit**. The Spirit is thus responsible for more than the *charismata* and signs and wonders. Something as seemingly mundane as hope is experienced only by virtue of his power.

That Paul aims to highlight the effusive and abundant blessings that come from God is evident from the words **fill**, **all**, and **overflow**. God does more than merely give these blessings. He *fills* us with them, *all* of them. We don't simply have or possess them; we *overflow* with them. Paul's emphasis is on the generous, expansive, overflowing, and measureless way in which God answers prayers.

Paul's Confidence in the Maturity of the Church in Rome (15:14–17)

Paul says quite clearly in verse 14 that he is confident of his addressees' spiritual maturity and the goodness of their hearts. He wants them to know how blessed he is with their spiritual progress. He mentions their morality: they are **full of goodness** (v. 14a); their mentality: they are **filled with all knowledge** (v. 14b ESV; the NIV omits *pasēs*, **all**); and their maturity: they are **competent to instruct one another** (v. 14c). But this doesn't mean that they no longer need instruction or rebuke or encouragement. No matter how much success we have in our Christian growth, there is always room for much more.

In numerous texts in the previous fourteen chapters Paul has written **quite boldly** (v. 15) to the church in Rome. This reminder is itself a reminder to us that we must never think that we have arrived theologically, that we know it all and no longer have any need to revisit and rehearse the great truths of the gospel. And lest they think that he is speaking from his own authority, he says very clearly that his approach in this letter is the result of the grace God gave him, an obvious reference to his calling as an apostle (see Rom. 1:1, 5–6).

In addition, he has been called and empowered with a **priestly duty** not solely to see Gentiles come to saving faith in Christ but also to see them **sanctified**, made experientially holy, gradually transformed ever more increasingly into the very image of Jesus himself (v. 16b). The **offering acceptable to God** is not something that they, the Gentiles, bring to God. Paul says that *he* is **offering** the Gentiles to God in fulfillment of his priestly service. He is declaring that these non-Jewish Christians who were excluded from the temple in Jerusalem and had no part in the sacrifices offered there are themselves, by God's grace, an **acceptable** offering unto God by the sanctifying work of the Holy Spirit. In this way Paul emphasizes the unity of all ethnicities, whether Jew or Gentile, in Christ by faith, and unashamedly declares that he, literally, "has reason to boast" (**I glory**), but only **in Christ Jesus** (v. 17; cf. 2 Cor. 10:17; Gal. 6:14).[1]

Gospel Ministry in the Power of the Holy Spirit (15:18–19a)

Paul quickly reinforces his claim that whatever boasting he has in the success of his ministry (v. 17) is by virtue of **what Christ has accomplished through him to bring the Gentiles to obedience** (v. 18 ESV; cf. 1 Cor. 15:10). Paul mentions four important truths or primary instruments to account for the success of his evangelistic ministry. First, Paul points to the **word** he proclaimed (v. 18b ESV). He verbally declared the truth of who Jesus is and what he did. Second, his ministry was characterized by what he has **done** (*ergon*, "work"). This could conceivably include everything he did, be it acts of mercy or generosity or compassion or serving the poor. But the more likely reference is to the **signs and wonders** (v. 19) that he was enabled to perform, which is the third expression of his evangelistic ministry. Fourth, he accomplished all this—word and deed, signs and wonders—**through the power of the Spirit of God** (cf. 1 Cor. 2:1–5; 4:20).

Paul says not that he proclaimed the gospel but that he has **fulfilled** [*peplērō-kenai*] **. . . the gospel of Christ** (Rom. 15:19b ESV). His work in relation to the gospel involved not only words or propositions but also actions or deeds empowered by the Spirit, in particular, miracles. For Paul, the gospel was a combination of both the audible message and the tangible presence of God's power. The gospel was both human words about Christ Jesus and divine power through the Holy Spirit.

1. Observe the latent trinitarianism in verse 16: "The good news of which Paul is a minister has its origins in God [the Father]; in taking it to the Gentiles he is a 'priestly minister' of Christ Jesus, the content of this good news; the effectual appropriation of the good news in the lives of Gentiles is the working of the Holy Spirit" (Fee, *God's Empowering Presence*, 627).

Signs and wonders (v. 19a) are another way of referring to miracles, the latter having been subjected to a variety of different definitions. Max Turner's definition of a miracle is most apt: "(1) It is an extraordinary or startling observable event, (2) it cannot reasonably be explained in terms of human abilities or other known forces in the world, (3) it is perceived as a direct act of God, and (4) it is usually understood to have symbolic or sign value (e.g., pointing to God as redeemer, judge, and Savior)."[2]

In response to the argument that only apostles ministered in such power, one need only point to the seventy-two followers of Jesus (Luke 10:9, 17–19), believers present on the day of Pentecost (Acts 2:4, 17–18), Stephen (Acts 6:8), Philip (Acts 8:6–7, 13), Ananias (Acts 9:10–19), the anonymous disciples of John the Baptist (Acts 19:5–7), disciples in Tyre (Acts 21:4), Philip's four daughters (Acts 21:9), Christians in Rome (Rom. 12:6), the *charisma* of miracles (1 Cor. 12:10, 28), and the ministry of ordinary believers in the church at Galatia (Gal. 3:5).

Paul's Missionary Itinerary (15:19b–29)

Paul wants the Christians in Rome to understand why he has not come to them sooner, lest they draw the unwarranted conclusion that the Corinthians did, that Paul was unconcerned with them and was making selfish decisions for his own welfare rather than theirs. He had earlier reminded them of his intent to visit Rome (Rom. 1:13). He now, in verse 22, explains the reason for his failure to arrive there: he had a ministry to fulfill (v. 19). And that ministry, that holy ambition of his, was to preach the gospel where it had not yet been made known. And that region of ministry was **from Jerusalem all the way around to Illyricum** (modern-day Albania) (v. 19b). His failure to make his way to Rome was not because he didn't care for the Romans but because Christ had called him to preach the gospel in regions that had never heard the good news. He will go on to say that his work in that area is complete and he will soon make his way to Rome (vv. 23–24). His ambition to preach Christ where the gospel was unknown was more important than his desire to visit Rome. To make his

---

2. Turner, *The Holy Spirit*, 272n31. Helen Collins insists that we need "to broaden the definition of the word *miracle*. No longer can it mean the 'breaking of natural laws'; instead, a miracle can be anything that witnesses to God's mediated activity in the world." Thus miracles "testify to the Spirit's encompassing and sustaining of all of creation and mediate God to us." A miracle is a "sign or wonder that reveals God in the world in a particularly intense way" and manifests the presence and power of the kingdom of God (Collins, *Charismatic Christianity*, 61). Although her focus is on signs, wonders, and miracles in the Philippines, Lora Timenia provides helpful biblical and pastoral criteria for assessing all claims to what are called "manifestations" of the Spirit and extraordinary spiritual experiences. See Timenia, *Third Wave Pentecostalism*.

point, Paul quotes Isa. 52:15 (Septuagint) in verse 21: **Those who were not told about him will see, and those who have not heard will understand.**

Thus far Paul has proclaimed the gospel from Jerusalem north through Syria, then farther north and west through the provinces of Asia Minor (modern-day Turkey). He would then cross the Aegean Sea and enter Greece on the east side and up the west to northern Italy where Albania is today. And **now that there is no more place for** him **to work in these regions** (v. 23a), he hopes to make his way to Rome. Paul does not mean that he preached to every living soul in those regions, far less that all of them came to saving faith in Jesus. He is saying that his

---

BIBLICAL BACKGROUND

The Journeys of the Apostle Paul

In Rom. 15:22–29 Paul labors to explain his movements in light of the difficult relationship he sustained with the church in Corinth. The latter had accused the apostle of deceiving them about his travel plans. His enemies in Corinth took advantage of this in their efforts to undermine his credibility and to cause the Corinthians to question whether he was a genuine apostle of Jesus Christ (see 2 Cor. 1:15–19, 23–24).

Paul had hoped to visit the Corinthians twice: first, on his way *to* Macedonia, and second, on his way *back from* Macedonia (see 2 Cor. 1:15–16). This changed when Timothy arrived in Corinth bearing the letter we know as 1 Corinthians and communicated how bad things were. Upon hearing of this, Paul immediately made an urgent visit to Corinth, a visit that was confrontational, as well as humiliating and bitter for him (cf. 2 Cor. 2:1). He quickly returned to Ephesus and determined not to make another painful visit to Corinth. Therefore, he called off the two stops he had earlier planned. It was this alteration in his plans that opened him up to the charge of being fickle and unstable. This apparently arbitrary change of plans, they insisted, was motivated by self-interest and a lack of concern for the Corinthians themselves. He was accused of making plans like a worldly person, according to the mood of the moment (see 2 Cor. 1:17), to which he responds in 2 Cor. 1:18–19.

Having already dealt with this sort of problem once, in his relationship with the Corinthians, Paul is now faced with it again in his relationship with the Romans. So, he slows down, as it were, here in Rom. 15:22–29, to explain to them very clearly why he made his decisions regarding when and why he would visit them.

work in those regions is that of a frontier or pioneer missionary. Once churches had been planted in these regions, his work was done. He would now depart and let the believers in those regions continue the work that he initially established.

Paul does not specify what **hindered** him from coming to Rome (v. 22), but it was likely imposed by God and pertained to the call on Paul's life to take the gospel to heretofore unreached people. But he also wants them to know that Rome is not his final destination. He feels the urge to pass through Rome on his way to Spain (v. 24). We don't know if Paul ever made it to Spain, but it seems unlikely. However, before making his way to Rome, he must first go to Jerusalem (v. 25).

This is an incredibly arduous task. If Paul wrote Romans while in Corinth, it would entail a thousand-mile detour, east, in the opposite direction from Rome. Thus, before traveling to Rome, Paul says, he must first travel a thousand miles to Jerusalem, then a thousand miles back to Corinth, and then on to Rome. Paul describes in verse 25 what prompted him to make such an indescribably long, demanding, and dangerous journey of an additional two thousand miles. It was to serve **the Lord's people there** by bringing them financial assistance to help alleviate their poverty.

Paul tells us in verses 25–28 why he had to put off his visit to Rome and to Spain. The churches in Macedonia and Achaia (both the northern and southern parts of Greece, primarily Philippi and Corinth, where he had planted churches) were determined to do their part in sending money to their poverty-stricken brothers and sisters in Jerusalem. Paul's appeal to the church in Corinth to participate in this ministry is described in 2 Cor. 8–9. The Gentile believers in Macedonia and Achaia felt themselves spiritually indebted to the Jewish Christians in Jerusalem (Rom. 15:27). It was from Jerusalem and the Jewish believers there that the gospel had spread to the Gentiles. So, says Paul, **if the Gentiles have shared in the Jews' spiritual blessings, they owe it to the Jews to share with them their material blessings** (v. 27).

Why didn't Paul commission someone else to take the money to Jerusalem? Remember that Paul himself had raised this money from the churches in Philippi and Corinth, and his reputation was at stake if all of it didn't arrive. In 2 Cor. 9:13 Paul connects this offering to the Jerusalem church with the gospel itself: "Because of the service by which you have proved yourselves, others [the poor saints in Jerusalem] will praise God for the obedience that accompanies your [the Gentiles'] confession of the gospel of Christ." If this financial offering were embezzled or lost on its way to Jerusalem, it would undermine the truth of the gospel, which Paul refuses to permit. It may also be that Paul is honoring the request of the other apostles and felt an obligation to see it through personally (see Gal. 2:9–10).

Then there is the issue of Jewish and Gentile unity. By personally taking the money from Gentile Christians to the Jewish believers in Jerusalem, Paul was making a statement about the unity and oneness of the two in the gospel. It was his way of reminding every Gentile believer that their salvation is due to their being grafted into the one olive tree, the covenant that God made with Abraham. And Paul wanted every Gentile Christian never to forget this.

Twice, in verses 26 and 27, Paul says that the Gentile believers in Macedonia and Achaia **were pleased** to give generously to the needs of the saints. It's entirely possible that Paul wanted the saints in Jerusalem to clearly see and know that he too was pleased to participate in their relief, that it wasn't a perfunctory gesture that for the sake of his own safety he authorized a secondary party to fulfill. Then, on his way to Spain, he will stop in Rome (vv. 24, 28). His purpose for doing so is threefold. In Rom. 1:11 he said he hoped to "impart" to them "some spiritual gift" to strengthen them. He also desired that they and he be "mutually encouraged by each other's faith" (1:12). Finally, he says in 15:24 that he hopes that they will **assist** him on his **journey there**. This undoubtedly means that he was hoping that they would provide not only spiritual sustenance but also financial support for his continued missionary efforts. Assuring them that he will come in **the fullness of the blessing of Christ** (v. 29 ESV) may simply be another way of referring to the "spiritual gift" in 1:11 or perhaps be a summary of each of the blessings just noted.

Paul's Plans, Prayer, and the Providential Will of God (15:30–33)

Paul knew that his proposed journey to Jerusalem, then to Rome, and eventually to Spain was dependent on God's sovereign will (v. 32; cf. Acts 18:21; Rom. 1:9–10; 1 Cor. 4:19; 16:7; Phil. 2:24). But he also knew that God has chosen to accomplish his will for us in response to the prayers that we bring to the throne of grace on behalf of one another. This is why he writes what he does in verses 30–33.

The basis for his appeal is **by our Lord Jesus Christ and by the love of the Spirit** (v. 30). This may simply mean, "Because of what Jesus has done for us, join me in prayer." That is, because the life, death, and resurrection of Jesus have opened a door into heaven and to the throne of grace itself, Paul asks that they join him in praying. Or it may be that he means "for the sake of Jesus Christ" or "for the glory and praise of Jesus." But I think that he appeals to Jesus as **Lord** because he knows that the risen Christ exercises absolute sovereignty over the lives and wills of humans. Jesus can respond to the prayers of his people to accomplish otherwise seemingly impossible things. Paul knows that Jesus has the right and the power to orchestrate events and turn the will of government leaders and religious zealots to do whatever he pleases. And that is precisely what he asks for in verse 31.

He also bases his appeal on **the love of the Spirit**. This is the only place in Paul's writings where this precise phrase is found. Does he mean "because of the love that the Holy Spirit has for you and me"? Or is he referring to the love that the Spirit has created or engendered in our hearts for one another? The second option is more likely (cf. Gal. 5:13, 22; Col. 1:8).

Why is prayer a **struggle** (v. 30; see also Col. 4:12)? The struggle isn't with God, as if he could be cajoled or bullied into giving us what we want; nor are we striving to overcome his reluctance to help or to persuade him to change his mind and do things our way. The obstacles to prayer against which we strive find their origin in us and in our Enemy. So, at minimum Paul would be referring to demonic forces that seek to hinder and undermine our prayers. Paul said that our "struggle" is against "the rulers, against the authorities, against the powers of this dark world and against the spiritual forces of evil in the heavenly realms" (Eph. 6:12).

But we also strive against distractions and the laziness of our souls. Perhaps the greatest threat to persistence in prayer is a perceived track record of unanswered prayer. There is also a sense in which we must strive against the sin in our lives that may prove to be a hindrance to prayer (cf. Ps. 66:18). We must strive against unbelief, the doubts we have about God's goodness and power. Whatever the obstacle, Paul's appeal is clear. We must strive against everything that causes us to cease praying (cf. Dan. 9:3, 17–19; Col. 1:29; Heb. 4:16).

Paul clearly believed that his success in life and ministry depended on the prayers he prayed and that others prayed for him (see, e.g., 2 Cor. 1:8–11; Phil. 1:18–19; Philem. 22). He confesses that he does not know whether or not it is God's sovereign will that he finally make his way to Rome (see also Acts 18:21; Rom. 1:9–10; 1 Cor. 4:19; 16:7; Phil. 2:24; James 4:13–15).

He first asks them to pray that he **may be delivered from the unbelievers in Judea** (v. 31a ESV). The need arose from Paul's experience of facing opposition everywhere he traveled. This prayer was answered, but not in the way he and the Roman Christians might have expected. When Paul arrived in Jerusalem, the Jews from Asia stirred up the whole crowd and "seized him" (Acts 21:27). Later, "the whole city was aroused," and "seizing Paul, they dragged him from the temple" (Acts 21:30). So how was Paul saved? Luke tells us that "news reached the commander of the Roman troops" (Acts 21:31). The Roman soldiers rushed to the scene, rescued him, and put him in jail. The prayers of the church in Rome that Paul be **kept safe** from unbelievers in Judea were answered when God responded to their request by making certain that this "news" came to the tribune of the cohort. We don't know who delivered the report. What we do know is that by God's sovereign providential oversight of the situation, in response to the prayers of the Roman church, Paul was protected! The prayers of the Roman Christians 1,400 miles away were answered as God influenced the will of someone to inform the tribune, whose will God influenced to rush to the scene and rescue Paul.

That was only the first answer to their prayers. While Paul was in jail, "some Jews formed a conspiracy and bound themselves with an oath not to eat or drink until they had killed Paul" (Acts 23:12). But somehow Paul's nephew heard of the plot and informed the Roman tribune, who immediately dispatched two hundred soldiers with seventy horsemen and two hundred spearmen to escort Paul to Caesarea (Acts 23:16–24). All this was likely God's doing in response to the faithful, fervent prayers of the Roman Christians.

Second, Paul asks them to pray that **the contribution** he would **take to Jerusalem may be favorably received by the Lord's people there** (v. 31b). Paul was aware that some Jewish Christians in Jerusalem still didn't fully trust him and were suspicious of the gospel he preached and mistakenly assumed that he was trying to undermine Jewish traditions. Perhaps they would look on the financial gift as a bribe, an attempt by Paul to win their favor and good standing. If they refused to receive the gift or interpreted it as an attempt by Paul to purchase their affirmation, it would only widen the rift between Gentile and Jewish believers. Remember: the gift to the Jewish believers in Jerusalem came from Gentile believers in Corinth and Philippi.

This prayer was also answered. For one thing, we don't read anything in Scripture to suggest that the monetary gift was rejected. But we do read in Acts 24:17 Paul's statement, "After an absence of several years, I came to Jerusalem to bring my people gifts for the poor and to present offerings." If this had been turned down, we would expect something to be said to that effect. So, once again, God answered the prayers of Christians in Rome regarding events in Jerusalem!

Third, and finally, Paul wants them to pray so that he may come to them **with joy, by God's will**, and in their **company be refreshed** (v. 32). He has in mind the joy and mutual encouragement and love that come from Christian fellowship described earlier in Rom. 1:11–12.

ROMANS 16

Greetings, a Warning, and a Closing Doxology

Greetings from the Apostle Paul (16:1–16)

How could Paul have known these people, given the fact that he had never traveled to Rome? When the emperor Claudius expelled all Jews from Rome in AD 49, many would have landed in cities that Paul visited on his missionary journeys. When Claudius rescinded his decree in AD 54, many would have returned to Rome. It is likely, then, that most of the people in this list were those Paul had previously met while on his many evangelistic journeys.

There are nine women mentioned in the list of those to whom Paul sends his greetings, eight by name and one who is called the **sister** of Nereus (v. 15). The fact that Paul lists so many women in this passage testifies to the vital role that women play in the life and ministries of the local church.[1] Perhaps the most important of this group is **Phoebe** (vv. 1–2). She is a person worthy of commendation and deserving of loving acceptance by the church in Rome. There is no indication that she is coming to Rome after the letter had already arrived, and thus most scholars believe that it is Phoebe who is carrying the Letter to the Romans from Paul to the church in that city. She is the only person in this long

---

1. For a wide-ranging survey of the role of women in the ancient world and in the church, see Cohick, *Women in the World of the Earliest Christians*. A contemporary focus on women in ministry, in particular the wives of pastors in evangelical megachurches, is ably provided by Bowler, *The Preacher's Wife*. She includes discussion of women from both Black churches and other ethnic minorities. For a careful study of the role of African American women in ministry, see Butler, *Women in the Church of God*.

list that wasn't already living in Rome, being a native of Cenchreae, a port city on the eastern side of Corinth. This is most likely where Paul was living when he wrote Romans. Phoebe was a **deacon** of the church at Cenchreae.

Paul refers to Phoebe as **our sister** (v. 1), not "my" sister, which is Paul's way of saying that she is part of our spiritual family. We all have the same spiritual Father. So, **help her in whatever she may need from you** (v. 2 ESV), probably a reference to housing and food and perhaps connections with people who will assist her in whatever ministry she undertakes.

Phoebe probably was quite wealthy, as she is described as being **the benefactor** [*prostatis*, "financial supporter"] **of many people**, including Paul (v. 2). Craig Keener suggests that "she likely hosts the house congregation" in Cenchreae.[2] Her courage and commitment to the Lord Jesus Christ and his people are evident from the fact that she willingly took on the arduous task of traveling all the way from eastern Corinth to Rome. We don't know if she traveled alone or in the company of others, but apparently she was asked by Paul to carry this epistle to Rome and she happily took on the task.

Prisca, also known as **Priscilla** (v. 3; see Acts 18:2, 18, 26), was married to **Aquila**. She and her husband first lived in Rome until they were driven out of the city by the emperor Claudius in AD 49, together with all the Jews who resided there. They obviously were not strangers to persecution. After Paul left Athens and went to Corinth, "he met a Jew named Aquila, a native of Pontus, who had recently come from Italy with his wife Priscilla, because Claudius had ordered all Jews to leave Rome" (Acts 18:1–2). They then traveled to Ephesus, where they hosted a church in their house (Acts 18:26; 1 Cor. 16:19). They evidently returned to live in Rome and once again hosted a church in their home (see Rom. 16:5a). We later read in 2 Tim. 4:19 that they finally settled in Ephesus. So, this couple lived in Rome, Corinth, Ephesus, back in Rome, then back again in Ephesus. And everywhere they went, they opened their home for the church (v. 5).

Priscilla and Aquila were quite well educated in the Scriptures and could articulate and teach biblical truth to others, as they together "explained . . . the way of God more accurately" to Apollos, who himself was "a learned man, with a thorough knowledge of the Scriptures" (Acts 18:24–26). As eloquent and competent as Apollos was, both Priscilla and Aquila were more skilled and more knowledgeable. They were both **co-workers** (v. 3) alongside Paul and **risked their necks** for him (v. 4a ESV). We don't know precisely what risks they took, but Paul appeals for all to express their profound gratitude to this lady and her husband. "I'm alive today," Paul is saying, "because of this woman and her husband."

---

2. Keener, *Romans*, 183.

Women Deacons?

Although there is some dispute as to whether women served as deacons in the early church, the evidence appears to show that they did. When the generic meaning of *diakonos* is intended, the text usually reads, "servant of the Lord" or something similar. Romans 16:1 is the only place where Paul speaks of someone being a *diakonos* of a local church. Tychicus is called a "minister [servant] in the Lord" (Eph. 6:21), Epaphras is named a "minister [servant] of Christ" (Col. 1:7), and Timothy is labeled a "servant of Christ Jesus" (1 Tim. 4:6). Because only Phoebe is specifically said to be a servant of a local congregation (the church at Cenchreae), it is likely that she was a "deacon" of her church.

Furthermore, when this particular Greek construction, found in Rom. 16:1, with a present participle is used (*ousan*, "being" or "who is" [NASB], words omitted in the NIV), it identifies a person's performance of some office in the New Testament. Examples of this usage are found in John 11:49 ("who was high priest that year") and Acts 18:12 ("Gallio was pro-consul of Achaia") (cf. Acts 24:10).

In 1 Tim. 3:8–13 the question is whether Paul is referring to the "wives" (v. 11 [ESV]) of deacons or to "women" (v. 11 [NIV]) as those who, much like men, can be appointed to this office. The evidence seems to be evenly weighted in this debate, but the arguments for women as deacons are more persuasive.

First, contrary to the ESV translation, the possessive pronoun "their" at the start of 1 Tim. 3:11 does not appear in the Greek text. The insertion of this word reflects the view of the translators that the females in view here are the "wives" of the male deacons. If Paul had wanted to speak unmistakably of the wives of deacons, it seems reasonable to think that he would have included the possessive pronoun. It speaks loudly that he didn't.

Second, Paul introduces the office of elder and its qualifications in 1 Tim. 3:1–7. He then introduces the office of deacon in verse 8 with the phrase "in the same way [*hōsautōs*], deacons." He begins verse 11 in virtually identical terms, suggesting that he is introducing yet another office, that of deaconess. He writes in verse 11, "In the same way [*hōsautōs*], the women . . ."

Third, although there is evidence for both sides, the word translated as "women" (*gynaikas*) in verse 11 (or "wives" in the ESV) can refer either to females generally or to wives in particular. The word itself does not provide decisive proof of either translation.

Fourth, a fact that carries much weight is that Paul says nothing about the qualifications of elders' wives. Why would he list qualifications for the wives of deacons but say nothing at all about the wives of elders, especially given the fact that being an elder carried far more spiritual authority and responsibility than being a deacon? Why would Paul hold the wives of deacons to a higher standard than the wives of elders?

Therefore, it seems reasonable to conclude that there are two offices in the New Testament—elder and deacon—and that the latter may be filled by both qualified men and women. Should we then refer to a female deacon as a "deaconess"? Although that is surely permissible, it isn't helpful. In the one text where a woman is specifically said to be a deacon (Rom. 16:1), the masculine form of the Greek noun is used, not the feminine form. So, there are not three offices in the local church— elder, deacon, and deaconess—but only two.

In Rom. 16:1–16 twenty-seven people are mentioned by name, together with numerous others who remain anonymous. There were undoubtedly many in **the church** that met in the **house** of Priscilla and Aquila (v. 5a). The families of **Aristobulus** (v. 10b) and **Narcissus** (v. 11b) are mentioned as a group. Then there are the **mother** of **Rufus** (v. 13a), unnamed **brothers and sisters** (v. 14b), the **sister** of **Nereus** (v. 15a), and **all the saints who are with them** (v. 15b ESV).

We should note the various designations by which Paul identifies them: **sister** (v. 1), **deacon** (v. 1; **servant** [NIV margin]), **saints** (v. 2 ESV; **his people** [NIV]), **benefactor** (v. 2), **co-workers** (vv. 3, 9), **beloved** (vv. 5, 9, 12 ESV; **dear friend** [NIV]), **convert** (v. 5), **fellow Jews** (vv. 7, 11; **kinsmen** [ESV]), **fellow prisoners** (v. 7 ESV), **dear friend** [**beloved** (ESV)] **in the Lord** (v. 8), one who is **approved in Christ** (v. 10 ESV; **fidelity to Christ** [NIV]), **women who work hard in the Lord** (v. 12), **chosen in the Lord** (v. 13), **mother** (v. 13), and **brothers and sisters** (v. 14).

Another recurring characteristic that Paul highlights is the relationship that these people have with Jesus. What unites them all isn't their ethnicity, country of origin, gender, occupations, size of their families, personal wealth, or physical characteristics. What unites them, and what Paul highlights, is their relationship to Jesus. Note the repeated references to the Lord Jesus Christ. Welcome Phoebe **in the Lord** (v. 2). Many are described as co-workers **in Christ Jesus** (vv. 3, 9). Epenetus was the first convert **to Christ** in Asia (v. 5). Andronicus and Junia

Women in Public Ministry in the Pentecostal-Charismatic World

The divisive controversy over the role of women in public ministry contin-ues unabated. Leah Payne, in her book *Gender and Pentecostal Revival-ism: Making a Female Ministry in the Early Twentieth Century*, provides insight into the way two women in particular emerged as celebrity minis-ters in a world dominated by men. The two are Maria Woodworth-Etter (1844–1924) and Aimee Semple McPherson (1890–1944). Payne seeks to account for how women became powerful female revivalist ministers during the 1890s–1920s, "an era in which public leadership was seen as naturally, 'instinctively' male." More specifically, her book "asks how two Pentecostal women—Woodworth-Etter and McPherson—overcame not only their gender, but also the taints of divorce, single motherhood, and public scandal to become authoritative revivalist pastors." In addi-tion, Payne investigates "what it is about Pentecostalism that allowed for such talented (albeit scandalous) women to rise so remarkably within the movement."[a]

a. Payne, *Gender and Pentecostal Revivalism*, 1.

were **in Christ** before Paul was (v. 7). Ampliatus is described as Paul's friend **in the Lord** (v. 8). Apelles is **approved in Christ** (v. 10 ESV). It is those of the family of Narcissus who are **in the Lord** whom Paul greets (v. 11). Tryphena, Tryphosa, and Persis have worked hard **in the Lord** (v. 12). Rufus is chosen **in the Lord** (v. 13). He may have been the son of Simon of Cyrene, the man who was compelled to carry the cross of Jesus when our Lord buckled under the weight of that instrument of crucifixion (Mark 15:21). The mother of Rufus was a **mother** also to Paul (v. 13). Evidently, she had befriended Paul in a special way and filled a place in his life that Paul's mother either couldn't or wouldn't.

There are two crucial issues in verse 7. First, if **Junia** is feminine, then she and Andronicus are most likely husband and wife. Recent examination of extensive Greek literature outside the Bible gives little help. The word "Junia" turns up only twice as a woman's name and only once as a man's name. Second, the NIV translates the phrase in question as **outstanding among the apostles**, while the ESV renders it as **well known to the apostles**. The former would suggest that Andronicus and Junia themselves were apostles, well known in that unique circle of believers. The latter would suggest that the apostles, such as Paul, knew these two people quite well. Grammatical analysis of this text shows no signs of abating.[3] If Junia and Andronicus were apostles, the question remains whether they functioned authoritatively, as did Paul, or more as ambassadors or representatives of a local church (see 2 Cor. 8:23; Phil. 2:25).

This list of Christian men and women extends to the lowest ranks of society as well as the highest. The names **Ampliatus**, **Urbanus**, and **Stachys** (vv. 8–9) were common slave names at that time, but that didn't prevent Paul from honoring them, as they were truly beloved by Paul and faithful followers of Jesus. Paul also mentions a man named **Aristobulus** (v. 10), who many think was the grandson of Herod the Great. If so, the gospel clearly had penetrated into the imperial, royal household.

Paul refers to Phoebe as **our sister** (v. 1) in a spiritual sense. Most likely she was a Gentile convert to Christ, as a Jewish female would never have been given this name. "Phoebe" is a name derived from pagan mythology, related to Artemis, the moon goddess. But there were also physical sisters in the church at Rome. **Tryphena** and **Tryphosa** (v. 12) likely were twins. Their names mean something like "Dainty" and "Delicate." However, they were anything but dainty and delicate, as Paul describes them as women who **work hard in the Lord**.

There was not one, large, local church in Rome that met in a single large venue, but rather there were multiple, smaller, local churches that at this time in history met in private homes. There was a church that met in the house of Priscilla and Aquila (v. 5a). The fact that Paul mentions **brothers and sisters** who were **with** five individuals noted in verse 14 suggests that these composed yet another house church. Again, in verse 15 Paul greets **all the saints** (ESV) who are **with** those named in that verse.

Thirteen times in the span of sixteen verses Paul tells his addressees to greet this or that person. We know from Rom. 1:7 that Paul addressed this letter to all the Christians in Rome. But I assume that he intended for the leaders of the many churches to extend his greetings to those he mentions by name. Four times Paul mentions the love he has for these people in Rome. Although Paul surely loved them all, he goes out of his way to refer to several of them as **beloved** (*agapētos*) (vv. 5, 8, 9, 12 ESV; **dear friend** [NIV]). In verse 16 Paul exhorts them, **Greet one another with a holy kiss**. We find a similar exhortation elsewhere in 1 Cor. 16:20; 2 Cor. 13:12–13; 1 Thess. 5:26; 1 Pet. 5:14 ("kiss of love"). As an expression of family affection among those who were redeemed by Christ, this kiss was **holy**, not sexual.

---

3. See Burer and Wallace, "Was Junias Really an Apostle?" and the response by Belleville, "Ἰουνιαν."

Paul's Urgent Warning (16:17–20)

Here the apostle Paul tells us that some people are evil, cause divisions, and believe things that are contrary to the true doctrines that he himself has been teaching in Romans. He speaks directly and without apology to the fact that some people are deliberately deceitful and are to be avoided.

Paul is insistent on unity in the church (e.g., Rom. 15:5), but some people create **obstacles** (v. 17) and by doing so cause disunity. Some divisions are inevitable and come as a result of standing firmly on the truth. But divisions not in accord with the gospel are to be avoided. And yet, in verse 17b he issues an exhortation that on the surface appears to intensify disunity and division. He tells them to **keep away from** (NIV) or **avoid** (ESV) certain people. Don't greet them with a holy kiss (v. 16). Sometimes, in order to maintain unity and peace in the body of Christ, you have to avoid and steer clear of certain individuals. When you identify people who are causing divisions, divide from them. When you see people in the local church who are bent on creating disunity, avoid them. In order to maintain unity, sometimes there has to be disunity!

When Paul says that such people create obstacles **contrary to the doctrine that you have been taught** (v. 17 ESV), he undoubtedly has in mind the many doctrinal truths that he has expounded in the previous fifteen chapters of this letter. Some who cause division can be approached and won over, when shown the error of their ways. But Paul has in mind stubborn, recalcitrant, defiant, unrepentantly divisive people who when confronted push back and argue without biblical grounds for doing so. There is a standard of biblical truth to which we have been called (cf. Rom. 6:17; Acts 20:27; 2 Tim. 1:13–14; Jude 3). If someone in the church persists in causing division and creating obstacles by their denial of these truths, Paul's counsel is unmistakable: "Avoid them!"

Such divisive people **are not serving our Lord Christ, but their own appetites** (v. 18). Their motivation isn't to glorify Jesus or to uphold truth but to promote themselves and advance their personal agendas. It is their own personal praise and not that of Jesus that is uppermost in their minds. The reference to their **appetites** may be a way of saying that they are primarily interested in satisfying their own fleshly pleasure.

Furthermore, they engage in **smooth talk** and **flattery** (v. 18b [the latter translates *eulogia*, from which we derive our term "eulogy"]). Most false teachers in the course of church history have been extremely eloquent. But we are to test a person by their content, not by their oratorical talents. Most false teachers are undeniably nice. Their politeness and carefully chosen words are designed to put us at ease so that we will lower our guard and swallow the horrific ideas they are promoting.

Satan's Demise

In Rom. 16:20 Paul says that God "will soon crush Satan." Satan's demise comes in stages, the first being his defeat in the wilderness when Jesus resisted his temptations. The second stage came as Jesus delivered people from demonic influence. His casting out of demons was a major blow to Satan's kingdom. Yet a third stage came when Jesus authorized and empowered his followers to take authority over the demonic realm. We see this in Luke's Gospel where Jesus responds to the report from his disciples that "even the demons submit to us in your name," prompting Jesus to declare, "I saw Satan fall like lightning from heaven" (Luke 10:17–18).

The most decisive defeat of the devil came with the substitutionary sacrifice of Jesus on the cross. Speaking of his death on the cross, Jesus said, "Now is the time for judgment on this world; now the prince of this world will be driven out" (John 12:31). Paul speaks of this when he says that Jesus "disarmed the powers and authorities" and "made a public spectacle of them, triumphing over them by the cross" (Col. 2:15; cf. Heb. 2:14). When Jesus was raised from the dead, the Father exalted him "far above all rule and authority, power and dominion" and "placed all things under his feet" (Eph. 1:21–22). When Jesus died and was exalted and enthroned at the right hand of the Father, "the great dragon was hurled down—that ancient serpent called the devil, or Satan, who leads the whole world astray. He was hurled to the earth, and his angels with him" (Rev. 12:9).

Yet another stage in the defeat of Satan comes every time Christians, in the power of the Spirit, resist Satan and his temptations (cf. James 4:7). And the final stage in his defeat, the ultimate and everlasting overthrow of Satan, happens when he is "thrown into the lake of burning sulfur" to "be tormented day and night for ever and ever" (Rev. 20:10).

The aim of such divisive individuals is to **deceive the minds** [literally, **hearts** (ESV)] **of naive people** (v. 18c). Rarely will these deceivers be so blatant as to openly deny that Jesus is God incarnate. But they have a way of endorsing damnable heresies by couching them in words that sound, at least on the surface, orthodox. Simply put, "The Romans must be on guard because the opponents are urbane, witty, and sophisticated. They will not be unattractive boors."[4]

4. Schreiner, *Romans*, 778.

Here, once again (see 15:14), Paul praises the Roman believers for their spiritual growth and rejoices in their obedience. Their reputation for obedience had spread widely, so that **it is known to all** (v. 19a ESV). Nevertheless, they are to **be wise about what is good, and innocent about what is evil** (v. 19). He's talking specifically about how they respond to the divisive false teachers in verses 17–18, but the principle applies more broadly and encompasses everything in the Christian life and in the believer's response to the surrounding world.

Although Paul referred to "angels" and "demons" and "powers" in Rom. 8:38, verse 20 is the first and only explicit reference to **Satan** in this epistle. And the one thing Paul says about him is that he is soon destined for doom. In somewhat ironic fashion, it is the God of **peace** who will **crush** Satan. The only way to maintain peace is to destroy its enemy.

So, when and in what way will God **crush** Satan under the feet of Christians? It will happen **soon** (v. 20). On the one hand, believers crush Satan every time they avoid false teachers who try to perpetuate and impose doctrines of demons. Evidently, Paul believes the false teachers of verse 17 to be instruments of the devil. To identify and resist false teachers and remain innocent **about what is evil** (v. 19) is to **crush** Satan repeatedly in the present day. The fact that Paul says Satan will be crushed under **your** feet—that is, the feet of the Roman believers in the first century—serves to confirm this first view.

Satan will also be crushed at the final judgment. But in what sense is that **soon**? In 2 Pet. 3:8 the apostle Peter tells us, "With the Lord a day is like a thousand years, and a thousand years are like a day." **Soon** for God could be either tomorrow or two thousand years in the future. The word **soon**, then, probably focuses less on the time of Satan's final defeat and more on the certainty of it. In what sense will it be **under** our **feet**? Paul doesn't say, but he does tell us in 1 Cor. 6:3 that "we will judge angels." Satan himself is an angel—a fallen angel, but an angel nonetheless.

Who Wrote Romans? (16:21–23)[5]

The most important thing in verses 21–23 is the identity of Tertius, who in verse 22 claims to be the man who **wrote this letter** (ESV). Tertius was an amanuensis, a secretary of sorts who took dictation from Paul. The Spirit revealed words to Paul. Paul spoke the words to Tertius. Tertius put pen to parchment, and from this we have the Letter to the Romans. Paul regularly wrote using a secretary, because at least four times he concludes a letter with a greeting that he says is

---

5. Some manuscripts include as verse 24, **May the grace of our Lord Jesus Christ be with all of you. Amen.**

in his own hand, implying that the rest is in the hand of his secretary (1 Cor. 16:21; Gal. 6:11; Col. 4:18; 2 Thess. 3:17; see also Philem. 19). Although Tertius is the one who actually writes down the words, those words and the theology they express come directly from Paul. And Paul's words and theology are themselves the words and theology of God the Holy Spirit (see 2 Tim. 3:16–17). The truth of biblical inspiration means that the Spirit, mysteriously but with utmost certainty, communicated to Paul precisely what God wanted made known. And Paul, on the basis of his education, experience, personality, and vocabulary, in turn spoke to Tertius the revelation that came from the Spirit. And Tertius, in turn, inerrantly recorded what Paul said.

A Concluding Doxology (16:25–27)

In this concluding doxology Paul highlights what is a consistent theme in the New Testament regarding the ability or power of God (see also Matt. 19:26; Mark 1:40; 9:22–23; Rom. 4:20–21; 2 Tim. 1:12; Heb. 11:19; see esp. Eph. 3:20; Jude 24). Paul breaks out in praise of **him who is able to establish** [*stērizō*; **strengthen** (ESV)] **you in accordance with my gospel** (v. 25). Paul intends for his concluding words to be a hymn or declaration or song of praise and adoration of the God who is able to do the incredibly glorious and majestic things that have been described in Romans.

Paul specifically highlights the way in which the gospel strengthens weak people, something that he himself experienced firsthand (cf. 1 Cor. 2:3). The gospel strengthens the believer in the midst of suffering (cf. 1 Pet. 2:18–25; 3:17–18). When battling pride, call to mind the humble, self-sacrifice of God the Son (Phil. 2:6–11). When feeling weak and inadequate to love one's spouse, recall that "Christ loved the church and gave himself up for her" (Eph. 5:25). When battling greed, find strength in the truth that Christ Jesus, "though he was rich, yet for your sake he became poor, so that you through his poverty might become rich" (2 Cor. 8:9; cf. 9:13). If you feel too weak to forgive another who has offended or abused or betrayed you, meditate on how God in Christ forgave you (Eph. 4:32; Col. 3:13). If you struggle to love the unlovely, find strength in the fact that "Christ loved us and gave himself up for us" (Eph. 5:2). When called on to serve others, reflect deeply on how Christ served his disciples by washing their feet and eventually suffering in their stead (John 13:1–20). Simply put, there is great strength and power in the truth of the gospel.

In keeping with repeated references to the Christ-centered focus of the gospel in Romans, Paul reaffirms at the end of chapter 16 the message that he proclaims about Jesus Christ, insisting that it is perfectly consistent with **the revelation** of the mystery that was kept secret for long ages but has now been disclosed and through the prophetic writings has been made known to all nations (vv. 25b–26a ESV). The good news is not *new* news; it was prophesied throughout the Old Testament. The preaching of Christ in the gospel is not the product of any human insight or energy, but rather is in accordance with **the command of the eternal God** (v. 26). The Christocentric nature of the gospel resides in the fact that in Christ "are hidden all the treasures of wisdom and knowledge" (Col. 2:3), as well as "every spiritual blessing" (Eph. 1:3). It is in the gospel that Paul preached that we find "the boundless riches of Christ" (Eph. 3:8): his immutability (Heb. 13:8), his empathy (Heb. 4:14–15), the fullness of his divine nature (Col. 2:9) as well as his genuine humanity (John 1:14). In Christ alone we find one who is truly "gentle and humble in heart" (Matt. 11:29), loving (John 13:1), eternal (John 8:58), kind (Eph. 2:7), compassionate (Mark 6:34), and holy (Mark 1:24), and who has all authority in heaven and earth (Matt. 28:18–20).

In keeping with his earlier statement in 1:5, Paul reaffirms the purpose of the gospel, which is **to bring about the obedience of faith** (v. 26 ESV). Paul then concludes with a declaration of praise: **To the only wise God be glory forever through Jesus Christ! Amen** (v. 27). There is no verb here in the Greek text. Literally, Paul is saying, "To him, glory!" When we glorify God, we are not adding to his majesty or making him more beautiful and honorable than he was before we decided to glorify him. We glorify God by declaring that he is glorious. We acknowledge his glory, prize it, and treasure it. God's glory cannot increase or decrease. It is eternally infinite, and our task is to make this known to the world by means of the person and work of Jesus Christ, whom we preach.

God's wisdom is seen when we think back over Romans and the multitude of things God has done to achieve our salvation. We can rest assured that the process he chose was the wisest and best way to secure our forgiveness and to exalt his own glory. There was no better way to save us than how he has saved us through Jesus.

To him be glory, forever, through Jesus Christ! Indeed!

Bibliography

Abasciano, Brian J. "Corporate Election in Romans 9: A Reply to Thomas Schreiner." *Journal of the Evangelical Theological Society* 49, no. 2 (2006): 351–71.

Belleville, Linda. "Ιουνιαν . . . επισημοι εν τοις αποστολοις: A Re-examination of of Romans 16.7 in Light of Primary Source Materials." *New Testament Studies* 51, no. 2 (2005): 231–49.

Bertone, John. "The Experience of Glossolalia and the Spirit's Empathy: Romans 8:26 Revisited." *Pneuma: The Journal of the Society for Pentecostal Studies* 25, no. 1 (2003): 54–65.

Bowler, Kate. *The Preacher's Wife: The Precarious Power of Evangelical Women Celebrities.* Princeton: Princeton University Press, 2019.

Bruce, F. F. *Paul: Apostle of the Heart Set Free.* Grand Rapids: Eerdmans, 1977.

Burer, Michael H., and Daniel B. Wallace. "Was Junias Really an Apostle? A Re-examination of Romans 16:7." *New Testament Studies* 47, no. 1 (2001): 76–91.

Butler, Anthea. *Women in the Church of God in Christ: Making a Sanctified World.* Chapel Hill: University of North Carolina Press, 2007.

Cohick, Lynn H. *Women in the World of the Earliest Christians: Illuminating Ancient Ways of Life.* Grand Rapids: Baker Academic, 2009.

Collins, Helen. *Charismatic Christianity: Introducing Its Theology through the Gifts of the Spirit.* Grand Rapids: Baker Academic, 2023.

Cottrell, Jack. *Romans.* 2 vols. College Press NIV Commentary. Joplin, MO: College Press, 1996.

Cranfield, C. E. B. *A Critical and Exegetical Commentary on the Epistle to the Romans.* 2 vols. International Critical Commentary. Edinburgh: T&T Clark, 1975–79.

Donfried, Karl P., ed. *The Romans Debate.* Revised and expanded ed. Peabody, MA: Hendrickson, 1991.

Doriani, Daniel M. *Romans.* Reformed Expository Commentary. Phillipsburg, NJ: P&R, 2021.

Dunn, James D. G. "Rom. 7,14–25 in the Theology of Paul." *Theologische Zeitschrift* 31, no. 5 (1975): 257–73.

———. *Romans 1–8*. Word Biblical Commentary 38A. Dallas: Word, 1988.

———. *Romans 9–16*. Word Biblical Commentary 38B. Dallas: Word, 1988.

Erickson, Millard J. *Christian Theology*. 3 vols. in 1. Grand Rapids: Baker, 1984.

Fee, Gordon D. *God's Empowering Presence: The Holy Spirit in the Letters of Paul*. Peabody, MA: Hendrickson, 1994.

Fitzmyer, Joseph A. *Romans: A New Translation with Introduction and Commentary*. Anchor Bible 33. New York: Doubleday, 1993.

Gillespie, Thomas W. *The First Theologians: A Study in Early Christian Prophecy*. Grand Rapids: Eerdmans, 1994.

Gundry, Robert H. "The Moral Frustration of Paul before His Conversion: Sexual Lust in Romans 7:7–25." In *Pauline Studies: Essays Presented to Professor F. F. Bruce on His 70th Birthday*, edited by Donald A. Hagner and Murray J. Harris, 228–45. Grand Rapids: Eerdmans, 1980.

Gundry-Volf, Judith M. *Paul and Perseverance: Staying In and Falling Away*. Louisville: Westminster John Knox, 1990.

Harcourt, Paul. Foreword to *The Church Who Hears God's Voice: Equipping Everyone to Recognise and Respond to the Spirit*, by Tania Harris. Milton Keynes, UK: Paternoster, 2022.

Harris, Tania. "The Place of Contemporary Revelatory Experiences in Pentecostal Theology." *Journal of the European Pentecostal Theological Association* 41, no. 2 (2021): 93–107.

Hays, Richard B. *The Faith of Jesus Christ: An Investigation of the Narrative Substructure of Galatians 3:1–4:11*. Society of Biblical Literature Dissertation Series 56. Chico, CA: Scholars Press, 1983.

Heiser, Michael. *Demons: What the Bible Really Says about the Powers of Darkness*. Bellingham, WA: Lexham, 2020.

Hendriksen, William. *Exposition of Paul's Epistle to the Romans*. New Testament Commentary. Grand Rapids: Baker, 1982.

Hodge, Charles. *Commentary on the Epistle to the Romans*. Grand Rapids: Eerdmans, 1974.

Johnson, S. Lewis, Jr. "Romans 5:12—An Exercise in Exegesis and Theology." In *New Dimensions in New Testament Study*, edited by Richard N. Longenecker and Merrill C. Tenney, 298–316. Grand Rapids: Zondervan, 1974.

Jones, Beth Felker. *God the Spirit: Introducing Pneumatology in Wesleyan and Ecumenical Perspective*. Wesleyan Doctrine Series. Eugene, OR: Cascade Books, 2014.

Kärkkäinen, Veli-Matti. "Pentecostal Pneumatology of Religions: The Contribution of Pentecostalism to Our Understanding of the Work of God's Spirit in the World." In *The Spirit in the World: Emerging Pentecostal Theologies in Global Contexts*, edited by Veli-Matti Kärkkäinen, 155–80. Grand Rapids: Eerdmans, 2009.

Keener, Craig S. *Romans: A New Covenant Commentary.* New Covenant Commentary Series 6. Eugene, OR: Cascade Books, 2009.

Klein, William. *The New Chosen People: A Corporate View of Election.* Grand Rapids: Zondervan, 1990.

Kruse, Colin G. *Paul's Letter to the Romans.* Pillar New Testament Commentary. Grand Rapids: Eerdmans, 2012.

Luhrmann, T. M. *When God Talks Back: Understanding the American Evangelical Relationship with God.* New York: Knopf, 2012.

Marston, V. Paul, and Roger T. Forster. *God's Strategy in Human History.* Wheaton: Tyndale House, 1974.

Martin, Brice L. "Some Reflections on the Identity of ἐγώ in Rom. 7:14–25." *Scottish Journal of Theology* 34, no. 1 (1981): 39–47.

Menzies, Robert P. *Christ-Centered: The Evangelical Nature of Pentecostal Theology.* Eugene, OR: Cascade Books, 2020.

Merkle, Ben L. "Romans 11 and the Future of Ethnic Israel." *Journal of the Evangelical Theological Society* 43, no. 4 (2000): 709–21.

Meyer, Jason C. *The End of the Law: Mosaic Covenant in Pauline Theology.* Nashville: B&H Academic, 2009.

Mitton, C. Leslie. "Romans vii. Reconsidered—II." *Expository Times* 65, no. 4 (1954): 99–103.

Moo, Douglas J. *Encountering the Book of Romans: A Theological Survey.* 2nd ed. Grand Rapids: Baker Academic, 2014.

———. *The Epistle to the Romans.* New International Commentary on the New Testament. Grand Rapids: Eerdmans, 1996.

Morris, Leon. *The Apostolic Preaching of the Cross.* Grand Rapids: Eerdmans, 1972.

———. *The Epistle to the Romans.* Grand Rapids: Eerdmans, 1988.

Murray, John. *The Epistle to the Romans.* 2 vols. in 1. New International Commentary on the New Testament. Grand Rapids: Eerdmans, 1971.

———. *Redemption: Accomplished and Applied.* Grand Rapids: Eerdmans, 1973.

Nicole, Roger R. "C. H. Dodd and the Doctrine of Propitiation." *Westminster Theological Journal* 17 (1955): 117–57.

Packer, J. I. *Knowing God.* Downers Grove, IL: InterVarsity, 1993.

———. "The 'Wretched Man' in Romans 7." In *Keep in Step with the Spirit*, 263–70. Old Tappan, NJ: Revell, 1984.

Payne, Leah. *Gender and Pentecostal Revivalism: Making a Female Ministry in the Early Twentieth Century.* New York: Palgrave Macmillan, 2015.

Piper, John. *The Justification of God: An Exegetical and Theological Study of Romans 9:1–23.* Grand Rapids: Baker, 1983.

Poloma, Margaret M. *Main Street Mystics: The Toronto Blessing and Reviving Pentecostalism.* Walnut Creek, CA: AltaMira, 2003.

Ridderbos, Herman. *Paul: An Outline of His Theology*. Translated by John Richard de Witt. Grand Rapids: Eerdmans, 1975.

Robertson, O. Palmer. "Is There a Distinctive Future for Ethnic Israel in Romans 11?" In *Perspectives on Evangelical Theology: Papers from the Thirtieth Annual Meeting of the Evangelical Theological Society*, edited by Kenneth S. Kantzer and Stanley N. Gundry, 220–27. Grand Rapids: Baker, 1979.

———. *The Israel of God: Yesterday, Today, and Tomorrow*. Phillipsburg, NJ: P&R, 2000.

Sanders, E. P. *Paul and Palestinian Judaism: A Comparison of Patterns of Religion*. Philadelphia: Fortress, 1977.

Schreiner, Thomas R. "Corporate and Individual Election in Romans 9: A Response to Brian Abasciano." *Journal of the Evangelical Theological Society* 49, no. 2 (2006): 373–86.

———. "Does Romans 9 Teach Individual Election unto Salvation? Some Exegetical and Theological Reflections." *Journal of the Evangelical Theological Society* 36, no. 1 (1993): 25–40.

———. *40 Questions about Christians and Biblical Law*. Grand Rapids: Kregel, 2010.

———. *Interpreting the Pauline Epistles*. Guides to New Testament Exegesis 5. Grand Rapids: Baker, 1990.

———. *Romans*. 2nd ed. Baker Exegetical Commentary on the New Testament. Grand Rapids: Baker Academic, 2018.

———. "'Works of Law' in Paul." *Novum Testamentum* 33, no. 3 (1991): 217–44.

Schreiner, Thomas, and Ardel Caneday. *The Race Set before Us: A Biblical Theology of Perseverance & Assurance*. Downers Grove, IL: InterVarsity, 2001.

Smith, James K. A. *Thinking in Tongues: Pentecostal Contributions to Christian Philosophy*. Grand Rapids: Eerdmans, 2010.

Stendahl, Krister. "Paul and the Introspective Conscience of the West." In *Paul among Jews and Gentiles and Other Essays*, 78–96. Philadelphia: Fortress, 1976.

Stott, John. *The Epistles of John: An Introduction and Commentary*. Tyndale New Testament Commentaries 19. Leicester, UK: Inter-Varsity, 1988.

———. *Romans: God's Good News for the World*. Downers Grove, IL: InterVarsity, 1994.

Tan-Chow, May Ling. *Pentecostal Theology for the Twenty-First Century: Engaging with Multi-faith Singapore*. Aldershot, UK: Ashgate, 2007.

Thielman, Frank. *Romans*. Zondervan Exegetical Commentary on the New Testament 6. Grand Rapids: Zondervan, 2018.

Timenia, Lora Angeline Embudo. *Third Wave Pentecostalism in the Philippines: Understanding Toronto Blessing Revivalism's Signs and Wonders Theology in the Philippines*. Baguio City, Philippines: Asia Pacific Theological Seminary Press, 2020.

Turner, Max. *The Holy Spirit and Spiritual Gifts: Then and Now*. Carlisle, UK: Paternoster, 1996.

Wallace, Daniel B. "Greek Grammar and the Personality of the Holy Spirit." *Bulletin for Biblical Research* 13, no. 1 (2003): 97–125.

———. *Greek Grammar beyond the Basics: An Exegetical Syntax of the New Testament.* Grand Rapids: Zondervan, 1996.

———. "The Witness of the Spirit in Romans 8:16: Interpretation and Implications." Bible.org, December 14, 2005, https://bible.org/seriespage/2-witness-spirit-romans -816-interpretation-and-implications.

Wellum, Stephen J. *God the Son Incarnate: The Doctrine of Christ.* Wheaton: Crossway, 2016.

Westerholm, Stephen. *Romans: Text, Readers, and the History of Interpretation.* Grand Rapids: Eerdmans, 2022.

Wiles, Gordon. *Paul's Intercessory Prayers: The Significance of the Intercessory Prayer Passages in the Letters of St. Paul.* London: Cambridge University Press, 1974.

Witherington, Ben, III. *Paul's Letter to the Romans: A Socio-rhetorical Commentary.* Grand Rapids: Eerdmans, 2004.

Wright, N. T. "The Law in Romans 2." In *Paul and the Mosaic Law*, edited by James D. G. Dunn, 131–50. Grand Rapids: Eerdmans, 2001.

———. "The Letter to the Romans." In vol. 10 of *The New Interpreter's Bible*, edited by Leander E. Keck, 395–770. Nashville: Abingdon, 2002.

Yong, Amos. *The Spirit Poured Out on All Flesh: Pentecostalism and the Possibility of Global Theology.* Grand Rapids: Baker Academic, 2005.

Index of Authors

Index of Scripture and Other Ancient Sources